NAPOLEON
THE LAST PHASE

NAPOLEON

THE LAST PHASE

by

LORD ROSEBERY

NEW YORK

JONATHAN CAPE AND HARRISON SMITH

PRINTED IN THE UNITED STATES BY THE VAIL-BALLOU PRESS
AND BOUND BY THE J. F. TAPLEY CO.

CONTENTS

PUBLISHERS seem to think that a book is not a book without an introduction. To this one there is indeed a preface; but it became, somehow, embedded in page 242, and cannot now be extricated. For this issue something more, or at any rate something else, seems to be demanded. The form of the work does, no doubt, require explanation. Some critics have, not without justice, advised readers to skip the first two chapters; others have recommended that these should be relegated to an appendix, which, after all, is much the same thing.

There is something to be said for this view, but I may be pardoned for thinking that it is unsound. Those two chapters are the necessary foundations of the book. It is true that the visitors to a house, to whom readers may be compared, do not think it necessary to explore its foundations before entering it; but it is not less true that wise visitors will not enter a house at all if they are doubtful about its security. Now, if one wishes to study seriously the life of Napoleon at St. Helena, it is necessary first to feel one's way through the maze of legendary literature to arrive at any chance or possibility of facts; it is necessary to discard copiously, until at last one may doubt if anything be left. The more one reads and sifts the more dubious become all these chronicles, the more questionable becomes every assertion in them; and in re-reading these two chapters my conviction is that they are unduly lenient to the records of the captivity.

So much for the preliminary necessity of discrimination.

As to the main purpose of the book, it is so obvious that it does not seem to need explanation; for the procession of Napoleon from the throne to the grave must always be a theme of historic and human interest. What the last phase might have been, how his later life might have developed under other circumstances, is a topic for idle but not wholly unfruitful speculation. At some cold interval of reflection he might have realized—what he knew with regard to others—that the war period in a man's life has its definite limits: he might have said "Enough!" and set himself to consolidate what he had won. Then that imperious but practical mind might have worked wonders of administration, have endeavoured to fascinate subject races by good government in lieu of crushing and bleeding them, and have made France forget the Revolution in the enjoyment of material prosperity and pride of dominion; while he himself remained the overshadowing authority of the Continent.

Liberty in the Anglo-Saxon sense he would never have conceded, for he misunderstood and distrusted it; but he would have contented by contrast those Frenchmen who remembered the selfish oppressions of the old monarchy and the unspeakable horrors of the Revolution. Of the working classes he and his nephew after him were always mindful. Frenchmen, too, he had studied closely and understood thoroughly. Other nations, except perhaps the English, he had never troubled himself to understand, and them he understood least of all. Had he wisely put war away from him, and rested on the terror of his name, he might have dispensed with this knowledge, for the internal administration of his empire would have sufficed for his energies, when the keen edge of youth, restlessness, and ambition had been removed.

Imagination can scarcely set limits to the beneficent possibilities of a Napoleon of peace, of that vast operative intellect absorbed in the problems of internal government: genius and energy and organizing power all devoted to the amelioration of a region already so favoured by Nature, and to laying deep and solid the foundations of a dynasty which should have had a title to existence in the obvious advantages it afforded as compared with all preceding governments. But, then, to do this he would have had to turn his back on himself, to retrace his steps, and to stay the waste of France. Others saw his opportunity, though he himself was too headstrong. "What a fall in history!" said Talleyrand, with an eloquence and elevation rare in him: "to give his name to adventures instead of giving it to his age!"

All this he might have combined with the kindred task of training his sons, of forming his heirs, and practically founding a beneficent succession. His son is now an object of renewed and pathetic interest, all the more pathetic because there is so little to say. But imagination cannot help dwelling on the child of so infinite a future and so sterile a reality, who clung as if by instinct to the Tuileries when it was sought to remove him, and who withered away among the enemies of his father and his race. And yet he was, perhaps, happy in his death, for had he lived he must have been practically a prisoner; utilized by Metternich as a piece on the European chessboard, and compelled to sustain the awful heritage of his dreaded name—intrigue, captivity, and revolution. He would in effect have been more formidable than his father, after so much of the Napoleonic glamour had been lost in Russia. For around that blameless figure played the aureole of the splendid tradition; passions and enthusiasms which Napoleon had inspired but alienated would have rallied to his son; the inevitable errors of other governments—legitimist, constitutional, or republican—would have added to their volume; and the youth would have been regarded as the Messiah of democracy on the one hand and as a prince within the mystic circle of hereditary sovereignty on the other.

If Napoleon III, the not unquestioned nephew of the Emperor, could fascinate the French with his name after the almost grotesque adventures of Strasburg and Boulogne, it seems impossible to measure the attractive force of the youth who was the very child of Cæsar, and who for three years had actually lived in Paris as a king.

His father in exile planned and pondered much over his son's future. What else had he to dream of or build upon? It was to him the redeeming fact of his captivity that it might appeal pathetically to the French people on behalf of his son, and that his sufferings might secure his dynasty. It was, as he said, his crucifixion. What he dreaded was that the boy might be compelled by his Austrian relatives to take orders and enter the priesthood, so as to remove him definitely from the dynastic arena. That, no doubt, was a contingency to be reckoned with. But the undoubted affection of Francis for his grandson, or the desire of Metternich to retain so precious a political asset, averted any such solution, and the future of the boy was unembarrassed by the cloister.

What were the chances of that future we may estimate by an incident. When Prince Napoleon, the son of Jerôme, was in Paris under the name of Montfort in 1845 he visited the Hôtel des Invalides. His resemblance to the founder of his house was striking, and the sentry on duty, after looking hard at him, in a moment of uncontrollable emotion presented arms. Some of the veterans came up. "It is a son of the Emperor, or at least a nephew of the Emperor." The news spread like wildfire, and the old men rushed like madmen to fetch General Petit, the Lieutenant-Governor—him of the famous farewell in the courtyard of Fontainebleau. He came, and embraced the young man, as Napoleon had then embraced him, amid shouts of "Vive l'Empereur!" "Had it been in a barrack, not a hospital, no one knows what would have happened," says a contemporary chronicler. From which may be inferred not merely the force of the imperial tradition, thirty years after Waterloo, but also that had Louis Napoleon physically resembled his uncle he would have succeeded much sooner than he did in mounting the throne of France.

Surely, then, the son of the Emperor was happy in his death; for the saddest fate that can befall a prince is to be the passive tool and instrument of statesmanship, as the bitter experience of Djem and the Stewart pretenders sufficiently testifies. Moreover, the man has yet to be found who, for even a score of years, can rule the fierce equality of France as it has been since the Revolution.

But all these are bubbles, and this book is not intended to deal with speculations; its aim is to penetrate the deliberate darkness which surrounds the last act of the Napoleonic drama. In stage tragedy the catastrophe is, as a rule, decently concealed. One may see the headsman or the assassin or the funeral, but not the scaffold or the stab. For Napoleon there was no such close. Yet none the less was his exile a tragedy, and, as if from the custom and habit of tragedy, a curtain, though not wholly impenetrable, veils the fifth act. The victim will have it so; he shrouds himself and closes all the shutters; what is allowed to issue forth is calculated misrepresentation; to obtain a glimpse of the truth we are almost reduced, like the officer on guard at Longwood, to utilize the keyhole.

Further, the purpose of this book may be justified from another point of view. There is a natural curiosity to know how the rulers of mankind demean themselves when fortune turns, or when they turn their backs on fortune. To humanity at large they are, indeed, then more interesting than in their splendour.

We watch, with a personal emotion, Walpole at Houghton, unable to employ himself after his fall, for business has sterilized him, and he can no longer read; Charles V at Yuste endeavouring to persuade himself that he has done with the world, and to still an active mind with monastic observance; Mary Queen of Scots as she trails her fallen fortunes from prison to prison; Charles XII at Demotika, taking to his bed in the dumb fury of defeat; Diocletian feining or finding happiness in his kitchen garden at Salona; Charles Albert as he rides away a citizen from the battlefield which he entered as a king, to hide his broken heart at Oporto; the two uncrowned Queens who pace the green but hopeless garden of Zell; Wolsey as he seeks in the ruin of his career the shelter of his monks; Charles as he walks across the park from one of his palaces, to have his head cut off in front of the other. Napoleon was well aware of this curiosity, never keener than about himself. No one, perhaps, since Julius Cæsar concentrated on himself the personal and familiar devotion of so many hundreds of thousands. None, perhaps, had ever excited so much visible consternation. There had never been a more meteoric rise or a more terrible fall. On no captive, then, could the attention of the world be more fixed. But for that reason he was resolved not to gratify the inquisition. He knew that he was slowly dying; he knew that he was politically dead. He would fold his mantle around him as he passed; he would not expose his captive majesty, like Samson or Jugurtha, to the idle wonder of the crowd. And so, when he lost what slender hopes of release he may have had, if he ever entertained any, he made himself invisible.

It was well done—better done than in the first months when he exposed himself to the Governor and to the tourists—but it only increases our curiosity. Had he lived in the eye of the world no languid hand would have turned the pages of his meagre court circular. His conversations of parade in adversity would have been even less interesting than his conversations of parade in prosperity. Had he come to England, as he wished, he would, no doubt, have tried to play the part of a country squire. He might have attempted to solace himself with the ambitions, at once petty and solid, of a gentleman farmer; have punched his cattle or weighed his pigs, and simulated satisfaction with his lot. That, perhaps, had been the worst ending of all; for no one would have believed in it. Other men could pass from lofty station to agricultural absorption without suspicion. Althorp, for example, could exchange the leadership of the House of Commons for the cultivation of shorthorns without fear and without reproach. Washington, a born country gentleman, could step down from the highest office and resume rural pursuits with dignity and satisfaction. But Napoleon in such guise would have deceived no one, least of all himself. His shepherds would have been suspected of intrigue, his bailiff would have been treated as a diplomatist, his oil-cake would have been probed for despatches. And in the midst of the byre would have been Napoleon, with some Poppleton in attendance, suspected of meditating, and no doubt meditating, very different things.

It must, indeed, be conceded that it was not possible for him to live in England. There, to say the least, he would have been the figure-head of faction both in Britain and abroad. Napoleon in the Tower of London would have been an anachronism,—and, even there, an unexploded shell. He would have been under the very eye of France, an eye which was always turning restlessly away from the Bourbons; he would have been a cause of unrest and agitation in England; he would have enjoyed in his prison the sympathy of Whigs like Sussex or Holland, and the enthusiasm of Radicals like Hobhouse. Men who are not old have seen how the support of portions of our community may be enlisted on behalf of enemies much less attractive and illustrious than Napoleon. He would have been the stock subject of parliamentary inquiries; and even the fierce bull-dog hostility of the mass of the nation would have served the captive in producing reaction both in Britain and on the Continent:—in fine, it would have become at last impossible to keep him in and impossible to let him out. And all these drawbacks would have been multiplied a hundredfold had he been allowed to be comparatively at large under supervision; even had the Confederate Powers agreed to such an arrangement, which, after the experience of Elba, we may be sure was out of the question. On the Continent, outside France and Italy, he could have lived under custody of some kind with no such danger; the risk would have been rather to himself than to peace. This might well have been urged by our Government as a reason why Austria, Prussia, or Russia should undertake the burden. There was no danger of his escaping from the affectionate solicitude of his father-in-law, or the vindictive vigilance of Prussia, or the outraged territory of Russia.

That, again, is not the main issue so far as this book is concerned. Granted, as it must be granted, that Napoleon was destined after the collapse of Waterloo to eat his heart out somewhere till released by death, it was its purpose to try and ascertain the truth as to this final scene.

And in attempting this much it is not intended to maintain that Napoleon should not have been kept in strict custody, but to express regret that the ungracious responsibility should have devolved on Great Britain, and that it should not have been discharged with more consideration and less crudeness. It should be remembered that, although Napoleon had surrendered himself to Great Britain, he was in effect the prisoner of the Allies, and we cannot help wishing that his confinement had been under the auspices of some other Power. Absolute security from further intervention by Napoleon in its affairs was justly and imperatively demanded by the world; it was its reluctant and unconscious tribute to the man. But it would have been fully consistent with security to lodge the Emperor decently; to give him practically the full liberty of the island —if St. Helena were the choice of the confederates for his residence; to assign to him a custodian who should have veiled his functions with something of courtesy and tact. For we were guarding at St. Helena not merely a renowned conqueror, not merely one who had been for a decade the paramount sovereign of Western Europe and had received the homage and adulation of almost all kings and rulers, but one of the supreme figures of history, whom, though it was necessary to control, it was not possible to obliterate. It should have been flattering to our pride to remember this; for we had dealt him the final blow at Waterloo, and he had surrendered to us. It was in our national interest, therefore, rather to magnify than to diminish the greatness of our charge. It should, then, have been at the least a matter of expediency for us to remember that our relations with the former conqueror would be recorded by history in characters both dispassionate and ineffaceable, that our debit and credit account in that matter would be graven on tablets of brass. Our relation to him should have been that of the chivalrous conqueror to the illustrious vanquished. And this we could easily have achieved without sacrificing security and without unfaithfulness to our odious duty.

One strange question does, somehow, arise—a sort of historical freak. Suppose the boot, to use an expressive vulgarism, had been on the other leg. Suppose that, instead of the Allied Sovereigns capturing Napoleon, Napoleon had, as was possible in 1813 or 1814, captured the Allied Sovereigns? Here there comes in the difference between the hereditary and the self-made monarch, between the founder and the heirs of a dynasty. Every dynasty must have a beginning, but woe to the founder if he fails.

There would have been no question of Napoleon's immuring or exiling the sovereigns of Austria, Prussia, or Russia; their countries would not have endured it. Their subjects would have ceded provinces and fortresses, and regained their masters in exchange.

But Napoleon did not belong to that sacred race, he had made himself imperial; he had no hereditary rights of kingship: France divested herself of him without qualm or difficulty. And yet he had claims on her; claims of admitted fealty, claims of conquest on her behalf. But he had not the special indefinable traditional birthright. He had the claim of a Pepin, not the claim of a Dagobert; and so in defeat he had to go out into the wilderness, much as a detected adventurer who has intruded into polite society.

He knew and recognized the difference. He well understood his relation to the world. When he had asked his courtiers what would be the effect of his disappearance, and they in reply had exhausted themselves in hyperbole: "Bah!" he said, "there will be a great 'Ouf!' of relief." He played his stake, lost it, and went his way.

For Alexander and Francis and Frederic William it was

different. Had Darius captured Alexander, the defeated Macedonian would, no doubt, have been paraded in chains of gold. But some two thousand years had elapsed since then, and an hereditary king, even though a barbarian, could no longer be so treated. Vienna and St. Petersburg and Berlin would have made the necessary sacrifices, and have welcomed their released monarchs with wreaths and arches and tears of joy. A not less characteristic and peculiar sense of propriety despatched the parvenu sovereign—although he had been crowned in Paris and Milan, anointed by the Pope and affirmed by countless treaties—to a desolate rock as General Bonaparte.

It would be well if the sombre episode of St. Helena could be blotted out of history in the interests both of Great Britain and Napoleon; it is not a bright page for either; it consorts with the dignity of neither. But the imperial verdict of posterity, when given—and is still in suspense—must, whatever its import, record that Napoleon was then stripped and power-less, while Britain was triumphant and overwhelmingly strong.

CHAPTER ONE
The Literature

★

WILL there ever be an adequate Life of Napoleon? Hitherto it has been scarcely worth while to ask the question, as we have been too near the prejudices and passions of his time for any such book to be written. Nor are we as yet very remote, for it may be noted that Queen Victoria was all but two years old when Napoleon died, and that there may still be in existence people who have seen him. Moreover, the Second Empire revived and reproduced these feelings in almost their original force, and the reaction from the Second Empire prolonged them. So we are still, perhaps, not sufficiently outside Napoleon's historical sphere of influence for such a book to be written.

Nor until recently did we possess sufficient materials for the work. The pages and pages that follow Napoleon's name in library catalogues mainly represent compilations, or pamphlets, or lives conscientiously constructed from dubious or partial authorities, meagre bricks of scrannel straw. But now, under a Government in France which opens its records freely, and with the gradual publication of private memoirs, more or less authentic, we are beginning to see new possibilities of definite veracity. The issue of the suppressed correspondence removes a reproach from the official collection, and fills its blanks. And the mania for Napoleonic literature which has prevailed for some years past, unaccompanied, strangely enough, by any sign of the revival of Bonapartism as a political force, has had the effect of producing a great supply to meet a greedy demand—a supply, indeed, by no means always unquestionable or unmixed, but at any rate out of the harvest of its abundance furnishing some grains of genuine fact.

The material, then, varied and massive as it is, seems to be almost ready for the hand of the destined workman, when he shall appear. And even he would seem not to be remote. In the great *Narrative* of the relations of Napoleon and Alexander of Russia we wish to see his shadow projected. Is it too much to hope that M. Vandal will crown the services that he has rendered to history in that priceless work by writing at least the Civil Life of Napoleon? Might not he and M. Henry Houssaye, who has also done so much so well, jointly accomplish the whole? Of the intimate details of his private life M. Masson is the recognized master.

We speak of a partnership, as we do not conceive it to be possible for any one man to undertake the task. For the task of reading and sifting the documents would be gigantic before a single word could be written. Nor, indeed, could any one man adequately deal with Napoleon in his military and his civil capacities. For Napoleon, as was said by Metternich, a hostile judge, was born an administrator, a legislator, and a conqueror; he might have added, a statesman. The Conqueror of 1796–1812, and, it may be added, the Defender of 1813 and 1814, would require a consummate master of the art of war to analyze and celebrate his qualities. Again, Napoleon the civilian would have to be treated, though not necessarily by different hands, as the statesman, the administrator, the legislator. Last of all there comes the general survey of Napoleon as a man, one of the simplest character to his sworn admirers or sworn enemies, one of the most complicated to those who are neither.

And for this last study the most fruitful material should be furnished in the six years that he spent at St. Helena, when he not merely recorded and annotated his career, but afforded a definite and consecutive view of himself. "Now," as he said there himself, "thanks to my misfortune, one can see me nakedly as I am." What he dictated in the way of autobiography and commentary has never perhaps received its just measure of attention. Some one has said somewhere that the memoirs he produced himself appear to be neglected because they are the primitive and authoritative documents, so far as he is concerned, of his life. People prefer to drink at any other source than the original; more especially do they esteem the memoirs of any who came, however momentarily, into contact with him. What the man himself thought or said of himself seems to most of those who read about Napoleon a matter of little moment. What they want to read is Bourrienne, or Rémusat, or Constant, or the like. They may, no doubt, allege that Napoleon's own memoirs are not so spicy as those of some of his servants, and that they are by no means to be relied upon as unbiassed records of fact. Still they remain as the direct deliberate declarations of this prodigy as to his achievements, and they contain, moreover, commentaries on the great captains of the past—Cæsar, Frederick, and Turenne—which cannot be without serious interest to the historian or the soldier.

Nor must this indifference to truth count for too much in an estimate of Napoleon's character. Truth was in those days neither expected nor required in Continental statesmanship —so little, indeed, that half a century afterwards Bismarck discovered it to be the surest means of deception. Napoleon's fiercest enemies, Metternich and Talleyrand, have now given us their memoirs. But we should be sorry to give a blind credence to these in any case where their personal interest was involved. Napoleon at St. Helena was, as it were, making the best case for himself, just as he was in the habit of doing in his bulletins. His bulletins represented what Napoleon desired to be believed. So did the memoirs. They are a series of Napoleonic bulletins on the Napoleonic career, neither more nor less.

But there is one distinction to be drawn. In writing his bulletins, Napoleon had often an object in deceiving. At St. Helena his only practical aim was to further the interests of his dynasty and his son. So that where these are not directly concerned rather more reliance may be placed on the memoirs than on the bulletins.

The literature of St. Helena is fast accumulating, and must be within a measurable distance of completion. Eighty-four years have elapsed since a greedy public absorbed five editions of Warden's *Letters* in five months: seventy-eight since the booksellers were crowded with eager purchasers for O'-Meara's book. It is perhaps not too much to hope that his manuscript journal, which now sleeps in California, may soon be published in its entirety, for it is said to be full of vivid and original matter; [1] while it might throw light on the discrepancies between his *Voice from St. Helena* and his private communications to the English officials at the Admiralty and at Plantation House. Then we have had the voluminous batteries of Gourgaud, Montholon, and Las Cases (whose suppressed passages might also be safely produced, if indeed they exist or ever existed) met by the ponderous defence of Forsyth and the more effective abstract of Seaton. We have had, too, the light artillery of Maitland and Glover, and Cockburn and Santini, and the madcap "Miss Betsy," who became Mrs. Abell. We have the histories of St. Helena by Barnes and Masselin. And in 1816, a former Governor, General Beatson, availed himself of the sudden interest in the island to launch on the public a massive quarto detailing its agricultural features with a minuteness which could scarcely be justified even in the case of the Garden of Eden. We have the tragedy of Antommarchi, whatever that effort may be worth. Recently, too, the Commissaries have taken the field; Montchenu, Balmain, and Sturmer have all yielded their testimony. So has Madame de Montholon. Napoleon, indeed, urged his companions to record his utterances in journals, and frequently alluded to the result. "Yesterday evening," says Gourgaud, "the Emperor told me that I might turn my leisure to profit in writing down

---

[1] See O'Meara's mysterious notification in his *Voice*, ii. 419. Since this was written portions have been published in the *Century* magazine, which makes it abundantly clear that O'Meara skimmed off all the valuable matter for the *Voice*.

his sayings: I would thus gain from 500 to 1000 louis a day."
He was cognizant of the journal of Las Cases, which was dictated to or copied by St. Denis, one of the servants, whom Napoleon would sometimes question as to its contents.[1] O'Meara's journal was read to him. He took it for granted that they all kept journals, and he was right. For, except the faithful Bertrand, and the wife who divided with the Emperor his affection, none of the actors in that dreary drama have held their peace.

Lately, however, there have appeared two further contributions; and it may be considered that, while both are striking, one exceeds in interest all the previous publications of St. Helena, from the light that it throws on Napoleon's character. Lady Malcolm's *Diary of St. Helena* gives a vivid account of the Emperor's conversations with Sir Pulteney, and an impartial account of Lowe, which seems to turn the balance finally against that hapless and distracted official. But the second publication is in some respects not merely the most remarkable book relating to Napoleon at St. Helena, but to Napoleon at any time. It is the private diary of Gourgaud written entirely for his own eye, though the editors seem to think that the latter part at any rate may have been prepared for the possible detection of Lowe. But the great bulk was obviously prepared for no one except Gourgaud; since it could please no one else, and scarcely Gourgaud. It embodies, we believe, the truth as it appeared to the writer from day to day. It throws a strange light on the author, but a still newer light on his master. But when we have read it we feel a doubt of all the other records, and a conviction that this book is more nearly the unvarnished truth than anything else that has been put forth.

For there is one rule to which we fear we can scarcely make an exception, which applies to all the Longwood publications: they, none of them, to put it mildly, contain the exact truth. If we did make an exception it would certainly be in favour of Gourgaud. And it may further be said that their veracity in-

---

[1] Las Cases, vi. 241.

creases in proportion to the remoteness of their publication
from the events to which they relate. Gourgaud, who is published in 1898, is more truthful than Montholon, who publishes in 1847; and Montholon, again, is more truthful than
Las Cases, who publishes in 1823. Least of all, perhaps, to be
depended on is O'Meara, who published in 1822. In all these
books, except perhaps the latest, there are gross instances of
misrepresentation and fabrication. And yet to accuse all these
authors of wanton unveracity would not be fair. It was rarely
if ever wanton. Partly from idolatry of Napoleon, partly to
keep up a dramatic representation of events at St. Helena
and so bring about his liberation, facts were omitted or dis-
torted which in any way reflected on their idol or tended to
mar the intended effects. There seems to have been something in the air of St. Helena that blighted exact truths; and he
who collates the various narratives on any given point will
find strange and hopeless contradictions.[1] Truth probably
lurks in Forsyth, but the crushing of the ore is a hideous task;
and, for various other reasons, it is equally difficult to find
in the more contemporary narratives. There is a strange mil-
dew that rests on them all, as on the books and boots in the
island. One has to weigh each particle of evidence and bear
in mind the character of the witness. Sometimes, indeed, we
may be charged with having quoted from sources which we
have described as tainted. We could scarcely quote from any
others. But where the testimony seems of itself probable, and
no object but truth is perceptible in it, we have no choice
but to cite from what documents there are.

[1] Take, as a trivial example, the ice-machine sent to Napoleon by
Lord and Lady Holland. Lord Holland says (*For. Rem.* 20) that
'Lady Holland suggested the purchase to the British Government.'
The machine, however, was neither purchased nor sent. But Gour-
gaud (i. 236), Las Cases (v. 248), Lady Malcolm (p. 48), and Mon-
tholon (i. 353) all record its arrival, though the last says that it was a
gift of the Prince Regent. Las Cases says that it came from Lord and
Lady Holland. Lord Holland says expressly that none was sent.

THE LITERATURE

One striking circumstance remains to be noticed. Of the last three years of Napoleon's life we know scarcely anything. From the departure of Gourgaud, in March 1818, to the end in May 1821, we know practically nothing. We know what the English reported from without. We have an authorized but not very trustworthy record from within. But, in reality, we know nothing or next to nothing.

CHAPTER TWO

Las Cases, Antommarchi, and Others

★

THE BOOK of Las Cases, which is the most massive, and perhaps the most notorious, is not without a certain charm of its own. First published in eight volumes, it was subsequently compressed, and under the title of *Memorial of St. Helena*, adorned with the quaint and spirited designs of Charlet, has obtained a world-wide circulation. Las Cases is said, indeed, though no doubt with much exaggeration, to have realized from it no less a sum than eighty thousand pounds.[1] It is alleged to have been written in daily entries, and to supply an exact report of Napoleon's conversation. Much, however, is declared by the author to have been lost, partly from want of time for transcription; something, perhaps, from the vicissitudes of his papers. What he narrates is told with spirit and even eloquence, and when corroborated by other authority may be taken to be a faithful transcript of the Emperor's talk as Napoleon wished it to be reported, or at any rate of his dictations. But, when uncorroborated, it is wholly untrustworthy. For, putting on one side the usual exaggerations about diet, restrictions, and so forth, and making full allowance for the fact that the author was too completely dazzled by Napoleon (whom he sincerely adored) to see quite clearly, there is a fatal blot on his book. It is an arsenal of spurious documents. How this has come about, whether from the fertile invention of Las Cases, or by the connivance and inspiration of Napoleon, it is not possible definitely to pronounce, though suspicion may well amount to conviction. At any rate, four concocted letters are printed at length in Las Cases' book, and he must be held responsible for a fifth, which is nowhere printed, and which probably had but a transient existence.

The mythical character of the first of these has been clearly and categorically set forth by Count Murat in his excellent

[1] *Nouvelle Biographie Générale*, Art. "Las Cases."

book, *Murat, Lieutenant de l'Empereur en Espagne*.[1] The charge is there established that Las Cases, in order to lay the blame of his hero's Spanish policy on Murat, inserted in his book a spurious letter under the date of March 29, 1808. By whom this was composed does not appear. But that it is a fabrication is certain, and the responsibility for its production rests on Las Cases.[2] Count Murat accumulates damning proofs. He points out the irresolution of its style, and the orders that the French armies should perpetually retreat before the Spaniards, as wholly alien to the Napoleonic character. He points out the incessant inconsistencies with passages of authentic despatches written at the same time. On the 27th of March Napoleon had written to Murat to bid him make an imposing display of force in Madrid. In the spurious despatch, dated the 29th, he disapproves of his being in Madrid at all. It is known, moreover, that the news of Murat's occupation of Madrid did not reach the Emperor till the 30th. The form is not that in which Napoleon addressed Murat. The drafts, or minutes, of practically all Napoleon's letters are in existence. There is no minute of this. Napoleon in his other despatches never alludes to this one. Murat never acknowledges its receipt. Murat's minute register of letters received and sent contains no allusion to it. How, in any case, did it suddenly make its appearance at St. Helena?

It seems useless to accumulate proofs that a more audacious concoction has seldom been published as an original document. The editors of the imperial correspondence, indeed, blush as they print it, for they append a note stating that neither the draft, nor the original, nor any authentic copy is discoverable.

[1] Chapter III.
[2] Las Cases, iv. 214. In the first edition I followed Thiers, who says it was first printed by Las Cases. But I have now found it in vol. ii. p. 246, of a book called *Introduction à l'histoire de l'Empire Français* (Paris, 1820). Las Cases published the *Memorial* in 1823. But he returned to Europe in 1816.

Savary, Beausset, and Thibaudeau accept the letter on the authority of Las Cases. Méneval, who was at the time Napoleon's private secretary, anticipates the doubts of Count Murat, and details some material circumstances which vitiate the letter, one of them being that though the letter is dated from Paris, Napoleon at that time was at St. Cloud. Méneval says that he cannot solve the mystery, though his arguments all point irresistibly to an historical fraud; his only argument the other way—a very dangerous one—is that no one but Napoleon could have composed it.[1] The perplexity of Méneval, when his confidential position is considered, is extremely significant, if not conclusive. Thiers thinks that Napoleon wrote it, and wrote it on the professed date, but admits that the letter was never sent.[2] His reasons for this strange theory cannot be examined here, but they appear to be the mere result of a desperate effort to prove the authenticity of the letter, in spite of overwhelming difficulties stated by himself. Montholon prints it among a number of other letters which he says were handed to him by the Emperor.[3] This either casts doubt on the narrative of Montholon, or proves the complicity and even authorship of Napoleon himself.

It is indeed true that this document was not first, as Thiers asserts, published by Las Cases. It is to be found in the *Introduction à l'histoire de l'Empire Français*, a book published in 1820, whereas the *Memorial* was published in 1822–23. But it can scarcely be doubted that it was supplied by Las Cases, who was charged to get it somehow passed into history. It appears in this book, without any particular reason, inserted as if by a happy accident, not long after Las Cases returned from St. Helena. It was never published before that return, and we cannot dissociate the responsibility of its publication from Las Cases. It is a little unfortunate that he piqued himself on his skill in composition. He tells us that he drew up

[1] Méneval, ii. 155–6.   [2] Thiers, viii. 547, 671–9.
[3] Montholon, ii. 444–51.

28

Napoleon's protest at Plymouth.[1] He drew up innumerable protests of his own. "Once a correspondence established with Sir H. Lowe," he says, with ominous pleasantry, "I did not remain idle." [2] He rained documents on the Governor. Deported to the Cape, he never stopped writing: the Governor of that settlement, the Ministers, the Prince Regent—all had to endure him. Returning to Europe he bombards every Sovereign or Minister that he can think of. Last of all, the patient reader who ploughs through his eight volumes has ample reason to feel that Las Cases would like nothing better than to pen a few Napoleonic despatches to keep himself in exercise. We should not, perhaps, on this instance alone, definitely pronounce that Las Cases deliberately composed the letter to Murat; for it might have been an academical exercise, or there might have been confusion among his papers, or lapse of memory. There are strange freaks of this kind on record.

But, unfortunately, this is by no means the only effort or lapse of Las Cases in this direction. In the fifth part of his journal he gives in much the same way a letter from Napoleon to Bernadotte, dated August 8, 1811.[3] It is entirely ignored by the editors of the imperial correspondence. It is, however, inserted in the *Lettres inédites de Napoléon Ier*, but "with every reserve," for the editors do not know its source. Had they known its origin they would no doubt have rejected it, as had the former editors. They take it at second hand from Martel's *Œuvres littéraires de Napoléon Bonaparte*. Martel, who does not name his authority, evidently took it from Las Cases.

Again, in his sixth volume, Las Cases generously produces from his occult and unfailing store another State document. This time it is a letter addressed by Napoleon to his brother, Louis, King of Holland, on April 3, 1808, from the Palace of Marrac.[4] It bears all the mint marks of the others. It is

[1] Las Cases, i. 66.   [2] *Ibid.* vii. 283.
[3] *Ibid.* v. 157.   [4] *Ibid.* vi. 199.

found for the first time in Las Cases' book. No draft of it is in existence, a fact which is in itself fatal. Unluckily, too, Napoleon did not arrive at Marrac till fourteen days after April 3. The editors of the Emperor's correspondence print it with this dry remark, and with an ominous reference to Las Cases as the sole authority. M. Rocquain, in his *Napoléon et le Roi Louis*,[1] unhesitatingly dismisses it as in the main, if not wholly, a fraud. We see no reason for accepting any part as genuine, nor indeed does M. Rocquain supply any.

In his seventh volume, again, there is a fourth letter, of the authorship of which it may confidently be said, "Aut Las Cases, aut Diabolus." It purports to be instructions for an anonymous plenipotentiary on a mission in Poland, and it is dated April 18, 1812.[2] This composition is absolutely ignored by the official editors of the imperial correspondence. It is, as usual, suddenly produced by Las Cases as a revelation of the real motives of the Russian expedition. The real motive of that disastrous war, it seems, was the reconstitution of the ancient kingdom of Poland. When we consider that at that juncture, when the revival was passionately sought by the Poles, eagerly desired by his own army and by some of his most devoted servants, when it was vital to his strategy and to his policy, when it was clearly dictated by the commonest gratitude and humanity towards Poland, Napoleon resolutely refused it, we may judge of the value and authenticity of this document.[3]

The fifth fabrication, which we are not privileged even to see, is the most remarkable and the most impudent of all. In a moment of disinterested friendship, Las Cases drew from his manuscript hoards, to show to Warden, a letter from the Duc d'Enghien to Napoleon which was written on the eve of his execution, and which, according to Las Cases, was suppressed by Talleyrand for fear Napoleon should be moved by it to spare him. Las Cases appears to have had a monopoly

[1] P. 166, note.   [2] Las Cases, vii. 5.
[3] Villemain, i. 165–71, 189–92. Broglie, *Souvenirs*, i. 178.

of this document, for no one except himself and those to whom
he showed it ever had the singular good fortune to see or even
to hear of it. His own statement with regard to the Enghien
affair is perhaps the most nebulous in his whole book, and he
only makes a timid and transient [1] allusion to the letter which
he had shown so exultantly to Warden. Warden's language
is so remarkable that it deserves quotation: "I saw a copy of
this letter in possession of Count de Las Cases, which he
calmly represented to me *as one of the mass of documents
formed or collected to authenticate and justify certain mysterious parts of the history* which he was occasionally employed
in writing under the dictation of the hero of it." [2]

Let us follow up for a moment the subsequent history of the
letter of the Duc d'Enghien intercepted by Talleyrand and
providentially preserved by Las Cases. In the *Letters from the
Cape,* composed, inspired, or revised by Napoleon, this letter
is mentioned, for the author had "frequent opportunities of
cursorily running over manuscripts of the greatest interest relative to the memorable events of the last twenty years, a part
of which was even written from the dictation of *Napoleon*
himself;" [3] in other words, Napoleon, who is the author of the
Letters, has access to manuscripts dictated by himself. "When
the Duc d'Enghien had arrived at Strasburg, he wrote a letter
to Napoleon, in which he stated 'that his rights to the crown
were very distant: that for a length of time his family had lost
their claims: and promised, if pardon was granted to him, to
discover everything he knew of the plots of the enemies of
France, and to serve the First Consul faithfully.' This letter
was not presented by Talleyrand to Napoleon until it was too
late. The young prince was no more." [4] The author goes on
to say that in the manuscript, which he had been privileged

[1] Las Cases, vii. 249, 250, 258.
[2] Warden, p. 151. Cf. Montholon, i. 281, and Las Cases, iii. 301,
and note.
[3] *Letters from the Cape,* 3.   [4] *Ibid.* pp. 147–8.

to see, Napoleon states that "perhaps, if this letter had been presented in time, the political advantages which would have accrued from his declarations and his services, would have decided the First Consul to pardon him." [1] This extract is interesting as containing the only portion of the text of this remarkable document which has been preserved.

Rumours of this precious letter appear to have been cautiously spread about Longwood, and to have excited the curiosity of that portion of the household which had not been admitted to the confidence of Las Cases. O'Meara appears especially to have distinguished himself by a pertinacious spirit of investigation. In January 1817, he represents himself as asking the Emperor questions with regard to it. "I now asked if it were true that Talleyrand had retained a letter from Duc d'Enghien to him until two days after the Duke's execution? Napoleon's reply was: 'It is true; the Duke had written a letter, offering his services, and asking a command in the army from me, which that *scelerato* Talleyrand did not make known until two days after his execution.' I observed that Talleyrand by his culpable concealment of the letter was virtually guilty of the death of the Duke. 'Talleyrand,' replied Napoleon, 'is a *briccone*, capable of any crime.' " [2]

Two months later, in March, O'Meara mentions to Napoleon that a book has been published respecting him, by Warden, which was exciting great interest. This book had not then arrived, but there were extracts from it in the newspapers. Napoleon sits down to read the newspapers, asks the explanation of a few passages, and at once inquires what Warden had said of the affair of the Duc d'Enghien. "I replied that he asserted that Talleyrand had detained a letter from the Duke for a considerable time after his execution, and that he attributed his death to Talleyrand. 'Di questo non c' è dubbio' (Of this there is no doubt), replied Napoleon." [3] La-

[1] *Letters from the Cape*, p. 148.   [2] *Voice*, i. 335.   [3] *Ibid.* i. 410.

ter in the month Napoleon reiterates this statement to O'Meara. "When he (the Duc d'Enghien) arrived at Strasburg, he wrote a letter to me in which he offered to discover everything if pardon were granted to him, said that his family had lost their claims for a long time, and concluded by offering his services to me. The letter was delivered to Talleyrand, who concealed it until after his execution." [1] This seems succinct enough, but O'Meara wished to make assurance doubly sure. So in May, he tells us: "I asked Napoleon again, as I was anxious to put the matter beyond a doubt, whether, if Talleyrand had delivered the Duc d'Enghien's letter in time to him, he would have pardoned the writer. He replied, 'It is probable that I might, for in it he made an offer of his services; besides, he was the best of the family.' " [2] It is noteworthy that although Napoleon speaks more than once to Gourgaud about the Enghien affair he never mentions the letter to that critical and incredulous officer.

Finally, the whole bubble, blown assiduously by Warden, O'Meara, and the *Letters from the Cape,* ignominiously bursts. The letter disappears, and with it the charge against Talleyrand. The narrative is brought back to historical truth by placing on record the well-known note of the Duc d'Enghien written on the report of his trial. Montholon has to engineer this remarkable metamorphosis. It is, of course, impossible to perform this task with success, but the hapless equerry extracts himself from it with something less than grace or probability. He tells us that after O'Meara's departure the surgeon's journal was left with him, and that he was in the habit of reading it aloud to his master. The Emperor, he says, pointed out some errors in the manuscript. And it seems a pity that Montholon does not place on record what these errors were, for the only statement which is corrected is that thrice solemnly made by O'Meara on the authority of Napoleon himself. We must quote textually what is said about

[1] *Voice,* i. 454.   [2] *Ibid.* ii. 58.

it. "M. O'Meara dit que M. de Talleyrand intercepta une lettre écrite par le Duc d'Enghien quelques heures avant le jugement. La vérité est que le Duc d'Enghien a écrit sur le procès verbal d'interrogatoire, avant de signer: 'Je fais avec instance la demande d'avoir une audience particulière du premier consul. Mon nom, mon rang, ma façon de penser et l'horreur de ma situation, me font espérer qu'il ne refusera pas ma demande.'" This, of course, is what the Duc d'Enghien did actually write. Then Montholon proceeds, "Malheureusement l'Empereur n'eut connaissance de ce fait qu'après l'exécution du jugement. L'intervention de M. de Talleyrand dans ce drame sanglant est déjà assez grande sans qu'on lui prête un tort qu'il n'a pas eu." [1]

We regret to declare that we do not consider this contradiction as any more authentic than the letter from the Duc d'Enghien, written at Strasburg, offering his services, and asking for a command in the army, which Talleyrand intercepted for fear it should melt Napoleon's heart. The fact and purport of that letter are clearly set forth by Warden, who saw the letter; by Las Cases, who showed it to him; by O'Meara, who twice asked Napoleon about it; by Napoleon himself, in the *Letters from the Cape*; and the main point of the story is not the appeal of the Duke, but the infamy of Talleyrand, who suppressed it. Warden produced the first statement in 1816; the *Cape Letters* appeared in 1817; O'Meara in 1822; Las Cases in 1822–3. At last, in 1847, thirty years after the statement had been first promulgated, appears Montholon's book. By this time the whole story had been hopelessly exploded. A host of elucidatory pamphlets has been published. What has not transpired is the document itself, which, though so assiduously advertised, has never seen the light. So Montholon has to make the best of a bad job, and get rid somehow of this

[1] Montholon, ii. 315. Cf. ii. 86. See, too, Montholon's dubious report (i. 217–8) of Napoleon's secret intention of pardoning Enghien and making him Constable of France!

abortive fiction. As we have said, he conjures up an episode in which he reads O'Meara's composition to the Emperor, when the Emperor corrects several errors. Montholon, however, records only one correction, which is not a correction at all, but an absolute denial of the whole story, and an explicit acquittal of Talleyrand. The statements in Warden's book, which form the text for Napoleon's remarks to O'Meara in March 1817, and the categorical assertion in the *Letters from the Cape*, which were composed by Napoleon himself, Montholon does not and cannot touch. It is no doubt true that Napoleon did not see the last words which Enghien wrote before his execution took place. But these were not a letter written from Strasburg, nor were they an application for a post in the French army, nor were they intercepted by Talleyrand. It is noteworthy that, so far from the Duc d'Enghien soliciting employment under Napoleon, we know from Savary that the Duke's fatal admission at his trial was that he had asked to serve in the British army. We may admire Montholon's loyal spirit, but we think he might have effected the retreat from an impossible position with something more of skill, and veiled it with more probability.

As to Talleyrand, his share in the Enghien affair, though no doubt obscure, is certainly not open to this particular charge. Strangely enough, and most unfortunately for Las Cases, Napoleon in his own hand left an express acquittal of Talleyrand. Méneval transcribes from the autograph notes of Napoleon on the *History* of Fleury de Chaboulon the following lines: "Prince Talleyrand behaved on this occasion as a faithful Minister, and the Emperor has never had any reproach to make to him with regard to it." [1] Talleyrand's complicity or connivance does not fall to be discussed here; that is a very different matter. But this note expressly contradicts the charge of perfidy which we are discussing, and which is the essence of the charge preferred by Las Cases.

[1] Méneval, i. 304.

Finally, it is to be noted that on his death-bed the Emperor, provoked by an attack in an English review on Savary and Caulaincourt in connection with this incident, calls for his will, and inserts in it the following sentence: "I had the Duc d'Enghien arrested and tried because it was necessary for the safety, interest, and honour of the French people, when the Comte d'Artois was, avowedly, maintaining sixty assassins in Paris. Under the same circumstances, I should do the same again." This we believe to be the truth, though not perhaps the whole truth.

We have, then, we confess, a profound distrust of this mass of illustrative documents collected by Las Cases. We cannot, indeed, call to mind a single letter (except the various protests) which is given by Las Cases and which is genuine, except the farewell letter of Napoleon to Las Cases himself. Strangely enough, such is the fatality attaching to letters in this collection, Gourgaud gives a totally different version even of this one; yet Gourgaud read it under circumstances that would have stamped it on his memory. In this case, however, the version of Las Cases is supported by Lowe, and is no doubt the true one.

Whence came all these manuscripts? When and where was "the mass of documents formed or collected to justify certain mysterious parts of the history" of the Emperor's reign? Are we to understand that Napoleon hurriedly culled them at the Elysée or Malmaison after Waterloo—a letter to Louis, a letter to Murat, a letter to Bernadotte,—from his enormous correspondence? We know that the letters which he considered at that time of most importance he confided to his brother Joseph: they were bound in volumes.[1] How, then, did he come to have these sparse but notable despatches about him? Las Cases could only, if they were genuine, have obtained them from Napoleon, and Las Cases was not in the confidence of Napoleon till long after the Emperor was cut off from his

[1] Las Cases, i. 114, and note.

papers. Whence, then, come these casket letters? Las Cases could tell us, but does not: and no one else can. The only hint we obtain is from Gourgaud, who, speaking of some false statement of Warden's, says that it is probably "une partie du journal faux de Las Cases," [1] from which we may conclude that Las Cases kept an ostensible record for the information of curious strangers and the public, and that this was known at Longwood.

And here we must say, with deep regret, that we wish we could clear Napoleon of complicity with this manufacture. Could we shut our eyes to the evidence of the authorship of the *Letters from the Cape*, or did we choose to take that pamphlet as a sort of trial-balloon sent forth by the Emperor but not intended to carry his authority, there would be, perhaps, no absolutely certain or direct evidence of connection. Unfortunately, there is no doubt as to the authorship of the *Letters from the Cape*. Montholon, moreover, gives the letter to Murat in the midst of a narrative of Spanish affairs dictated by Napoleon. Napoleon is recorded as saying: "On the 29th of May I wrote to the Grand Duke of Berg." And then follows the spurious letter. If, then, we can trust Montholon, Napoleon declared the letter to be genuine. But we cannot in such a matter trust Montholon. We have, however, described the relations of Napoleon, as set forth by the chroniclers, to the imaginary Enghien letter. We can hardly, then, acquit Napoleon of having been at the least cognizant of these documents.

Las Cases, in his Journal, constantly treats us to comet showers of asterisks, which he assures us represent conversations with Napoleon of the utmost moment and mystery.[2] Possibly mystifications may have been concocted at these dark interviews, and if Las Cases kept any record of what then passed it would be well to publish it. Nor is it easy to under-

[1] Gourgaud, i. 525.
[2] Las Cases, ii. 298; iii. 206; v. 52, 148; vi. 7, 90, 91, 220, 233, 275–279.

NAPOLEON: THE LAST PHASE

stand that the idolater would venture to take such liberties without at least a sign from the idol. It must, moreover, be mentioned that an officer on board the *Northumberland* records that Napoleon was heard in dictation to Las Cases saying that he had received proofs of Enghien's innocence and an application from Enghien for employment, after the Duke's execution. Thiers, again, following the less emphatic opinion of Méneval, positively declares that there can be no doubt, from the evidence of the style, that the letter to Murat was composed by the Emperor. This is a damning admission if the authority of Thiers be accepted, for no one can now believe that that letter was written on the alleged date. On the other hand, Thiers is by no means infallible. Moreover, is it possible, to put things on the lowest ground, that Napoleon would associate himself with tricks so certain of discovery? Unless, indeed, what is not impossible, in a desperate mood he allowed them to be launched, careless of the future or of the verdict of history, in order to produce a momentary impression in his favour; just as he is said in the days of his power to have published in the *Moniteur* fictitious despatches from his marshals.

We offer no judgment: we care to go no further: our object is not to follow up the track further than to demonstrate the untrustworthiness of Las Cases. And we think we have said enough to show that these various fabrications lie like a bend sinister athwart the veracity of his massive volumes,[1] and make it impossible to accept any of his statements, when he has any questionable object in making them.

This being so, it is not necessary to point out minor and less elaborate inaccuracies. Pasquier, for example, complains that Las Cases gives a wholly imaginary account of the interview which Pasquier had with Napoleon on becoming Prefect of Police.[2] But the responsibility for this misstatement does

[1] See, too, what Gourgaud says (i. 523) about the "journal faux de Las Cases," and (i. 530) about his "plan."
[2] Pasquier, i. 410.

not probably lie with Las Cases. He also signalizes two other misrepresentations of the same kind.[1] But it is scarcely worth while to multiply instances.

We have, however, a further, though very minor, objection to this author, in that he is a bookmaker of an aggravated description. No sort of padding comes amiss to him. And yet the book is not without interest, and even value; for there are many cases in which he has no interest to serve, and where he records at length habits and remarks of Napoleon which we find nowhere else, the genuineness of which must be decided by internal evidence or probability. Las Cases, too, is by far the most Boswellian of the biographers, the most minute, the most insensible to ridicule, and in that respect affords some amusement. Some, indeed, of his flights towards the sublime hover perilously near the other extreme; as, for example, when he feels an indescribable emotion on seeing Napoleon rub his stomach. The Emperor has some coffee for breakfast, which he enjoys. "Quelques moments plus tard il disait, en se frottant l'estomac de la main, qu'il en sentait le bien là. Il serait difficile de rendre mes sentiments à ces simples paroles." [2]

Again, Napoleon tells him that when speaking to Lowe he became so angry that he felt a vibration in the calf of his left leg, which is one of his portentous symptoms, and one which he had not felt for years.[3]

Again, Las Cases records, in the true Boswellian strain, that Napoleon had called him a simpleton, consoling him with the assurance that he always meant the epithet as a certificate of honesty.[4]

Again, Las Cases speaks with rapture of the absence of all personal feeling in Napoleon. "He sees things so completely in the mass, and from so great a height that men escape him. Never has one surprised him in any irritation against any of those of whom he has had most to complain." [5] Were it possible

---

[1] Pasquier, i. 445–84, note.   [2] Las Cases, i. 348.
[3] Ibid. iii. 291.   [4] Ibid. vi. 157.   [5] Ibid. i. 359.

on other grounds to give complete credit to the narrative of Las Cases this stupendous assertion would make us pause.

The memoirs of Montholon are, like the author, eminently suave and gentlemanlike. O'Meara accuses him, in private letters to the English staff, of being untruthful,[1] and O'Meara should be a good judge. It must, too, be mentioned that as to one crucial and capital fact Montholon comes into direct collision with Bertrand. Each of them declares that he, having received the Emperor's solemn injunctions to do so, closed Napoleon's eyes after death. We are bound to confess that it would take much to make us distrust Bertrand on such a question. Nor can it be doubted that where Montholon's memoirs bear upon the general strategy of Longwood they are of little value, like all the publications within thirty years of Napoleon's death—though it should be remembered that they appeared late, not till 1847. Nor are the dates given always exact; and this inaccuracy gives the impression that the entries may have been written up some time afterwards. It is sufficiently obvious, indeed, that portions of the book are insertions long subsequent to the exile. We cannot, therefore, accept Montholon's unsupported statement as sufficient authority for any fact of importance. For example, he explicitly states that he closed Napoleon's eyes after death. Bertrand not less circumstantially states that he performed this pious office. Both allege that they acted on the Emperor's express injunction. We are compelled to believe one or the other, and we have no difficulty in believing Bertrand, who has not made other statements to which it is impossible to give credence. But, then, what of Montholon? We can only commend his tone, which is due, no doubt, to the date of publication. A quarter of a century had cooled many passions and allayed many feuds. Gourgaud had ceased to rage, and had amicably co-operated with Montholon in the production of the Emperor's memoirs. Hence, Montholon has not a word in his diary against Gour-

[1] Forsyth, i. 72, 184, 186; cf. Didot, p. 86, Gourgaud, ii. 195.

gaud, or even reflecting on Gourgaud, at a time when that
fretful porcupine must have been making his life almost intolerable. Indeed, at the time of Gourgaud's challenge, there is
simply a blank of ten days. Whether this judicious reticence
is due to anguish of mind; or whether, what is not impossible,
the whole transaction was what our ancestors would have
called a flam; or whether, on consideration, the entries were
cancelled, it is impossible now to say. We incline to the last
hypothesis, and regret, now that Gourgaud's journal is published, that Montholon's cannot as a counterblast be given in
its entirety. We know that he left in manuscript a great mass
of notes of conversation. One at least of these, the record of a
monologue of Napoleon's on March 10, 1819, has been published, and exceeds in interest anything in Montholon's book.
It is greatly to be desired that these notes should be unreserv-
edly given to the world. Were this done, we might have a
record not inferior in interest to that of Gourgaud. What we
chiefly regret about the book as it stands are the obvious
insertions and suppressions, due, no doubt, to blind veneration
for Napoleon's memory, and to solicitude for the political interests of Napoleon's nephew. There is, as is said of pictures,
a want of atmosphere—that is, of the atmosphere of St.
Helena. There is too much of the political colouring of Paris
or Ham. It languishes, moreover, just when it would have
been most fruitful—that is, after the departure of the other
chroniclers, Las Cases, O'Meara, and Gourgaud, when we
have nothing else to depend upon, except the imaginative
excursions of Antommarchi.

For, in the last days of all, we are left mainly to Antommarchi, and no one of the chroniclers is less veracious. He
was a young Corsican anatomist of some distinction, and
arrived at St. Helena eighteen months before Napoleon's
death. On his way through London he consulted Sir H. Holland on Napoleon's symptoms. As a Corsican, selected by
Cardinal Fesch, he should have been agreeable to the Em-

peror. But he was unlucky, for on several occasions he was absent when Napoleon wanted his aid.[1] Moreover, his illustrious patient, who in any case did not love physicians, thought him too young and inexperienced.[2] And, according to Montholon, Antommarchi treated the illness of Napoleon as trifling, and even feigned. Yet Montholon speaks well of him, as "an excellent young man," [3] and has no conceivable object for misrepresenting him. When, in March 1821, Napoleon complains of feeling internal stabs, as of a pen-knife, caused by the hideous disease which had then almost killed him, Antommarchi laughs.[4] Nothing, says Montholon, will make him believe, within seven weeks of the end, in the gravity, or even in the reality, of Napoleon's condition.[5] He is persuaded that the illness is only a political game, played with the intention of persuading the English Government to bring the Emperor back to Europe.[6] He declares, with a smile of incredulity, on March 20, that Napoleon's pulse is normal,[7] although on March 17 he had written a letter, printed by O'Meara with great unction, giving "undoubted facts" with regard to the perilous condition of the Emperor's health, which could only be amended by his removal. On March 21, however, he recognizes the seriousness of the situation, and declares that he sees undeniable signs of gastritis.[8] Napoleon thereupon consents, with great reluctance, to take some lemonade with an emetic. Next day, therefore, a quarter of a grain of tartar emetic was administered in some lemonade. The patient was violently sick, and rolled on the earth in agony. What the agony must have been, when we remember the ulcers which were internally devouring him, we can scarcely conceive. Antommarchi says that the effect is too strong, but that it is a necessary remedy. Napoleon, however, absolutely refuses any further medicine of the kind.[9] Next day he ordered his servant to

[1] Montholon, ii. 487–8, 507. [2] See Henry, *Events, etc.*, ii. 76–7.
[3] Montholon, i. 360. [4] *Ibid.* ii. 486. [5] *Ibid.* ii. 488. [6] *Ibid.* ii. 489.
[7] *Ibid.* ii. 490. [8] *Ibid.* ii. 491. [9] *Mémoirs du Roi Joseph* X, 261.

bring him a glass of lemonade; but the young doctor was on the watch, and craftily inserted the same dose of his favourite remedy.[1] Napoleon smelt something strange, and gave it to Montholon, who in ten minutes was horribly sick. The Emperor was naturally furious, called Antommarchi an assassin, and declared that he would never see him again.[2]

For some time past the young Corsican had been weary of his confinement, and his attendance on one whom he considered an imaginary invalid. He spent much of his time in Jamestown, or outside the limits, to the disgust of the orderly who was forced to accompany him.[3] Finally, in January 1821, he signified to Sir Thomas Reade his intention of leaving the Emperor's service and the island.[4] On January 31, 1821, he wrote to Montholon that he desired to return to Europe, and that he felt with regret his inability to gain the Emperor's confidence. Napoleon at once gave his consent in a letter which Montholon truly characterizes as "bien dure." We quote the concluding paragraph: "During the fifteen months that you have spent on the island you have not made His Majesty feel any confidence in your moral character; you can be of no use to him in his illness, and so there is no object in prolonging your stay here."[5]

In spite of this scathing sentence, Bertrand and Montholon patched up a reconciliation, and on February 6 Antommarchi was permitted to resume his service.[6] On March 23, as we have seen, there was another quarrel, and Montholon records that on March 31 Napoleon refused to allow his name to be even mentioned.[7] However, on April 3, he was allowed to be present at Dr. Arnott's visit.[8] On April 8, being again absent when summoned, he is formally told that the Emperor will never see him again.[9] On April 9 he went to Sir Hudson Lowe to request permission to return to Europe,—twenty-six days

[1] Montholon, ii. 498. [2] Forsyth, iii. 266. [3] Montholon, ii. 428.
[4] Ibid. ii. 479. [5] Ibid. ii. 481-2. [6] Ibid. ii. 482.
[7] Ibid. ii. 502. [8] Ibid. ii. 504. [9] Ibid. ii. 507.

before Napoleon's death. Lowe said that he must refer the matter to England.[1] On April 16, Arnott insisted that Napoleon should once more receive Antommarchi.[2] On April 17 Napoleon dictates a letter which he insists on Antommarchi signing as a condition of remaining, as the doctor had been accused of idle gossip and jests as to his master's habits.[3] On April 18 he is once more allowed to accompany Arnott to the patient's room.[4] On April 21, however, the English doctors hold a consultation without him;[5] and when Montholon wishes to summon him on April 29, Napoleon twice angrily refuses.[6] For the first five days of May, the last five days of life, he is allowed to watch in the room adjacent to the sick-room.[7] In the last agony, whenever he tries to moisten the lips of the dying man, Napoleon repels him and signs to Montholon.[8] Finally, on May 5, Napoleon dies, and, alone of all his attendants, omits Antommarchi from his will; though, it may be incidentally mentioned, Antommarchi produces an eighth codicil in his own favour which does not appear to have been recognized.

Why recall all this so minutely? For the simple reason that there is not a word of it in Antommarchi's book. That work, on the contrary, records nothing but the single-minded devotion of the physician, and the affectionate gratitude of the patient. For example, on the day on which Napoleon twice refused to see him, he records that the patient reluctantly accepted one of his remedies, and declared, "You can measure by my resignation the gratitude I feel for you." Napoleon, declares the doctor, added confidential directions about his funeral,—that it was to be, failing Paris, at Ajaccio, and, failing Ajaccio, near the spring in St. Helena.[9] On the 26th of March, when Napoleon would have none of him, Antommarchi represents himself as persuading Napoleon to see Arnott.[10] Montholon says that it was on the 31st that Napoleon first consented that Arnott

---

[1] Forsyth, iii. 275–7.   [2] Montholon, ii. 516.   [3] *Ibid.* ii. 516.
[4] *Ibid.* ii. 528.   [5] *Ibid.* ii. 529.   [6] *Ibid.* ii. 545.   [7] *Ibid.* ii. 546.
[8] *Ibid.* ii. 549.   [9] Antommarchi, ii. 143–4.   [10] *Ibid.* ii. 57.

should be sent for, and adds, "As for Antommarchi, he persists
in forbidding that his very name should be mentioned." [1]
Daily he records minute symptoms, and elaborate affectionate
conversations with his patient. But not a word of his being
forbidden the door, or of his contemptuous dismissal, or of his
efforts to leave the island. Yet the two volumes which contain
his record of eighteen months would have sufficed to find room
for this. It is not possible that Montholon should be guilty of
gratuitous falsehood with regard to him. Montholon is well
disposed towards Antommarchi; his statements are supported
both by documentary evidence and by the testimony of Lowe.
How, under these circumstances, these grave omissions and
assertions, can we put any confidence in the doctor's statements? No; we must take the Antommarchian narrative for
what it is worth, and that is little or nothing. For our own part,
we accept with great misgiving any of his uncorroborated statements. How, for example, can we credit that, in the midst of
this period of distrust and aversion, Napoleon should have
harangued him in this fashion: "When I am dead, each of you
will have the sweet consolation of returning to Europe. You
will see again, the one your relations, the other your friends,
and I shall find my braves in the Elysian Fields. Yes," he continued, raising his voice, "Kléber, Desaix, Bessières, Duroc,
Ney, Murat, Massena, Berthier, all will come to meet me: they
will speak to me of what we have done together. I will narrate
to them the later events of my life. In seeing me they will
become mad with enthusiasm and glory. We will talk of our
wars to the Scipios, the Hannibals, the Cæsars, the Frederics,
etc." [2] This fustian, of which Napoleon could scarcely have
been guilty before his delirium, is supposed to have been delivered to an audience of two, Antommarchi and Montholon:
—Antommarchi, who was in disgrace, and Montholon, who,
though he hung on his master's words, does not even mention
so remarkable a speech. We may safely aver that this is not

[1] Montholon, ii. 502. [2] Antommarchi, ii. 118.

what Napoleon said, but what Antommarchi considers that Napoleon ought to have said.

One service Antommarchi rendered, which almost outweighs his worthless and mendacious book. He produced a cast of Napoleon's face after his death, though even with regard to this his veracity is by no means uncontested. The original of this, now in England, represents the exquisite and early beauty of the countenance, when illness had transmuted passion into patience, and when death, with its last serene touch, had restored the regularity and refinement of youth. All who beheld the corpse were struck by this transformation. "How very beautiful," was the exclamation of the Englishmen who beheld it.[1] But Antommarchi had to fight even for the authenticity of his cast. The phrenologists fell on him and rent him. They declared the the skull had not the bumps, or the bony developments, requisite for a hero. Others averred that it was rather the face of the First Consul than of the Emperor, which is true. Others remembered that Antommarchi had not produced the cast till late in 1830.[2] Indeed, did he take it at all? Dr. Burton, the surgeon of the 66th Regiment, claimed that the cast was genuine, but that he had taken it, and that Antommarchi had nothing to do with it. We can only sum up our conclusions by declaring that we believe in the cast, but that if it be not more authentic than the book, we agree with the phrenologists.[3]

Warden's book consists of letters, addressed to the lady he afterwards married, vamped up by "a literary gentleman."[4] It bears, in passages, too obvious marks of the handiwork of the literary gentleman, who puts into Warden's mouth meditations of deplorable bathos. But in any case the book is of little value, for a simple reason. Napoleon knew no English, Warden knew no French, and their interpreter was Las Cases.[5] But we can-

[1] Henry, ii. 81.   [2] *Nouv. Biog. Générale*, Art. "Antommarchi."
[3] See as to the cast and its producer, *Annual Register*, Sept. 6, 1821.
[4] *Dict. Nat. Biog.*, Art. "Warden."
[5] Warden, p. 131. Gourgaud, i. 530.

not help wondering who translated two of Warden's tactful remarks to Napoleon. The latter had asked which was the more popular in England, the Army or the Navy. Warden replies in the noblest style, and ends, "Such a field as that of Waterloo can hardly find adequate gratitude in the hearts of Englishmen!" [1] To this Napoleon made no reply. On another occasion, Warden addressed the Emperor as follows: "The people of England appear to feel an interest in knowing your sentiments respecting the military character of the Duke of Wellington. They have no doubt that you would be just; and perhaps they may indulge the expectation that your justice might produce an eulogium of which the Duke of Wellington may be proud." Again Napoleon did not answer. [2] But we incline to hope and believe that the strain of translating these two observations was not placed on any interpreter, but that they proceed from the fertile resources of the "literary gentleman," who was not, however, equal to inventing the reply.

If anyone, however, should be inclined to give credit to this narrative, he should examine the letter of Sir Thomas Reade (head of Lowe's staff at St. Helena), which sets down three-fourths of the book as untrue. Reade adds, we think correctly, that on certain specified points, such as the death of Captain Wright, and the execution of the Duc d'Enghien, Las Cases was ordered to make explanations to Warden which could be published in Europe. [3]

Napoleon's reply to Warden was published in a little book called *Letters from the Cape*. These letters are addressed to a Lady C., who was, no doubt, Lady Clavering, a Frenchwoman who had married an English baronet, and who was a devoted adherent of the Emperor's, as well as a very intimate friend of Las Cases. They were addressed to her, and dated from the Cape in order to make the world believe that Las Cases, then at the Cape, had written them. The importance of this book arises from the fact that it is considered by the official editors of

[1] Warden, p. 186.   [2] *Ibid.* p. 196.   [3] Montholon, i. 281.

Napoleon's correspondence to be his composition, and they print it among his works. This is high authority, and is supported by the fact that a first proof of these letters is in existence with numerous corrections and additions in Napoleon's autograph. But, apart from these indications, it is abundantly clear, on the testimony both of Gourgaud and of Montholon, that the Emperor dictated these letters himself.[1] Who translated them into English, however, does not appear. If this was performed on the island, it was probably by Madame Bertrand, for O'Meara does not seem to have been in the secret of them. "The Emperor," says Gourgaud, "tells me that he does not intend to reply to Warden, but that Las Cases, now at the Cape, will reply." Gourgaud bluntly answers that he himself has seen more than ten letters dictated by Napoleon to Bertrand for publication. One, indeed, is on the table at the moment.[2] The Emperor no longer denies the authorship, and Gourgaud is taken into his confidence with regard to their composition. The letters are given to him for correction and annotation. On August 16, 1817, he reads his observations on them to Napoleon, and many of them are adopted.[3] On August 22, Montholon and Gourgaud both record that Napoleon finished the evening by having read to him the 5th, 6th, 7th, and 8th letters in reply to Warden.[4] The exiles do not admire them. The Montholons think that the Emperor in these letters puts ridiculous speeches into their mouths,[5] and Madame de Montholon goes so far as to say that they are badly written, full of "sottises" and personalities. She is vexed that the name of her husband should be cited in them. "It is all dirt," she says, "and the more you stir it up the worse it will smell"; and she believes that this pamphlet will occasion much hostile criticism.[6] It is indeed, only a pamphlet for contemporary consumption, with statements in it intended to influence public

---

[1] Gourgaud, ii. 155; Montholon, ii. 93, 171.   [2] Gourgaud, ii. 151.
[3] *Ibid*. ii. 246.   [4] *Ibid*. ii. 260; Montholon, ii. 171.
[5] Gourgaud, ii. 262.   [6] *Ibid*. ii. 268.

opinion. It has no value except from its authorship and the statement made in it of the spurious letter of the Duc d'Enghien, the existence of which the pamphlet explicitly asserts.[1]

O'Meara's *Voice from St. Helena* is perhaps the most popular of all the Longwood narratives, and few publications ever excited so great a sensation as that produced by this worthless book.[2] For worthless it undoubtedly is, in spite of its spirited flow and the vivid interest of the dialogue. No one can read the volumes of Forsyth in which are printed the letters of O'Meara to Lowe, and retain any confidence in O'Meara's facts. He may sometimes report conversations correctly, or he may not, but in any doubtful case it is impossible to accept his evidence. He was the confidential servant of Napoleon; [3] unknown to Napoleon he was the confidential agent of Lowe; and behind both their backs he was the confidential informant of the British Government, for whom he wrote letters to be circulated to the Cabinet.[4] Testimony from such a source is obviously tainted.

The book of Santini is a pure fabrication. It was written by Colonel Maceroni,[5] an Anglo-Italian follower of Murat's, who has left some readable memoirs. Santini, who had indeed little time for composition, being Napoleon's tailor, haircutter, and gamekeeper,[6] has, however, his episode in the history of the captivity. As he was waiting at dinner one night Napoleon burst forth at him, "What, brigand, you wished to kill the Governor! you villain! If you have any such notions again, you will have to deal with me." And then the Emperor explains to his guests that Santini, who had been of late on long solitary excursions with a double-barrelled gun, had admitted to another Corsican that he intended one barrel for the Governor, and the other for himself. It seemed quite natural to Santini. He wished to rid the world of a monster. "It needed all my imperial, all my pontifical, authority," said Napoleon, " to re-

[1] P. 147.   [2] Henry, ii. 41; Forsyth, i. 77, 81.   [3] Henry, ii. 41.
[4] Forsyth, i. 301-2; *Voice*, i. xiii.
[5] Maceroni, ii. 425. Cf., however, Gourgaud, ii. 94. [6] Forsyth, ii. 71.

NAPOLEON: THE LAST PHASE

strain him." [1] Santini, who was deported from the island by Sir Hudson Lowe, is said to have learned by heart Napoleon's great protest to the Powers, and so first brought it to Europe. Maceroni declares that this Corsican factotum was seized on Dutch territory by a force of Prussian cavalry and never seen again.[2] This is, of course, a fiction. Santini was harassed enough without so awesome a fate. He was hunted and spied on until he was allowed to live under surveillance at Brunn. Thence he finally returned to Paris, and ended his life, not unsuitably, as custodian of his master's tomb in the Invalides.[3]

The value of Lady Malcolm's book consists, as has been said already, in the vivid reports of Napoleon's conversations, which bear the impress of having been dictated, so to speak, red hot, by the Admiral; and in the picture it gives us of Lowe. Malcolm pleased the Emperor,[4] though on one stormy occasion he did not escape being called a fool ("Malcolm qui est un tsot"),[5] and Lady Malcolm was supposed, in her turn, to be fascinated.[6] Napoleon would talk to Malcolm three or four hours at a time; never, for reasons of etiquette, seated, or allowing a seat; both men standing or walking about, till at last they would lean against the furniture from fatigue.[7] The raciness of Napoleon's conversation, even in a translation, is notable. "I made Ossian the fashion," he exclaims.[8] "The income-tax is a good tax, for every one grumbles at it, which shows that every one pays it."[9] "Trifles are great things in France, reason nothing."[10] He tells the story of the Dey of Algiers, who, on hearing that the French were fitting out an expedition to destroy the town, said that, if the King would send him half the money that the expedition would cost, he would burn down the town him-

---

[1] Las Cases, v. 74–6; *Voice*, ii. 390; Montholon, i. 406.

[2] Maceroni, ii. 427.

[3] See *Le Tombeau de Napoléon Premier et son gardien Noël Santini*, Paris, 1857.

[4] Forsyth, i. 233; Montholon, i. 312; *Voice*, i. 65.

[5] Gourgaud, ii. 215.   [6] Didot, p. 58.   [7] Balmain, Sept. 8, 1816.

[8] Lady Malcolm, p. 22.   [9] *Ibid*. p. 20.   [10] *Ibid*. p. 97.

self.[1] It is scarcely necessary to say that Lowe disliked these
visits, for many reasons.[2] He had quarrelled with Napoleon,
therefore every one should quarrel with him. He could not
see Napoleon, therefore no one should see him.

It was now abundantly clear that the one supreme distinction at St. Helena was to obtain an interview with the Emperor;
it is also clear that this annoyed the ruler of St. Helena, with
whom no one endured an interview who could possibly avoid
it. Moreover, who could tell what terrible things might not be
said in conversation? Plans of escape might be concerted, messages might be transmitted, and, sin of sins, the Governor
might be criticized. So the person who had seen Napoleon was
expected to hurry to the Governor to report what had passed,
with the certain reward of being suspected of having suppressed something material.[3] An English lieutenant was sent
away from the island because he delayed for a few days to
report to the Governor a commonplace remark made by the
Bertrands, who had met him in a walk. Even the Admiral could
not be trusted. He soon ceased to be on speaking terms with
the Governor, but sedulously reported by letter his conversations with Napoleon. Sir Hudson's reply to the last report
charged the Admiral with suppressing matters of consequence,[4]
and "the Admiral now discovered that there was a system of
spies on the island, and that every trifle was reported to the
Governor. With open, candid Englishmen," continues the
ingenuous Lady Malcolm, "this is detestable, and must cause
incalculable evil." [5] An exchange of letters ensued between the
two high dignitaries, of so inflammable a character that their
destruction was suggested.[6] A previous correspondence has,
however, been preserved, eminently characteristic of Lowe,
whose share in it is tart, narrow, and suspicious.[7] No one who
reads it can fail to understand why he was an unfit representative of Britain in so delicate and difficult a charge.

[1] Lady Malcolm, p. 76.   [2] *Ibid.* p. 81.   [3] *Ibid.* p. 110.
[4] Lady Malcolm, p. 164; St. Cère, p. 118.
[5] Lady Malcolm, p. 166.   [6] *Ibid.* p. 165.   [7] *Ibid.* pp. 114–29.

CHAPTER THREE
Gourgaud

★

BUT the one capital and supreme record of life at St. Helena is
the private journal of Gourgaud, written, in the main at least,
for his own eye and conscience alone, without flattery or even
prejudice, almost brutal in its raw realism. He alone of all the
chroniclers strove to be accurate, and, on the whole, succeeded.
For no man would willingly draw such a portrait of himself as
Gourgaud has page by page delineated. He takes, indeed, the
greatest pains to prove that no more captious, cantankerous,
sullen, and impossible a being than himself can ever have
existed. He watched his master like a jealous woman:[1] as
Napoleon himself remarked, "He loved me as a lover loves his
mistress, he was impossible."[2] Did Napoleon call Bertrand an
excellent engineer, or Las Cases a devoted friend, or Montholon by the endearing expression of son, Gourgaud went off
into a dumb, glowering, self-torturing rage, which he fuses
into his journal; and yet, by a strange hazard, writing sometimes with almost insane fury about his master, produces the
most pleasing portrait of Napoleon that exists. The fact is, he
was utterly out of place. On active service, on the field of
battle, he would have been of the utmost service to his chief,
a keen, intelligent, devoted aide-de-camp.[3] But in the inaction
of St. Helena his energy, deprived of its natural outlet, turned
on himself, on his nerves, on his relations to others. The result
is that he was never happy except when quarrelling or grum-
bling. Napoleon himself was in much the same position. His
fire without fuel, to use Madame de Montholon's figure,[4] con-
sumed himself and those around him. But Napoleon had the
command of what luxury and companionship there was: the
others of the little colony had their wives and children. Gourgaud had nothing.

[1] Balmain, p. 653.   [2] Didot, p. 142.
[3] See De Sor, *Souvenirs du Duc de Vicence*, p. 220.   [4] *Souvenirs*, p. 67.

Napoleon seems to have been aware that Gourgaud was not the man for the place. He had originally selected Planat, a man of simple and devoted character, to accompany him.[1] Maitland had noticed on the *Bellerophon* the tears stealing down Planat's cheeks as he sat at breakfast the first day contemplating his fallen master, and had formed a high opinion of him.[2] Planat, indeed, at the moment of Napoleon's death was preparing with unshaken fidelity to proceed to St. Helena to take the place of Montholon.[3] But on his first nomination being communicated to Gourgaud there was such a scene of jealous fury that Gourgaud's name had to be substituted.[4] Gourgaud's wishes had thus been gratified, he was almost alone with the Emperor, his only resource was the Emperor, yet every day his sulkiness and susceptibility alienated the Emperor from him. We perceive in his own record constant hints from Napoleon that he had better go, which become broader and broader as time goes on. At last he departed, having first challenged Montholon. The Emperor intervened, and enveloped Montholon in his authority. Whether the duel was a comedy or not, it is impossible to say. The editors of his journal think that it was. Their case rests entirely on a document which they print in their preface from the original among Gourgaud's papers; a letter written by Montholon to Gourgaud a fortnight after the challenge, which shows that their relations were then not unfriendly, and that the departure of Gourgaud was either planned or utilized by the Emperor for purposes of his own. "The Emperor thinks, my dear Gourgaud," writes Montholon, "that you are overacting your part. He fears that Sir H. Lowe may begin to open his eyes." [5] We admit that if this letter were printed by Las Cases we should be inclined to doubt it; as it is, we have no ground for questioning its authenticity. But how much of Gourgaud's departure was dramatic and strategical, and how

[1] *Souvenirs*, p. 25. Cf. Las Cases, ii. 118.
[2] *Narrative*, p. 93.　　　　　[3] *Vie de Planat*, pp. 378–93.
[4] Maitland's *Narrative*, p. 193.　　　　　[5] Gourgaud, i. 15.

much due to profound weariness and vexation of spirit, we
cannot know: it was probably a compound. It is, however,
noteworthy that two months before the ostentatious rupture
Montholon records that the Emperor is determined to send
Gourgaud away in order to appeal to the Russian Emperor.[1]
And, according to Montholon, as will appear later, Gourgaud's departure is merely a mission to Russia. There is no
mention or question of a quarrel. This, however, is an omis-
sion probably due to the editing of 1847. Again Montholon
writes in 1841, when a prisoner at Ham, to the Chevalier de
Beauterne: "Gourgaud did not, as you think, abandon the Emperor. He left St. Helena with the consent of the Emperor,
and charged with an important mission." In fine, we believe
the truth to be this: Gourgaud was weary of the life at St.
Helena; Napoleon was weary of Gourgaud; so that Gourgaud's real and active jealousy of Montholon was utilized by
the Emperor as a means both of getting rid of Gourgaud and
of communicating with Europe through an officer who could
thoroughly explain the situation and policy of Longwood.

The value of Gourgaud's journal does not lie in the por-
trayal of himself, but of his master. Incidentally, however, it is
necessary to say much of Gourgaud as the foil who illustrates
a new view of his chief's character. Without this inducement,
we should soon have had enough of the brilliant young officer,
devoted to his master, with the unreasonable petulant jealousy
which made his devotion intolerable, but, above all, profoundly
bored. Bored with the island, bored with the confinement,
bored with the isolation, bored with celibacy, bored with court
life in a shanty involving all the burden without any of the
splendour of a palace, bored with inaction, bored with himself
for being bored. And so he is forced to sharpen his rusting
energies with quarrels, sulky rage with the Emperor, fitful
furies with Las Cases, and, when Las Cases is deported, animosity against Montholon, apparently because there is no one

else to quarrel with; for Bertrand is a laborious and futile peacemaker. The long moan of his life is Ennui. "Ennui," "Grand Ennui," "Mélancolie," "Tristesse," are his perpetual entries. Here is the sample record of a week. "Mardi 25, Ennui, Ennui! Mercredi 26, idem. Jeudi 27, idem. Vendredi 28, idem. Samedi 29, idem. Dimanche 30, Grand Ennui." [1] Again, "j'étouffe d'Ennui." [2] We fear, indeed, that, so far as Gourgaud is concerned, the compendious word Ennui would make an adequate substitute for the 1200 octavo pages of his journal. Fortunately it is not Gourgaud who is in question.

Let us confess that the more we see of him the better we like him. He first became familiar to us in warfare with Sir Walter Scott. Scott hinted that Gourgaud had acted a double part, and had been a sort of agent for the British Government. Thereupon, Gourgaud not unnaturally wished to fight Scott, and, denied the relief of pistols, betook himself to pamphlets. But to be a foe of Scott is to be the foe of Great Britain; and Gourgaud passed among us as a sort of swashbuckler of dubious reputation. As to Scott's charges we say nothing, because we know nothing, nor were they adequately dealt with by Gourgaud. All that he says which is pertinent to Scott's charge is, that never once while at Longwood did he speak to Sir H. Lowe, and that he defies anybody to show a single line in his handwriting which is not instinct with the devotion he felt for Napoleon. In making this challenge he must have been conscious that his own diary was in his own keeping, for it contains innumerable passages which would scarcely have stood his test. Moreover, he records in it more than one interview that he had with Lowe while he was at Longwood. But where at St. Helena was truth to be found? "Jesting Pilate" might long have waited for any local indication from that island.

It is alleged by Scott that "before leaving St. Helena he was very communicative both to Sir Hudson Lowe and Sturmer, the Austrian Commissioner, respecting the secret hopes and

[1] Gourgaud, i. 210.   [2] *Ibid.* i. 215.

plans which were carrying on at Longwood. When he arrived in Britain in the spring of 1818, he was no less frank and open with the British Government, informing them of the various proposals for escape which had been laid before Napoleon: the facilities and difficulties which attended them, and the reasons why he preferred remaining on the island to making the attempt." [1] Scott rests these statements on records in the State Paper Office, and on a report by Sturmer, which, with the adhesive disingenuousness of St. Helena, is not included in the French collection of Sturmer's reports, but which may be found, stripped of its date, in the gloomy recesses of Forsyth's appendix. We do not pretend or wish to adjudicate on this matter, but we do not believe that Gourgaud, an honourable and distinguished French General, long attached to the person of Napoleon, would wantonly reveal to Lowe, Bathurst, or Sturmer the real secrets of the Emperor's intimacy. We are rather inclined to believe that, either to obtain the confidence of these gentlemen, or to gratify his own sense of humour, or, most probable of all, to divert their suspicions from something else, he was mystifying them; and, perhaps, as Montholon says, over-playing his part. [2] When we read in Balmain's reports, "His denunciations of his former master are beyond decency," [3] or when he tells Balmain that he intended to shoot Napoleon on the battlefield of Waterloo and cannot understand why he failed to do so, [4] we seem to hear the warning voice of Montholon, "You are over-acting your part." His candour was at least suspicious; "ton de franchise suspect," [5] says the Russian Government in its memorial. We do not believe, for example, that it had been proposed to remove Napoleon in a trunk of dirty linen, or a beer cask, or a sugar-box, [6] or as a servant

---

[1] Cf. Ségur, vii. 288.
[2] Jackson, *Notes and Reminiscences of a Staff Officer*, p. 151.
[3] Balmain, Feb. 18, 1818. Cf. Forsyth, p. 256.
[4] Balmain, March 16, 1818.
[5] Didot, p. 302.   [6] *Ibid.*

carrying a dish.[1] Yet these, we are informed, were the revelations of Gourgaud. Across an abyss of eighty years we seem to see him wink. So too as to the £10,000 which Napoleon is said to have received in Spanish doubloons.[2] Such a parcel would be bulky and weighty:—the expenditure of such a coin would soon be traced; we know exactly the money left by Napoleon on his death, and there are no doubloons; they were, we are convinced, coined by Gourgaud for circulation to Lowe.

We think it very possible that the irritable officer did at St. Helena talk something at random, as Balmain says, in the madness of his jealous rage, and that, as Montholon says, he overdid his part. But we are convinced that he revealed nothing of the slightest importance either now or afterwards in London. Indeed, he was soon ordered out of England on account of his active devotion to the cause of his master.

It must, however, be admitted that on one occasion at St. Helena he used language which, to say the least, is ambiguous. We give it as recorded by himself. He is speaking to Montchenu, the old French Royalist Commissioner. "You are talking," says Gourgaud, "to a chevalier of St. Louis; whatever attachment I might still have felt (in 1814) for the Emperor, nothing could have made me fail in my duty to the King and my gratitude to the Duc de Berry. The proof of this is that my friend Lallemand thought me too much attached to this last prince to put me in the secret of his conspiracy. After the departure of the King and the dismissal of his household, I gave in my adhesion to the Chief of the French nation. I should always have remained faithful to the King had he remained with the army, but I thought that he abandoned us. On April 3 I was appointed by the Emperor his first orderly officer, and that is why I am here." [3] Men who use language of this kind cannot complain if they are misunderstood, or if they are held to be playing an ambiguous part.

[1] Scott's *Napoleon*, ix. 165.
[2] Forsyth, ii. 260. See, too, note.   [3] Gourgaud, i. 583.

Gourgaud was, it should be remembered, esteemed by all who knew him and did not have to live with him. But the curse of his temper was jealousy, which made him an impossible companion. It empoisoned his life at St. Helena. Long after his departure from St. Helena the success of Ségur's narrative of the Russian campaign maddened him and drove him to publishing a waspish, unworthy criticism of it in a thick volume, which has by no means attained the enduring fame of the history which it professes to review. By others whom his jealousies did not touch he was highly esteemed. Lowe, for example, always considered and described him as a gallant and loyal soldier who followed his Emperor in adversity, without mixing himself up in vexations and complaints. Jackson says the same thing. "He is a brave and distinguished officer," says Sturmer, "but no courtier;" [1] and this description sums him up exactly. He was so little of a courtier that the proceedings of courtiers irritate him. When Las Cases exclaims, on hearing some military narrative of Napoleon's, that it is finer than the *Iliad*, Gourgaud, like Burchell in the *Vicar of Wakefield*, says audibly, "Fudge," or its equivalent. The narrative had been dictated to and put in form by Las Cases; so Gourgaud grimly remarks, "I can see Achilles well enough, but not Las Cases as Homer." [2] He is so repelled by this sort of thing that Napoleon ceases to confide his compositions to him, and keeps them for the less formidable criticisms of Las Cases.[3] He had seen the brilliant side of Court life at the Tuileries when he had other things to think of than the relative favour of courtiers; now he sees nothing but the seamy side, and has nothing to think of but the confidence shown to others and the coldness to himself. He becomes more and more sullen, and, consequently, a less and less agreeable companion. Take, for example, this: Napoleon asks what time it is. "Ten o'clock, Sire." "Ah! how long the nights are!" "And the days, Sire?" [4] At last Napoleon says

[1] St. Cère, p. 164.   [2] Gourgaud, i. 235. Cf. Montholon, i. 351.
[3] Gourgaud, ii. 197, 192-3.   [4] *Ibid.* i. 342.

frankly to him: "What right have you to complain that I only
see and dine with Montholon? You are always gloomy and do
nothing but grumble. Be as gloomy as you please, so long as
you do not appear gloomy in my presence." [1] And, though we
cannot blame Gourgaud for being melancholy, we think
Napoleon was right. In a society of four men, one of whom, at
any rate, might well be held to require the anxious treatment
of a convalescent after a terrible fall, there should have been a
sustained effort in the common interest to combat depression.
Gourgaud made no such effort; he was the embodiment of
captious melancholy, yet he could not understand why his
bilious companionship was not eagerly sought. But to the
blank hopelessness of St. Helena a Knight of Sorrowful
Countenance was an intolerable addition. And indeed, on
more than one occasion, Gougaud embarrassed his master by
weeping in conversation. "Je pleure" is not an unfrequent
entry.[2]

Moreover, Gourgaud was not merely passively gloomy; he
became actively a bore. He began on every slight occasion to
detail his services and his claims, as a preface or an epilogue to
a long recital of his wrongs. Bertrand suffered much of this
with exemplary patience; for Gourgaud's conception of conversation with Bertrand is embodied in this entry: "He talks of
his worries, and I of mine." [3] But at last he told Gourgaud
that no longer, even on this mutual principle, could he be
wearied with Gourgaud's complaints.[4] One of Gourgaud's
great achievements was the having saved Napoleon's life at the
Battle of Brienne.[5] He was supposed, by Warden at any rate,
to have had his sword engraved with an account of this exploit.
This was all very well; but Napoleon heard too much of it,[6]

[1] Gourgaud, ii. 445, cf. 444.
[2] E.g. Gourgaud, i. 106, 429, 431; ii. 62, 290.
[3] Ibid. ii. 352.　　　　　[4] Ibid. ii. 372.
[5] Ibid. i. 2, 335; Warden, p. 208; Forsyth, i. 76.
[6] Napoleon contradicted the story to O'Meara also, Forsyth, ii. 135.
Montholon inserts (ii. 19) a dubious confirmation. Fain, who is trust-

and so the following scene occurred:—*Gourgaud:* "I never had engraved on my sword that I had saved your life, and yet I killed a hussar that was attacking your Majesty." *Napoleon:* "I do not recollect it." *Gourgaud:* "This is too much!" and so poor Gourgaud storms. At last the Emperor puts a stop to this outburst of spleen, by saying that Gourgaud is a brave young man, but that it is astonishing that with such good sense he should be such a baby.[1] And Gourgaud had good sense. With regard to the disputes with Sir Hudson, his good sense is nothing less than portentous. With regard to one letter of complaint, he declares boldly that "the less one writes about eating and drinking the better, as these sordid details lend themselves to ridicule." [2] Again, speaking of the Emperor, he says: "He is working at a reply to Lord Bathurst, but one cannot make a noble rejoinder out of the question of eatables." [3] He protests against the waste of the servants at Longwood, and makes the remark, full of the truest sense and dignity: "In our position the best course is to accept the last." [4]

On the whole position he writes with wisdom, and a conviction of what was the proper attitude of Napoleon. "The only law that the Emperor can follow, in my opinion, is neither to insult nor be friends with Hudson Lowe. It would be unworthy of His Majesty to be on cordial terms with that person. The Emperor's position is so frightful that the only method of maintaining his dignity is to appear resigned, and to do nothing to obtain any change in the restrictions. We must endure everything with resignation. If His Majesty had all the island to himself, it would be nothing compared to what he has lost." [5] Would that Napoleon had followed his counsel.

The household at Longwood was not, and could not be, a

worthy, narrates the incident, *Manuscrit de 1814*, pp. 74-5. But I should judge that Fain depended much on Gourgaud for information here and elsewhere, as he looms large in Fain's books. Jackson saw the sword (p. 153). Cf. Pétiet, *Souvenirs Militaires*, p. 87 and note.

[1] Gourgaud, i. 531-2.   [2] *Ibid.* i. 186.   [3] *Ibid.* ii. 99.
[4] *Ibid.* i. 213.   [5] *Ibid.* i. 324.

happy family; [1] but it might have been much happier than it
was. It could not be happy, in the first place, of course, because of the prodigious vicissitude.[2] But, secondly, a collection
of Parisians could not be cheerful, perched like crippled sea-
birds on a tropical rock. St. Helena had been chosen because it
was one of the remotest of islands; for that reason it was antipathetic to the whole lives and nature, and to every taste, of
these brilliant people. There was no space, no society, no
amusement. There was a meagre shop, but even there they
were refused credit by order of the Governor.[3] All things considered, they bore this fate, so irksome to anyone, so terrible
to them, with fortitude and philosophy.

The jealousies which haunt a court forbade them to be a little
less unhappy than they were. For them, at this petty court,
where neither fortune nor places could be awarded, there was
only one dignity, only one consolation—the notice of the Emperor, which alone gave rank and consideration.[4] Hence anger,
envy, and tears. Bertrand had soon remarked them: "His
Majesty," he said, in April 1816, "is the victim of intriguers.
Longwood is made detestable by their disputes." [5] As a rule
Bertrand comforts himself by declaring that the Emperor is
just at bottom, and that though intriguers sometimes get the
upper hand for a moment, he always in the long run returns to
sound judgment. But jealousy began with the very first night
on the island. In Napoleon's limited lodging he had room for
only one companion, and he chose Las Cases: Las Cases, a
mere acquaintance, as it were, of the eleventh hour. Las Cases
at once became the enemy of the human race, so far as his
colleagues were concerned. And so they hated him until he
was removed, when they all fell on his neck and forgave him.[6]

[1] Forsyth, i. 230; Las Cases, ii. 37; vi. 76.
[2] Montholon, i. 305   [3] Gourgaud, i. 171; Forsyth, i. 165.
[4] Gourgaud, i. 222.   [5] *Ibid*. i. 152.
[6] Las Cases, viii. 32. See Napoleon's appeasing discourse to his
suite in Las Cases, iii. 95, and his remarks, vi. 76.

Then Montholon and Gourgaud fell out, till Gourgaud departed. Then, when two out of the four had gone, the other two seemed to have remained in peace of some kind, but we may gather that the preference shown to Montholon was the source of some soreness to Bertrand.

Another subject of discussion was money.[1] They speculated about the Emperor's supposed hoards with the subtle suspicion of heirs in a miser's sick-room.[2] He has given so much to one; it is untrue; he gives another a double allowance; he does not; how does another pay for dress and luxury? They torment themselves and each other with questions like these. The Emperor, with all the malice of a testator, encourages these surmises. "I have no one," he says, "to leave my money to, but my companions." [3] And this question of money has much to do with Gourgaud's furious jealousies. He is always mounting on a pinnacle whence he declares that he will take nothing from the Emperor; but he is always descending and accepting. Through a whole volume there run the narrative and variations of his mother's pension.[4] Gourgaud will not ask for one; he does ask for one; he will not take it; he will take it; and so forth: until the reader is left wondering whether Gourgaud's mother, through all these susceptibilities and delicacies, constantly aroused and constantly overcome, ever secured anything at all. In any case she and her pension became a nightmare to Napoleon, who was irritated by so much filial solicitude for the mother whom his follower had left behind in France.

Gourgaud did, indeed, air this devotion a little too often, and this irritated the Emperor. In the first place, Napoleon suspected, we think, and perhaps not unjustly, that the frequent mention of the mother and of her needy circumstances was meant as an appeal for his assistance,[5] which he was will-

---

[1] Gourgaud, i. 83, 453; Forsyth, iii. 221.
[2] Forsyth, iii. 221–2.   [3] Gourgaud, ii. 201.
[4] Gourgaud, i. 188, et passim. Cf. Montholon, ii. 143/147–8.
[5] Gourgaud, ii. 429.

ing to give, but not under pressure; so he gave it at last, irritably and ungraciously. Secondly, this good son caused some inconvenience by painting everything at St. Helena in rose-colour so as to cheer his parent.[1] His letters of this deceptive character were read by Lowe, or by Bathurst, or both, and gave them the most sensible pleasure, as affording an authoritative contradiction to Napoleon's complaints. Bathurst and Lowe henceforward cherished a sort of affection for Gourgaud.[2] This fact, and these dutifully mendacious letters, could not be agreeable to Napoleon. Thirdly, the Emperor could not bear that anyone who was devoted to him should be devoted to anyone else.[3] He required a sole and absorbing allegiance. Bertrand's wife and Gourgaud's mother offended him. "You are mad to love your mother so," said Napoleon to Gourgaud. "How old is she?" "Sixty-seven, Sire." "Well, you will never see her again; she will be dead before you return to France." Gourgaud weeps.[4]

But Napoleon's brutality was only a passing expression of annoyance at a devotion which he considered he should absorb. Napoleon made no secret of this,[5] he avowed it to Montholon. "Every one," he says, "has a dominant object of affection, and to those whom I like and honour with my confidence, I must be that object: I will share with nobody." [6] On other occasions he was even more cynical:—"Princes," he said, "only like those who are useful to them, and so long as they are useful." [7] Again, he says to Gourgaud: "After all, I only care for people who are useful to me, and so long as they are useful." [8] His followers were well aware of this guiding principle in Napoleon's relations to mankind. Bertrand in a moment of irritation confides to Gourgaud the astonishing discovery that for some

---

[1] Gourgaud, i. 221, ii. 466; Las Cases, ii. 70, note.
[2] Forsyth, ii. 467; Gourgaud, ii. 392; *Voice*, ii. 75.
[3] *E.g.* Montholon, ii. 60.   [4] Gourgaud, i. 106.
[5] Rémusat, ii. 170.   [6] Montholon, ii. 412.
[7] *Ibid.* ii. 247, 485.   [8] Gourgaud, ii. 444.

time past he has been aware that the Emperor is an egotist.[1] He only, says Bertrand, cares for those from whom he expects some service.[2] Another day he goes further. "The Emperor is what he is, my dear Gourgaud; we cannot change his character. It is because of that character that he has no friends, that he has so many enemies, and, indeed, that we are at St. Helena. And it is for the same reason that neither Drouot nor the others who were at Elba except ourselves (Madame Bertrand and himself) would follow him here." [3] Bertrand was no doubt right in saying that Napoleon had no friends, for the friends of his youth were dead; and, in the days of his power, he had denied himself that solace and that strength. "I have made courtiers; I have never pretended to make friends," he would say.[4] His imperial ideas of state and aloofness, indeed, made any idea of friendship impossible. Now the retribution had come; when he wanted friends he found only courtiers. Painfully and laboriously he endeavoured to resume the forgotten art of making friends. It was only fair, and in the nature of things, that he should be but partially successful.

It is not a pleasant trait in Napoleon that he should expect the blind renunciation of every human tie and human interest that a Messiah alone may exact; that he should desire his followers to leave all and follow him. But much excuse must be made for an egotism which was the inevitable result of the prolonged adulation of the world.

And although Gourgaud had much to bear—chiefly from the torture he inflicted on himself—we gather from his own account that the balance is largely in his favour, and that he made his companions suffer much more. Of all these, Napoleon, if he may be called a companion, had by far the most to endure.

For, as we have said, the real value of Gourgaud's book does not lie in the portraiture, interesting though it be, of himself.

[1] Gourgaud, i. 110.   [2] *Ibid.* i. 582.
[3] *Ibid.* i. 223.   [4] Chaptal, p. 251.

What is profoundly interesting is the new and original view
that it afforded of Napoleon's own character, and the faithful
notes of Napoleon's conversation in its naked strength. We
dwell on Gourgaud, not for the sake of Gourgaud, but for the
sake of Napoleon. Napoleon is the figure, Gourgaud is the foil.

We are all apt to fancy that we thoroughly understand Napoleon's disposition. Selfish, domineering, violent, and so forth.
But in this book we see a new Napoleon; strange, and contrary to our ideas: a Napoleon such as few but Rapp have hitherto presented to us. Rapp, indeed, the most independent and
unflattering of all Napoleon's generals, and who, as his aide-
de-camp, was constantly by his side, says of his master: "Many
people describe Napoleon as a harsh, violent, passionate man.
It is because they never knew him. Absorbed as he was in affairs, opposed in his plans, hampered in his projects, his humour was sometimes impatient and fluctuating. But he was so
good and so generous that he was soon appeased: though the
confidants of his cares, far from appeasing, would endeavour to
incite his anger." [1] The austere and upright Drouot constantly
averred when at Elba that the Emperor's anger was only skin-
deep.[2] "I always found him," says his private secretary, "kind,
patient, indulgent." [3] Testimonies of this kind might be multiplied from more dubious sources. But Gourgaud was certainly
one of the confidants described by Rapp. He unconsciously depicts himself as petulant, sulky, and captious to the last degree,
while we see Napoleon gentle, patient, good-tempered, trying
to soothe his touchy and morbid attendant,[4] with something
like the tenderness of a parent for a wayward child. Once, indeed, he calls Gourgaud a child.[5] Gourgaud is furious. "Me a
child! I shall soon be thirty-four. I have eighteen years of
service; I have been in thirteen campaigns; I have received
three wounds! And then to be treated like this. Calling me a

[1] Rapp, p. 7.   [2] Pons, *Souvenirs de l'Île d'Elbe*, iii.
[3] Méneval, i. 402.   [4] *E.g.* Gourgaud, i. 246.
[5] More than once. See Gourgaud, i. 268-9.

child is calling me a fool." All this he pours forth on the Emperor in an angry torrent.

The Napoleon of our preconceptions would have ordered a subordinate who talked to him like this out of the room before he had finished a sentence. What does this Napoleon do? Let us hear Gourgaud himself. "In short, I am very angry. The Emperor seeks to calm me; I remain silent: we pass to the drawing-room. His Majesty wishes to play chess, but places the pieces all awry. He speaks to me gently: 'I know you have commanded troops and batteries, but you are, after all, very young.' I only reply by a gloomy silence." [1] The insulting charge of youth is more than Gourgaud can bear. This is our Gourgaud as we come to know him. But is this the Napoleon that we have learned? Not crushing or rebuking his sullen and rebellious equerry, but trying to soothe, to assuage, to persuade.

There was no one at St. Helena who had more to endure and more to try him than the Emperor, no one whose life had been less trained to patience and forbearance, but we rise from the study of Gourgaud's volumes with the conviction that few men would have borne so patiently with so irritating an attendant. Sometimes he is so moved as to speak openly of the disparity of their burdens. Gourgaud speaks of his "chagrin." The Emperor turns upon him with pathetic truth: "You speak of sorrow, you! And I! What sorrows have I not had! What things to reproach myself with! You at any rate have nothing to regret." [2] And again: "Do you suppose that when I wake at night I have not bad moments—when I think of what I was, and what I am?" [3]

On another occasion Napoleon proposes a remedy, or a sedative, for Gourgaud's ill-humour—unique perhaps among moral and intellectual prescriptions. He suggests that the general shall set himself to translate the *Annual Register*

---

[1] Gourgaud, i. 320–1. [2] *Ibid*. ii. 340.
[3] *Ibid*. ii. 340; cf. ii. 57–8; i. 340.

into French: "You should translate the *Annual Register*, it would give you an immense reputation." To which the hapless Gourgaud replies: "Sire, this journal has no doubt merits, but—" and so deprecates the glorious task.[1] This seems to us one of the few humorous incidents in the annals of the captivity. Sometimes the Emperor builds castles in the air to cheer his sulky follower. In England, "where we shall be in a year," he will find a bride in the city for Gourgaud, with a fortune of, say, £30,000: he will visit the happy couple and enjoy fox-hunting.[2] For the meditations of the Emperor constantly turn to a suitable marriage for Gourgaud: sometimes English, sometimes French, sometimes Corsican, but always with an adequate dowry.[3]

The revelation of this book is, we repeat, the forbearance and long-suffering of Napoleon.[4] The instances of Gourgaud's petulance and insolence are innumerable. One day the Emperor orders him to copy a letter on the subject of his grievances, which was to be launched above the signature of Montholon. "I am not the copyist of M. de Montholon," replies Gourgaud. The Emperor truly says that he is wanting in respect, and he has the grace to acknowledge that he is uneasy all night.[5] Then, when Las Cases goes, the Emperor writes him a letter too warm for Gourgaud's taste. Irritated by Gourgaud's criticism and sulks, Napoleon signs it "votre dévoué." Then Gourgaud breaks out. The Emperor invites him to play chess, and asks why he is so out of temper. "Sire, I have one great fault, I am too much attached to your Majesty; I am not jealous, but I feel bound to say that this letter is not worthy of you. Good God! I see that my poor father was too honest a man. He brought me up on much too strict principles of honour and virtue. I know now that one should never tell the

---

[1] Gourgaud, ii. 262.   [2] *Ibid.* ii. 176.
[3] *Ibid.* ii. 174; i. 124, 581; ii. 85, 174, 202, 365–6, 406, 411; Montholon, ii. 233.
[4] *E.g.* Gourgaud, i. 426–31; ii. 174–6.   [5] *Ibid.* i. 241.

truth to sovereigns, and that flatterers and schemers are those who succeed with them. Your Majesty will come to understand some day what a hypocrite is this man." Napoleon replies, half wearily, half pathetically, "What do you mean? that he betrays me? After all, Berthier, Marmont, and the rest on whom I have heaped benefits, have all done it. Mankind must be very bad to be as bad as I consider it." [1]

This scene rankles, and leaves Gourgaud for a long time in so diabolical a mood that the Emperor is forced from mere weariness of these outbursts of temper to confine himself to his room.[2] When Gourgaud hears this, he immediately, by way of allaying the strain on their common life, challenges Montholon.[3] Things get worse and worse, until Gourgaud remonstrates with the Emperor on the double allowance that he gives Montholon. Napoleon points out that Montholon has a wife and family, which Gourgaud has not.[4] Still Gourgaud grumbles. At last Napoleon loses patience, and says frankly that he prefers Montholon to Gourgaud. Then, indeed, there is an explosion. Gourgaud is choked with tears, says that all the generals who have distinguished him must have been mistaken, and so forth. "Not at all," replies the Emperor; "they saw you on the field of battle, brave and active [5]—they did not," he implies, "see you as you are now." All that the reader can gather from Gourgaud's own record is that it is scarcely possible that Montholon should have been so disagreeable as not to be a preferable companion to Gourgaud. And so the incessant and wearisome scenes go on. The Emperor patient [6] and friendly: the aide-de-camp fretful, sullen, even insulting. One day, for example, he says: "Yes, Sire, provided that History does not say that France was very great before Napoleon, but partitioned after him." [7] Even

---

[1] Gourgaud, i. 315–6. [2] Ibid. i. 330–1.
[3] Ibid. i. 332. Montholon, i. 305, appears to mention an earlier challenge.
[4] Ibid. i. 553. [5] Ibid. i. 555–6. [6] Ibid. i. 246.
[7] Ibid. ii. 346.

this taunt does not ruffle his master. Another time, after a tiresome wrangle, the Emperor tells him good-humouredly to go to bed and calm himself. To which Gourgaud replies, that if he had not more philosophy and strength of mind than Napoleon he would not be able to get through the night.[1] A few weeks after this remarkable statement our diarist shows his philosophy and strength of mind by informing Bertrand that his patience is at an end and that he must box Montholon's ears.[2]

On another occasion Napoleon utters a few gloomy words. "I," he said, "though I have long years of life before me, am already dead. What a position!" "Yes, Sire," says Gourgaud, with patronizing candour, "it is indeed horrible. It would have been better to die before coming here. But as one is here, one should have the courage to support the situation. It would be so ignominious to die at St. Helena." The Emperor, in reply, merely sends for Bertrand as a more agreeable companion.[3] On yet another day the Emperor groans, "What weariness! What a cross!" Gourgaud is at once ready with his superior compassion. "It pains me, me, Gourgaud, to see the man who commanded Europe brought to this." [4] But on this occasion he keeps his pity for his journal.

This all seems incredible to us with our preconceived opinion of Napoleon, and as our business is with him, we only make these quotations to show the incessant irritations and annoyances to which he was exposed on the part of his own friends, and the unexpected gentleness and patience with which he bore them.

His companions, indeed, were not of very much comfort to him; Bertrand was much absorbed by his wife; Montholon was neither very able nor very trustworthy; Las Cases, who was an adroit and intelligent talker, was a firebrand to the jealousies of the others; Gourgaud was almost intolerable. Napoleon had to

[1] Gourgaud, ii. 356.   [2] *Ibid.* ii. 391.
[3] *Ibid.* ii. 85. Cf. Montholon, ii. 129.
[4] Gourgaud, ii. 440; Montholon, ii. 246.

make the best of them, to soothe them, to cheer them, to pay visits to Madame de Bertrand and to make presents to Madame de Montholon, to try and put Gourgaud to some mathematical and historical work which would occupy his mind. Or else the Emperor tries almost humbly to put Gourgaud into a better humour. Six weeks before the final crisis he comes beside his sulky follower, and, as this last admits, exerts himself to be agreeable. He pinches his ear—the well-known sign of his affection and good humour. "Why are you so sad? What is the matter with you? Pluck up and be gay, Gorgo, Gorgotto, we will set about a book together, my son, Gorgo." [1] "Gorgo, Gorgotto" does not record his reception of these advances. Next day, however, there is the same half-piteous appeal, "Gorgo, Gorgotto, my son." [2]

Sometimes, no doubt, Gourgaud records that the Emperor is or appears to be cold or in a bad temper. But this can generally be traced to some absorbing news, or to some behaviour or some allusion of the chronicler himself. Moreover, these occasions are rare, and we gather them only from Gourgaud's malign impressions, not from any proof of the Emperor's anger. Once in these last days there is a misunderstanding, notable only as showing Gourgaud's anxiety to misunderstand. "I shall die," says Napoleon, "and you will go away" ("vous vous en irez"). The general thinks he hears "vous vous en rirez" ("you will laugh at it"), and sees a halcyon opportunity for righteous wrath. "Although your Majesty is habitually harsh to me, this is too much. I trust you do not mean what you are saying." [3] Then there is an explanation, and the ruffled plumes are momentarily smoothed. So proceeds this one-sided, cat-and-dog life. Everything that Napoleon says and does is a grievance. When Las Cases has gone, the Montholons lurk behind everything, they are the root of all evil. Nothing can be more wearisome, more irritating than this wrong-headed record. So the reader welcomes the inevitable catastrophe.

[1] Gourgaud, ii. 419.   [2] *Ibid.* ii. 419.   [3] *Ibid.* ii. 439.

Here we must attempt to accept Gourgaud's narrative, though we confess that it appears to be mainly prepared for consumption abroad. He tells us that after one of these scenes, in which, on Gourgaud's own showing, he is entirely in the wrong, he begs Bertrand to "organize his departure." But still he delays. Before he goes he must challenge Montholon, and Madame de Montholon is so near her confinement, that he fears to agitate her. Within a week, however, of the request to Bertrand the child is born.[1] That very day Gourgaud declares to Bertrand that the moment has come to challenge Montholon. Nine years has he been with the Emperor (here follows the inevitable record of his services) and he is to be sacrificed to the Montholons. "Ah," he concludes, "the Emperor has been a great general, but what a hard heart!"[2] Still he waits a week. Then he has an interview with Napoleon, and declares his deadly intentions. "Behold my hair, which I have not cut for months, nor will cut until I am revenged." The Emperor says that he is a brigand, nay, an assassin, if he menaces Montholon, but that Montholon will kill him. "So much the better," says Gourgaud, "it is better to die with honour than to live with shame." "What do you want?" asks Napoleon; "to take precedence of Montholon, to see me twice a day—what is it?" Gourgaud sullenly replies that a brigand and assassin can ask nothing. Then the Emperor apologizes and begs him to forget those expressions. Gourgaud is mollified, consents to refrain from a challenge, if Napoleon gives him a written order to that effect, but, in a confused narrative, explains that he is resolved on leaving St. Helena.[3]

The obscurity is probably due to the fact, which we have already discussed, that the motives for his departure were mixed. It was impossible for him to continue on his present footing; he had become irksome to the Emperor, and the Emperor a torture to him: and yet, though leaving on these terms and for these causes, he was to be an agent for the

[1] Gourgaud, ii. 451.   [2] Ibid. ii. 453.   [3] Ibid. ii. 465, 466.

71

Emperor in Europe. We discern obscurely through the perplexed paragraphs that it is feared he may be suspected of being sent on a mission; that he must leave on grounds of ill-health, and with certificates of illness from O'Meara. Napoleon bids him farewell. "It is the last time we shall see each other." [1] They are destined, however, to meet again. As Gourgaud does not receive the written order, he calls out Montholon.[2] With his usual unconsciousness of humour, he sends with the challenge a gun and six louis which he had borrowed of his enemy.[3] Montholon replies that he has given his word of honour to his master not to fight under present circumstances.[4] Then Gourgaud doubles back again. The strange creature goes to Lowe, of all people, and asks his advice. Lowe says that some will think that the general is leaving because he is bored, some because he has a mission. Thereupon Gourgaud begs to be treated with extreme rigour,[5] and returns to Longwood to write a letter to Napoleon, asking leave to retire on the ground of illness. The Emperor grants permission, regretting with imperturbable gravity that the liver complaint indigenous to the island (and with which, for obvious reasons, he was always determined to credit himself) should have made another victim.[6] He receives Gourgaud once more. This last records, though, it may be presumed, very incompletely, what passes. The Emperor bids him see Princess Charlotte, on whose favour he reckoned. It may be noted, as a fair example of the difficulties that beset the seeker for truth in St. Helena, that Napoleon, when he is reported as saying this, had known for several days that she was dead.[7] He prophetically sees Gourgaud commanding French artillery against the English. "Tell them in France that I hate those scoundrels, those wretches, as

---

[1] Gourgaud, ii. 467.   [2] *Ibid.* ii. 468.   [3] *Ibid.* ii. 468.
[4] *Ibid.* ii. 526. For Gourgaud's challenge and rejoinder, see Didot, 128–30, and Forsyth, iii. 389–90.
[5] *Ibid.* ii. 469; Forsyth, ii. 247.   [6] *Ibid.* ii. 470, 529–30.
[7] *Ibid.* ii. 467; Montholon, ii. 248; *Voice*, ii. 366.

cordially as ever." (This was a gloss on the instructions he had dictated the day before, when he declared: "I have always highly esteemed the English people, and, in spite of the martyrdom imposed on me by their Ministers, my esteem for them remains.") [1] He gives the parting guest a friendly tap on the cheek. "Good-bye; we shall see each other in another world—embrace me." Gourgaud embraces him with tears, and so ends this strange, unhappy connection.[2] From another source we discover that the day before this farewell interview, the Emperor dictated to Montholon a long appeal to the Emperor of Russia, probably for the use of Gourgaud.[3] To this document we shall return later. Napoleon also gave definite instructions to Gourgaud as to his course on arriving in Europe. The general was to convey certain notes in the soles of his shoes: he was to take some of the Emperor's hair to Marie Louise.[4] There is nothing striking or particularly confidential in this paper. What was secret was probably oral.

But to return to St. Helena. There was, of course, the inevitable question of money: the usual offer and the usual refusal, the usual vagueness as to the ultimate result.[5] Then Gourgaud goes forth among the Gentiles; stays with Jackson, dines with Lowe and the Commissioners, abuses Napoleon, communicates cock-and-bull revelations, over-acts his part.[6] Meanwhile, we learn from Montholon that he is all the time secretly communicating to Longwood the result of his conversations with Sturmer and Balmain.[7] After a month of this sort of life he sails away, with the benedictions of his new friends, with letters of introduction from Montchenu,[8] with a substantial loan from Lowe in his pocket,[9] and with secret communications from Napoleon in the soles of his boots. A characteristic ending to his tormented exile.

[1] Montholon, ii. 253.   [2] Gourgaud, ii. 470–1.
[3] Montholon, ii. 251, 260.   [4] Gourgaud, ii. 531.
[5] *Ibid.* ii. 471, 482–3, *et passim.*   [6] *Ibid.* ii. 471, 484.
[7] Montholon, ii. 263.   [8] Gourgaud, ii. 484.   [9] Forsyth, ii. 259.

CHAPTER FOUR
The Deportation

★

WERE it possible, we would ignore all this literature, as it is peculiarly painful for an Englishman to read. He must regret that his Government ever undertook the custody of Napoleon, and he must regret still more that the duty should have been discharged in a spirit so ignoble and through agents so unfortunate. If St. Helena recalls painful memories to the French, much more poignant are those that it excites among ourselves.

In these days we are not perhaps fair judges of the situation, as it presented itself to the British Government. They were at the head of a coalition which had twice succeeded in overthrowing Napoleon. It had cost Great Britain, according to the spacious figures of statistical dictionaries, more than eight hundred millions sterling to effect Napoleon's removal to Elba. His return had cost them millions more, besides a hideous shock to the nervous system of nations. What all this had cost in human life can never perhaps be fairly estimated, not less than four millions of lives. The first main object, then, of the Allies—a duty to their own people, who had sacrificed so much—was to make it absolutely certain that Napoleon should never more escape. Our own view is that under no circumstances could Napoleon have ever again conquered or even resisted Europe; his energies were exhausted, and so was France for his lifetime. But the Allies could not know this; they would have been censurable had they taken such a view into consideration, and in any case, Napoleon, well or ill, active or inactive, if at large, would have been a formidable rallying-point for the revolutionary forces of Europe.

We may, therefore, consider it as admitted and established that Napoleon could never again be a free agent. It was hard for him, but he had been hard on the world. And in a sense it was the greatest compliment that could be paid him.

Napoleon surrendered himself to Great Britain, and the

Allies desired that Great Britain should be answerable for him. In what spirit did our Government accept this charge? "We wish," writes Lord Liverpool, Prime Minister, to Lord Castlereagh, Foreign Secretary, "We wish that the King of France would hang or shoot Buonaparte, as the best termination of the business." [1] To make his case clear he put it thus to Eldon:— Napoleon "must then revert either to his original character of a French subject, or he had no character at all, and headed his expedition as an outlaw and an outcast—hostis humani generis." [2] The option, as it presented itself apparently to Lord Liverpool at that time, was that Napoleon might either be handed to Louis XVIII as a subject to be treated as a rebel, or might be placed outside the pale of humanity and treated as vermin. Again he writes regretfully to Castlereagh that "if . . . the King of France does not feel himself sufficiently strong to treat him as a rebel, we are ready to take upon ourselves the custody of his person," [3] and so forth. It should in fairness be said that the Government in this matter represented a great mass, perhaps the majority, of the nation. The English people had been fighting Napoleon for a score of years, their sacrifices had been tremendous, hardly a home in Britain had escaped scatheless. Their resentment, the steadfast enmity which had carried them through, their exultation in triumph, were alike boundless. Moreover, the nature of the contest had kept them almost blocked out of Europe; and so a generation had grown up of insular narrowness, which saw no greatness in Napoleon, only the enemy of the human race. The gentry who ruled the country were all the stronger in action for their want of generosity. By a single-minded persistence they had worn down Napoleon. They were not Squire Westerns, but they were homely, determined folk; less elegant and enlightened perhaps, but perhaps more dogged and formidable than their successors. For them, if Napoleon were not to be knocked on the

[1] Yonge's *Liverpool*, ii. 199. See, too, p. 189.   [2] *Ibid.* ii. 201.
[3] *Ibid.* ii. 196.

head like a polecat, it was well that he should be clapped into
prison for life. Sir Walter Scott admits that in 1816 a considerable party in Britain still considered that Napoleon should have
been handed over to Louis XVIII to be dealt with as a rebel
subject.[1] Even so mild and excellent a person as Southey was
of that opinion, and thought that Napoleon should be put to
death.[2] Fortunately, though no thanks to our Ministers, we
are spared the memory of their having handed over Napoleon
to the French Government to be shot like Ney.

We see, then, that there was not the slightest hope of our
Government behaving with any sort of magnanimity in the
matter; though a British Prince, the Duke of Sussex, in combination with Lord Holland, recorded his public protest against
the course which was pursued.[3] Napoleon, who had thought
of Themistocles, and afterwards thought of Hannibal, had ap-
pealed, with not perhaps so much confidence as he professed, to
the hospitality of Great Britain. He had hoped, under the
name of Colonel Muiron, an early friend who had been killed
by his side, while shielding his body, at Arcola, and for whose
memory he had a peculiar tenderness, to live as an English
country gentleman.[4] This, we think, though we say so with
regret, was impossible. England was too near France for such
a solution. The throne of the Bourbons, which had become for
some mysterious reason a pivot of our policy, could never have
been safe, were it generally known that some score of miles
from the French coast there was a middle-aged French colonel who had been Napoleon. Not all the precautions that en-
closed Danae could have prevented commiseration and solicitation to so puissant a neighbour. Napoleon had been the
genius of unrest in Europe; the tradition and association
would have remained with Colonel Muiron, however respectable and domesticated that officer might be. And Napoleon, indeed, blurted out the truth at St. Helena in the pres-

[1] Scott, ix. 147. [2] Life and Letters, iv. 119, 153.
[3] Voice, i. 66, note. [4] Las Cases, i. 81.

ence of his little circle. He had just received a letter stating that there was a great change of opinion in France. "Ah!" he exclaims, "were we but in England!" [1] Moreover he would have been the innocent subject of all sorts of legal questions, which would have tormented the Government. As it was, Admiral Lord Keith was chased round his own fleet through an entire day by a lawyer with a writ, on account of Napoleon.[2]

Lastly, and we suspect that this weighed most with our rulers, he would have become the centre of much sympathy and even admiration in England itself. For Great Britain, though victorious, was by no means contented. When we recall her internal history from Waterloo till Napoleon's death, we can well understand that the presence within her United Kingdoms of the triumphant child of the Revolution would not have been considered by the Tory Ministry as a strength or support to their Government.[3] "You know enough," writes Liverpool to Castlereagh, "of the feelings of people in this country not to doubt that he would become an object of curiosity immediately, and possibly of compassion in the course of a few months." [4] The innumerable visitors who flocked to see him at Plymouth [5] confirmed the prescience of our Premier. There was indeed an extraordinary glamour about the fallen Monarch, of which he himself was quite aware. He said with confidence at St. Helena that had he gone to England he would have conquered the hearts of the English. He fascinated Maitland, who took him to England, as he had fascinated Ussher, who had conducted him to Elba. Maitland caused inquiries to be made, after Napoleon had left the *Bellerophon*, as to the feelings of the crew, and received as the result: "Well, they may

[1] Gourgaud, ii. 245.
[2] Maitland, 167–71; Scott, ix. 96; *Autobiography of the Rev. J. Hamilton Gray*, p. 335; Villemain, *Souvenirs*, ii. 514–5.
[3] Scott, ix. 287; Yonge's *Liverpool*, ii. cap. xxi.
[4] *Castlereagh Corresp*. x. 434.
[5] Maitland, pp. 117–38; Montholon, i. 105; Las Cases, i. 53–4; *Memoirs of an Aristocrat*, p. 243.

abuse that man as much as they please: but if the people of England knew him as well as we do, they would not touch a hair of his head." [1] When he left the *Northumberland*, the crew were much of the same opinion: "He is a fine fellow, who does not deserve his fate." [2] The crew which brought Montchenu held similar views.[3] When he had left the *Undaunted*, which conveyed him to Elba, the boatswain, on behalf of the ship's company, had wished him "long life and prosperity in the island of Elba, and better luck another time." [4] After two short meetings, both Hotham, the admiral, and Senhouse, the flag-captain, felt all their prejudices evaporate. "The Admiral and myself," writes Senhouse, "have both discovered that our inveteracy has oozed out like the courage of *Acres* in the *Rivals*." [5] There was a more sublime peril yet. "Damn the fellow," said Lord Keith, after seeing him, "if he had obtained an interview with His Royal Highness (the Prince Regent), in half-an-hour they would have been the best friends in England." [6] Napoleon was ultimately made aware of the danger that was apprehended from his living in England. A traveller had told him that the British Government could not suffer him there lest the Rioters should place him at their head.[7] Another had told him that he had heard Lords Liverpool and Castlereagh say that their main reason for sending him to St. Helena was their fear of his caballing with the Opposition.[8] It is unnecessary to expand. Napoleon in England would have been a danger to the Governments both of France and of Britain.

On the Continent of Europe he could only have lived in a fortress. In some countries he would have been a volcano, in others he could scarcely have escaped outrage or assassination.

[1] Maitland, pp. 233–4; *Memoirs of an Aristocrat*, p. 253.
[2] Didot, p. 49; Montholon, i. 126; Las Cases, ii. 108.
[3] Didot, p. 49.
[4] Scott, viii. 259, note. Cf. *Voice*, i. 478; Hobhouse, i. 11.
[5] Senhouse's Letters, *Macmillan's Mag.*, Sept. 1897.
[6] Maitland, p. 211.   [7] Gourgaud, ii. 259.
[8] O'Meara's *Voice*, i. 101.

In the United States he would have been outside the control of those Powers which had the greatest interest in his restraint, and, in a region where a Burr had schemed for Empire, a Napoleon would have been at least a centre of disturbance. Indeed, he frankly admitted that had he lived there he would not have confined himself like Joseph to building and planting, but would have tried to found a State.[1] Montholon avers that, as things were, the crown of Mexico was offered to Napoleon at St. Helena; [2] but this we take for what it is worth. Under these circumstances, however, it was not unnatural to select St. Helena as a proper residence for Napoleon. The Congress at Vienna, in 1814–15, had had their eye on the island [3] as a possible prison for the sovereign of Elba.[4] It was reputed to be a tropical paradise; it was remote; it possessed, said Lord Liverpool, a very fine residence which Napoleon might inhabit; [5]—as he might, no doubt, had not Lord Liverpool sent instructions that he was on no account to do so.[6] The Duke of Wellington, too, thought the climate charming,[7] but then he had not to go there; and he viewed the future of Napoleon with a robust philosophy, unmingled with any suspicion of altruism. There was, moreover, only one anchorage, and that very limited; vessels approaching the island could be descried from an incredible distance; and neutral vessels could be altogether excluded.[8]

The selection, we think, can fairly be justified, though it was a terrible shock to Napoleon and his attendants, who had hoped that at the worst their destination would be Dumbarton

[1] Montholon, ii. 197; Gourgaud, ii. 309.   [2] Montholon, ii. 63.
[3] As to removal from Elba, see *Corresp. de Talleyrand et de Louis XVIII*, pp. 43, 171.
[4] Holland's *Foreign Remin.* p. 194; Pasquier, iii. 120; *Mém. de Lafayette*, v. 345, note.
[5] Yonge's *Liverpool*, p. 199.
[6] Scott's *Napoleon*, ix. 117; Forsyth, i. 292.
[7] Stanhope's *Conversations with Wellington*, p. 137.
[8] Yonge's *Liverpool*, p. 199.

Castle or the Tower of London.[1] No good Frenchman appears to be long happy outside France, and St. Helena seemed to be the end of the world. Napoleon himself said at first that he would not go alive.[2] Eventually he recovered himself, and behaved with dignity and composure. From the very first he had much to bear. Savary and Lallemand were forbidden to accompany him, and their parting with him is described by stolid British witnesses as a scene of anguish.[3] They, with others of his suite, were shipped to Malta, and there interned. He himself was handed over to Cockburn, who seems to have entered with relish into the spirit of his instructions. Napoleon was now to be known as General Bonaparte, and treated with the same honours "as a British General not in employ." [4] He was soon made to feel that a British General not in employ was entitled to no peculiar consideration.[5] A cabin twelve feet by nine was assigned to him. When he attempted to use the adjacent room as a private study, he was at once made to understand that it was common to all officers. "He received the communication with submission and good-humour." [6] When he appeared on the deck bareheaded, the British officers remained covered.[7] Why, indeed, should they show courtesy to a half-pay officer? Napoleon, who had never been accustomed to sit at table more than twenty minutes, was wearied with the protracted English meal, and when he had taken his coffee went on deck: "rather uncivilly," thinks the Admiral, and desires every one to remain.[8] "I believe the General has never read Lord Chesterfield," [9] he remarks. This delicate irony was not lost on Napoleon's little court, one of whom was quick to retort with pertinence and effect.[10] She might have added that the Admiral could not himself have read Lord Chesterfield

[1] Montholon, i. 104–5.
[2] *Memoirs of Sir H. Bunbury*, pp. 297, 304.   [3] Maitland, p. 207.
[4] *Napoleon's Last Voyages* (1895), p. 96.   [5] Las Cases, i. 80.
[6] Cockburn, p. 6; Las Cases, i. 82.   [7] Cockburn, p. 11.
[8] *Ibid.* p. 12.   [9] *Voice*, i. 30.
[10] Forsyth, i. 146; Las Cases, i. 101.

with any great attention, as the practice of sitting over wine is one that that philosopher especially reprobates. "It is clear," notes the Admiral, "he is still inclined to act the Sovereign occasionally, but I cannot allow it." [1] Pursuing this course of discipline, he notes, a few days later, "I did not see much of General Buonaparte throughout this day, as, owing to *his appearing inclined to try to assume again improper consequence*, I was purposely more than usually distant with him." [2] A lion-tamer indeed! We were truly far removed from the days of the Black Prince and that captive sovereign of France of whom he was the guardian.

Even Montchenu, the French Commissioner, whose views as to the proper treatment of Napoleon were of the most austere character, thinks that Cockburn behaved somewhat too cavalierly to the captive. [3] He quotes Napoleon as saying: "Let them put me in chains if they like, but let them at least treat me with the consideration that is due to me." [4]

Cockburn, from his vantage-point of native chivalry, considers the "nature" of Napoleon as "not very polished," but that he is as civil as his "nature seems capable of." [5] So that the Admiral, on Napoleon's birthday, unbends so far as to drink his health, "which civility he seemed to appreciate." [6] Later again, Sir George states, with a proper appreciation of their relative stations in life, "I am always ready to meet him halfway, when he appears to conduct himself with due modesty and consideration of his present situation." [7] And at last so decently did he comport himself that he earned from the Admiral the tribute that "he has throughout shown far less impatience about the wind and the weather, and made less difficulties, than any of the rest of the party." [8]

And yet he and they had some cause for complaint. They were packed like herrings in a barrel. [9] The *Northumberland* had

---

[1] Cockburn, p. 13.   [2] *Ibid*. p. 19.   [3] Didot, p. 54.
[4] *Ibid*. p. 54.   [5] Cockburn, p. 20.   [6] *Ibid*. p. 20.
[7] *Ibid*. p. 25.   [8] *Ibid*. p. 79.   [9] *Madame de Montholon*, p. 28.

been fitted up in a desperate hurry for the reception of the
exiles; the water was so discoloured and tainted that, it was
alleged, it might well have come from India in the ship.[1]
They had the gloomiest prospect to face in the future. A little
fretfulness, then, would not have been inexcusable, at any
rate on the part of the two French ladies. But they appear to
have been fairly patient, and not to have attracted the particular censure of the fastidious Cockburn.

The Admiral himself cannot have been entirely at his ease.
His crew was in a state of scarcely suppressed mutiny. They
refused to get up anchor at Portsmouth, until a large military
force was brought on board to compel them. On the voyage
their language and conduct were beyond description; they
thought nothing of striking the midshipmen. A guard was
placed outside the Emperor's cabin to prevent communication
between the captive and the crew. Napoleon is said to have
told Cockburn that he did not doubt that he could get many
to join him.[2] What between teaching manners to Napoleon,
and discipline to his crew, Sir George's position can scarcely
have been a sinecure.

Napoleon landed at St. Helena exactly three months after
his surrender to Maitland. But he remained in charge of the
Admiral until a new governor should arrive, for the actual
Governor, Mr. Wilks, besides being the servant of the East
India Company, was not, it may be presumed, considered
equal to the novel and special functions attaching to his office,
though Wellington thinks that it would have been better to
keep him.[3] So Cockburn continued in office till April 1816,
when he was superseded by the arrival of Sir Hudson Lowe.

[1] *Madame de Montholon*, pp. 26, 30
[2] *Diaries of a Lady of Quality*, pp. 72, 75–6.
[3] Stanhope's *Conversations with Wellington*, p. 445.

CHAPTER FIVE

Sir Hudson Lowe

★

THERE are few names in history so unfortunate as Lowe's. Had he not been selected for the delicate and invidious post of Governor of St. Helena during Napoleon's residence, he might have passed through and out of life with the same tranquil distinction as other officers of his service and standing. It was his luckless fate, however, to accept a position in which it was difficult to be successful, but impossible for him. He was, we conceive, a narrow, ignorant, irritable man, without a vestige of tact or sympathy. "His manner," says the apologetic Forsyth, "was not prepossessing, even in the judgment of favourable friends." [1] "His eye," said Napoleon, on first seeing him, "is that of a hyena caught in a trap." [2] On another occasion, with even greater bitterness, he compared the aspect of the Governor to that of St. Helena. Lady Granville, who saw him two years after he had left St. Helena, said that he had the countenance of a devil. We are afraid we must add that he was not what we should call, in the best sense, a gentleman. [3] But a Government which had wished Napoleon to be hanged or shot was not likely to select any person of large or generous nature to watch over the remainder of his life; nor, indeed, had they sought one, were they likely to secure one for such a post. Lowe, however, was a specially ill choice, for a reason external to himself. He had commanded the Corsican Rangers, a regiment of Napoleon's subjects and fellow-countrymen in arms against France, and, therefore, from that sovereign's point of view, a regiment of rebels and deserters. This made him peculiarly obnoxious to the Corsican Emperor, who was not sparing of taunts on the subject. Nor was it any advantage to him to have been driven

[1] Forsyth, i. 135; cf. Seaton, pp. 105-9; Forsyth, iii. 347.
[2] Montholon, i. 244; *Voice*, ii. 154, 345.
[3] Walter Scott seems long ago to have arrived at this conclusion. See his *Letters*, ii. 203.

from Capri by General Lamarque. But not in any case, though we believe his intentions were good, and although he had just married a charming wife, whose tact should have guided him, could he ever have been a success.

In saying this we do not rely on our own impression alone. The verdict of history is almost uniformly unfavourable. We have met with only two writers who give a favourable account of Lowe, besides his official defenders. One is Henry, a military surgeon quartered at St. Helena, a friend and guest of Lowe, who gives, by the by, an admirable description of the reception of his regiment by Napoleon. Henry, throughout his two volumes, has a loyal and catholic devotion to all British governors, which does not exclude Lowe. He speaks of Sir Hudson as a much-maligned man, though he admits that his first impressions of the Governor's appearance were unfavourable, and alludes to the hastiness of temper, uncourteousness of demeanour, and severity of measures with which Lowe was credited. All these are counterbalanced in the author's mind by the talent which the Governor "exerted in unravelling the intricate plotting constantly going on at Longwood, and the firmness in tearing it to pieces, with the unceasing vigilance," [1] and so forth. No one denies the vigilance; but we have no evidence of plots at Longwood more dangerous than the smuggling of letters. The testimony, therefore, does not seem very valuable, but let it stand for what it is worth. The other authority is the anonymous author of a story called *Edward Lascelles*,[2] whose name is now known to have been Rowley Wynyard, a midshipman on board the *Menai*. Here the prejudices of the author are overcome by the hospitality of the Governor; and, in both cases, the charm of Lady Lowe seems to have been effectual. These, however, are slender bulwarks. On the other hand, we have Sir Walter Scott, with strong prepossessions in favour of High Toryism and the Liverpool Government. "It would require," says Scott, "a strong defence on the part of Sir Hudson Lowe

[1] Henry, ii. 9.   [2] *Edward Lascelles*, i. 78, etc.

himself . . . to induce us to consider him as the very rare and highly-exalted species of character to whom, as we have already stated, this important charge ought to have been entrusted." [1] Even Lowe's own biographer, whose zeal on the Government's behalf cannot be questioned by those who have survived the perusal of his book, is obliged to censure: on one occasion he says truly that one of Lowe's proceedings was uncalled for and indiscreet,[2] on others a similar opinion is not less manifest.[3] Alison, an ardent supporter of the same political creed, says that Lowe "proved an unhappy selection. His manner was rigid and unaccommodating, and his temper of mind was not such as to soften the distress which the Emperor suffered during his detention." [4] "Sir Hudson Lowe," said the Duke of Wellington, "was a very bad choice; he was a man wanting in education and judgment. He was a stupid man, he knew nothing at all of the world, and, like all men who know nothing of the world, he was suspicious and jealous." [5] Again: "I always thought that Lowe was the most unfit person to be charged with the care of Bonaparte's person." Finally, he sums the Governor up concisely: "As for Lowe, he is a damned fool." These judgments coming from Wellington, were remarkable, for he was not a generous enemy, and he thought that Napoleon had nothing to complain of. But, after all, there are certain witnesses of high character, well acquainted with Lowe, who were on the spot, whose testimony seems to us conclusive. We mean Sir Pulteney Malcolm (who was Admiral on the station) and the foreign Commissioners. Malcolm was in the same interest, was serving the same Government, and seems to have been heartily loyal to the Governor. But that did not prevent the Governor's quarrelling with him. Malcolm found, as we have seen, that the island was pervaded by the Governor's

[1] Scott, ix. 158.   [2] Forsyth, iii. 35.
[3] *Ibid.* i. 171, 199, note; iii. 279.   [4] Quoted in Forsyth, i. 124.
[5] Stanhope's *Conversations*, p. 90. See, too, Ellesmere's *Reminiscences*, p. 118.

spies, that Lowe did not treat him as a gentleman, that Lowe cross-questioned him about his conversations with Napoleon in a spirit of unworthy suspicion. They parted on the coolest terms, if on any terms at all.

The Commissioners were hostile to Napoleon, and anxious to be well with Lowe. But this was impossible. The Frenchman, Montchenu, was the most favourable, yet he writes: "I should not be surprised to hear shortly that his little head has succumbed under the enormous weight of the defence of an inaccessible rock, protected by land and sea forces. . . . Ah! What a man! I am convinced that with every possible search one could not discover the like of him." [1]

Sturmer, the Austrian, says that it would have been impossible to make a worse choice. It would be difficult to find a man more awkward, extravagant, or disagreeable.[2] "I know not by what fatality Sir Hudson Lowe always ends by quarrelling with everybody. Overwhelmed with the weight of his responsibilities, he harasses and worries himself unceasingly, and feels a desire to worry everybody else." [3] Again he writes of Lowe: "He makes himself odious. The English dread him and fly from him, the French laugh at him, the Commissioners complain of him, and every one agrees that he is half crazy." [4] Balmain, the Russian, was a favoured guest of Lowe, and ended by marrying his step-daughter. But he never ceases railing against that luckless official. "The Governor is not a tyrant, but he is troublesome and unreasonable beyond endurance." [5] Elsewhere he says, "Lowe can get on with nobody, and sees everywhere nothing but treason and traitors." [6] Lowe, indeed, did not love the Commissioners, as representing an authority other than his own. He would remain silent when they spoke to him.[7] He was inconceivably rude to

[1] Didot, p. 28.   [2] St. Cère, p. 181.   [3] Ibid. p. 178.
[4] Ibid. p. 202.   [5] Balmain, Oct. 1, 1817.
[6] Ibid. June 26, 1818.   [7] St. Cère, pp. 187–8.

them.[1] But that in itself seems no proof of his fitness for his post.

One of his freaks with regard to the Commissioners is too quaint to be omitted. He insisted on addressing them in English. Montchenu, who did not understand a word of the language, complained. Whereupon Lowe, who wrote French with facility, offered to correspond in Latin, as the diplomatic language of the sixteenth century.[2]

"The duty of detaining Napoleon's person," said Scott, ". . . required a man of that extraordinary firmness of mind, who should never yield for one instant his judgment to his feelings, and should be able at once to detect and reply to all such false arguments, as might be used to deter him from the downright and manful discharge of his office. But then, there ought to have been combined with those rare qualities a calmness of temper almost equally rare, and a generosity of mind, which, confident in its own honour and integrity, could look with serenity and compassion upon the daily and hourly effects of the maddening causes, which tortured into a state of constant and unendurable irritability the extraordinary being subjected to their influence."[3] This rather pompous and wordy definition does certainly not apply to Lowe. He was, in truth, tormented by a sort of monomania of plots and escapes: he was, if we may coin an English equivalent for a useful and untranslatable French word, meticulous almost to madness: he was tactless to a degree almost incredible. We believe that we can produce from the pages of his own ponderous biographer sufficient examples of his character and of his unfitness for a post of discrimination and delicacy.

Montholon offers Montchenu a few beans to plant, both white and green. To the ordinary mind this seems commonplace and utilitarian enough. But the Governor's was not an ordinary mind. He scents a plot: he suspects in these innocent

[1] St. Cère, pp. 189, 190, 191, 202. [2] Montholon, ii. 298, 299.
[3] Scott, ix. 150.

vegetables an allusion to the white flag of the Bourbons and the green uniform usually worn by Napoleon. He writes gravely to Bathurst: "Whether the haricots blancs and haricots verts bear any reference to the drapeau blanc of the Bourbons, and the habit vert of General Bonaparte himself, and the livery of his servants at Longwood, I am unable to say; but the Marquis de Montchenu, it appears to me, would have acted with more propriety if he had declined receiving either, or limited himself to a demand for the white alone." [1] "Sir H. Lowe," says Forsyth, "thought the matter of some importance, and again alluded to it in another letter to Lord Bathurst." [2] Even Forsyth cuts a little joke.

Take another example. A young Corsican priest is sent out to the exile. He is, like all the rest, much and necessarily bored —all the more since, as Lowe reports on the authority of Montholon, he could neither read nor write [3] when he arrived in St. Helena; an obvious exaggeration, which points, however, to a lack of intellectual resource. So he determines to try and ride, and he is naturally shy about being seen making the experiment. But he wears a jacket something like Napoleon's, though the rest of the costume is totally unlike the Emperor's. All this is reported in great detail to the Governor, and is called by Forsyth "an apparent attempt to personate Napoleon and thus deceive the orderly officer. . . . It was not an unimportant fact that Bonaparte did not leave the house that day at all." [4] We do not know the exact stress laid on this incident by Lowe. Judging from Forsyth's account it was considerable. The fact that the experimental ride of a young priest should be construed into an attempt to personate the middle-aged and corpulent exile shows the effect which an abiding panic may exercise on a mind in which suspicion has become monomania.

Bertrand's children go to breakfast with Montchenu. The little boy, on seeing a portrait of Louis XVIII, asks: "Qui est ce

[1] Forsyth, iii. 223.   [2] Ibid. iii. 224, note.
[3] Ibid. iii. 256.   [4] Ibid. iii. 232-4.

grospouf?" On being told, he adds, "C'est un grand coquin;" [1]
while his sister Hortense displays a not unnatural aversion to
the white cockade, the symbol of the party which had ruined
her family and condemned her father to death.[2] The artless
prattle of these babes is categorically recorded by the conscientious Governor for the instruction of the Secretary of State.

Balmain records an observation of Lowe, in the same strain
of exaggeration, which depicts the man. "Dr. O'Meara," says
the Governor, "has committed unpardonable faults. He informed the people there" (at Longwood) "of what was going
on in the town, in the country, on board the ships; he went in
search of news for them, and paid base court to them. Then
he gave an Englishman, on behalf of Napoleon, and secretly,
a snuff-box! What infamy! And is it not disgraceful of this
grandissime emperor thus to break the regulations?" [3] This is
not burlesque; it is serious.

The man seems to have become half crazy with his responsibility,[4] and with the sense that he was an object of ridicule both
to the French and to his colleagues, while his captive remained
the centre of admiration and interest, and, in the main, master
of the situation. He prowled uneasily about Longwood, as if
unable to keep away, though Napoleon refused to receive him.
They had, indeed, only six interviews in all, and those entirely
in the first three months of his term of office. For nearly five
years before Napoleon's death they never exchanged a word.

With regard to this question of interviews, Napoleon was
rational enough. Lowe was antipathetic to him as a man and as
his gaoler. Consequently, Napoleon lost his temper outra-
geously when they met, a humiliation for which the Emperor
suffered afterwards, and which he was therefore anxious to
avoid. Four days before their last terrible conversation of
August 18, 1816, Napoleon says, with perfect good sense and
right feeling, that he does not wish to see the Governor, be-

---

[1] *Ibid.* iii. 219.   [2] *Ibid.* iii. 226.   [3] Balmain, May 11, 1818.
[4] Scott, ix. 160: *Memoir of Hugh Elliot*, p. 413.

cause when they meet he says things which compromise his character and dignity.[1] On the 18th Lowe comes to Longwood. Napoleon escapes, but Lowe insists on seeing him, and the result fully justifies Napoleon's apprehension and self-distrust. As soon as it is over, Napoleon returns to his former frame of mind, and bitterly regrets having received the Governor, for the reasons he gave before, and determines to see him no more—a resolution to which he fortunately adhered.[2]

And yet, with all this mania of suspicion, it is curious to note that Lowe was unable to watch over those of his own household. Balmain was convinced, and brings instances to prove, that all that passed at Government House was promptly known at Longwood—perhaps through Lady Lowe's French maid.[3]

We have said that Lowe was incredibly tactless. One of his first acts was to ask Napoleon to dinner. We give the actual note as an admirable illustration of Lowe's lack of propriety and common sense. "Should the arrangements of General Bonaparte admit it, Sir Hudson and Lady Lowe would feel gratified in the honour of his company to meet the Countess at dinner on Monday next at six o'clock. They request Count Bertrand will have the goodness to make known this invitation to him, and forward to them his reply." [4] Bertrand did make the invitation known to the Emperor, who merely remarked, "It is too silly; send no reply." [5] The "Countess" was Lady Loudoun, wife of Lord Moira, Governor-General of India. A man who could ask one who, the year before, had occupied the throne of France, "to meet the Countess" at dinner, was not likely to discharge with success functions of extreme delicacy. Sir Hudson, however, regarded Napoleon as a British General not in employ, and thought it an amiable condescension to invite him to take his dinner with "the Countess." Moreover, to make his advances entirely acceptable, the Governor addressed

[1] Las Cases, v. 246.   [2] *Ibid.* v. 270, 272; Montholon, ii. 358.
[3] Balmain, March 18, 1819; Montholon, ii. 230; *Voice*, ii. 335, note.
[4] Forsyth, i. 168.   [5] Las Cases, iii. 239; Forsyth, i. 169.

Napoleon by a title which he well knew that the Emperor considered as an insult to France and to himself. With a spirit of hospitality, however, unquenched by his rebuff, Sir Hudson, three months afterwards, asked Bertrand to invite the Emperor, on his behalf, to his party on the Prince Regent's birthday, but Bertrand declined to give the message.[1] Lady Lowe, however, had the good sense to say gaily, "He would not come to my house, and I thought him perfectly right."[2]

It is unnecessary, we think, to multiply these examples, or to dilate further on the uncongenial subject of Lowe's shortcomings and disabilities. Justice, however, requires us to notice that Napoleon was avenged on his enemy by the ill-fortune which pursued Sir Hudson. He was coldly approved by his Government, but received little solace, in spite of constant solicitation. His rewards were indeed slender and unsatisfying. George IV, at a levee, shook him warmly by the hand,[3] and he was given the colonelcy of a regiment.[4] Four years later he was made commander of the forces in Ceylon.[5] This was all. Three years afterwards he returned to England in the hope of better things, visiting St. Helena on his way. He found Longwood already converted to the basest uses. The approach to it was through a large pig-sty: the billiard-room was a hay-loft: the room in which Napoleon died was converted into a stable. All trace of the garden at which the Emperor had toiled, and which had cheered and occupied his last moments, had vanished: it was now a potato-field.[6] Whatever may have been Lowe's feelings at beholding this scene of desolation and disgrace, he was not destined to witness a more cheering prospect in England. He first waited on his old patron, Lord Bathurst, who advised him at once to return to Ceylon.[7] He then went to the Duke of Wellington, and asked for a promise of the reversion of the governorship of Ceylon. The Duke replied

[1] Montholon, i. 348; Gourgaud, i. 233.
[2] Didot, p. 46.   [3] Forsyth, iii. 315.   [4] Ibid. iii. 316.
[5] Ibid. iii. 327.   [6] Ibid. iii. 330-1.   [7] Ibid. iii. 331.

that he could make no promise till the vacancy arose, but added, ambiguously enough, that no motive of policy would prevent him from employing Sir Hudson wherever that officer's services could be useful. Sir Hudson then pressed for a pension, but the Duke replied, unambiguously enough, that neither would Parliament ever grant one, nor would Mr. Peel ever consent to propose one to the House of Commons.[1] This was cold comfort from the Duke for the man whom the Duke professed to think hardly used.[2] And after the expiry of his appointment in Ceylon, he never received either employment or pension.[3] We do not know what his deserts may have been, but we think that he was hardly used by his employers.

When O'Meara's book came out, Sir Hudson had his opportunity. He determined to appeal to the law to vindicate his character. He at once retained Copley and Tindal, who bade him select the most libellous passages in the book for his affidavit in applying for a criminal information. This was easier said than done, "from the peculiar art with which the book was composed." . . . "Truth and falsehood," continued Lowe, "were so artfully blended together in the book, that he found it extremely difficult to deny them in an unqualified manner." He found it indeed so difficult that he took too long about it. O'Meara had published his book in July 1822. It was not till the latter end of Hilary Term 1823 that Lowe's counsel appeared in court to move for the criminal information. The judges held that the application was made too late. He had to pay his own costs, and his character remained unvindicated. Nor did he attempt any further efforts to clear himself, but, in the words of his admiring biographer, "he wearied the Government with applications for redress, when he had, in fact, in his own hands the amplest means of vindicating his own character." [4] These "ample means" apparently

[1] Forsyth, iii. 331–2.
[2] Stanhope's *Conversations*, p. 138.
[3] Forsyth, iii. 325, 335.   [4] *Ibid*. iii. 317, 324.

lurked in an enormous mass of papers, entrusted first to Sir Harris Nicolas, and then to Mr. Forsyth.

And when at length the vindication appeared, Sir Hudson's ill-fortune did not, in our judgment, forsake him. He himself had been dead nine years when the *Captivity of Napoleon at St. Helena*, by Forsyth, was published to clear his sore and neglected memory. It is in three massive volumes, and represents the indigestible digest of Sir Hudson Lowe's papers, extracted by that respectable author whom, in allusion to a former work, Brougham used to address as "My dearest Hortensius." [1] The result, it must be admitted, is a dull and trackless collection, though it embraces a period which one would have thought made dullness impossible. It is a dreary book crowned by a barren index. We are willing to believe that the demerits of the work are due rather to the hero than the biographer. With that question we are not concerned. But as a defence of Lowe it is futile because it is unreadable. And yet, with all its drawbacks, it renders two services to the student. For it is a repository of original documents bearing on the story: and it conclusively exposes the bad faith and unveracity of O'Meara.

[1] See Brougham's *Letters to Forsyth* (privately printed).

CHAPTER SIX
The Question of Title

★

A DISCUSSION of Lowe's character inevitably raises other questions: the nature of the grievances of which Napoleon complained, and the amount of responsibility for those grievances justly attaching to the Governor. The grievances may be ranged under three heads: those relating to title, to finance, and to custody. Of these the question of title is by far the most important, for it was not merely the source of half the troubles of the captivity,[1] but it operated as an almost absolute bar to intercourse and as an absolute veto on what might have been an amicable discussion of other grievances.

We have set forth at length the ill-advised note in which Lowe asked Napoleon to dinner. It was, in any case, a silly thing to do, but the Governor must have known that there was one phrase in it which would certainly prevent Napoleon noticing it; for in it he was styled "General Bonaparte." Napoleon regarded this as an affront. When he had first landed on the island, Cockburn had sent him an invitation to a ball directed to "General Bonaparte." On receiving it, through Bertrand, Napoleon had remarked to the Grand Marshal, "Send this card to General Bonaparte; the last I heard of him was at the Pyramids and Mount Tabor." [2]

But, as a rule, he did not treat this matter so lightly. It was not, he said, that he cared particularly for the title of Emperor, but that when his right to it was challenged, he was bound to maintain it. We cannot ourselves conceive on what ground it was disputed. He had been recognized as Emperor by every Power in the world except Great Britain, and even she had recognized him as First Consul, and been willing to make peace with him both in Paris and at Châtillon. He had been anointed Emperor by the Pope himself: he had been

---

[1] See, *e.g.*, Henry, ii. 59–61; Scott, ix. 143; *Voice*, i. 161.
[2] *Letters from the Cape*, p. 85.

twice solemnly crowned, once as Emperor, and once as King. He had received every sanction which tradition, or religion, or diplomacy could give to the imperial title, and as a fact had been the most powerful emperor since Charlemagne. In France the titles he had given, the dukes and marshals and knights whom he had created, all were recognized. The sovereign source of these was by implication necessarily recognized with them. The Commissioners appointed to accompany Napoleon to Elba were especially enjoined to give him the title of Emperor and the honours due to that rank. Wellington himself used to send messages to Joseph—the mere transient nominee of Napoleon—as to "the King." It seems impossible, then, to surmise why, except for purposes of petty annoyance, our rulers refused to recognize Napoleon's admission to the caste of Kings; for, as Consalvi remarked at Vienna in 1814, "It is not to be supposed that the Pope went to Paris to consecrate and crown a man of straw." [1] But that refusal was the keynote of their policy, vehement and insistent, and it affords an admirable object-lesson of the range and wisdom of that Ministry. In the Act which passed through Parliament "for the more effectually detaining" him "in custody," he is carefully called "Napoleon Buonaparté," [2] as if to deny that he had ever been French at all. This would be pitiable, were it not ridiculous.

Cockburn had on shipboard, as we have seen, resolutely inaugurated this solemn farce. And so soon as he landed he thus answered a note in which Bertrand mentioned the Emperor: "Sir, I have the honour to acknowledge the receipt of your letter and note of yesterday's date, by which you oblige me officially to explain to you that I have no cognizance of any Emperor being actually upon this island, or of any person possessing such dignity having (as stated by you) come hither with me in the *Northumberland*. With regard to yourself, and the other officers of distinction who have accompanied you

[1] Beausset, ii. 242.   [2] Forsyth, iii. 449.

here," and so he proceeds. Napoleon was one of these! Cockburn complacently sends the correspondence to Bathurst, with a note in which he speaks of "General Bonaparte (if by the term 'Emperor' he meant to designate that person)." This is too much even for Forsyth.[1]

Lowe carried on this puerile affectation with scrupulous fidelity. Hobhouse sent his book on the Hundred Days to Napoleon, writing inside it "Imperatori Napoleoni." This, though the inscription after all in strictness meant "To General Napoleon," the conscientious Lowe sequestrated.[2] And on this occasion he laid down a principle. He had allowed letters directed under the imperial title to reach Napoleon from his relations or his former subjects, "but this was from an English person."[3] The Hon. John Elphinstone, who was grateful for attentions paid to a wounded brother at Quatre Bras, sent him some chessmen from China. Lowe made difficulties about forwarding these because they bore N and a crown.[4] We feel tempted to ask if Napoleon's linen, marked as it was with the objectionable cipher, was admitted to the honours of the island laundry.

It would be easy to multiply instances of Lowe's childishness in this respect; but we will add only one more. Three weeks before his death the sick captive sent Coxe's *Life of Marlborough,* as a token of goodwill, to the officers of the 20th Regiment. These naturally welcomed the *Life* of the greatest of English, given by the greatest of French, generals.[5] But they reckoned without their Governor. On the title-page were written the words "l'Empereur Napoléon," though not, it is believed, in Napoleon's handwriting. Lowe insisted on this inscription being torn out. To this multilation the officers would not consent. So the book was sent to England for the supreme decision of the Duke of York as Commander-in-Chief. The Duke returned it to the regiment with the sensible

---

[1] Forsyth, i. 39, 41, 62.   [2] *Ibid.* i. 193.   [3] *Ibid.* i. 193.
[4] *Ibid.* ii. 154; Montholon, ii. 111.   [5] Forsyth, iii. 277, 279.

remark that "such a gift from Napoleon to a British regiment was most gratifying to him." What must Lowe have felt in discovering such heresy in high places, and on seeing the Emperor mentioned under the excommunicated name by a British prince?

It is humiliating to be obliged to add that this pettiness survived even Napoleon himself. On the Emperor's coffin-plate his followers desired to place the simple inscription "Napoleon," with the date and place of his birth and death. Sir Hudson refused to sanction this, unless "Bonaparte" were added. But the Emperor's suite felt themselves unable to agree to the style which their master had declined to accept. So there was no name on the coffin.[1] It seems incredible, but it is true.

What are the grounds on which the British Government took up so unchivalrous and undignified an attitude? They are paraded by Scott with the same apologetic melancholy with which his own Caleb Balderstone sets forth the supper of the Master of Ravenswood. They appear to be as follows:—

"There could be no reason why Britain, in compassionate courtesy, should give to her prisoner a title which she had refused to him *de jure*, even while he wielded the Empire of France *de facto*." [2]

The sentence would be more accurately put thus, and then it seems to answer itself: "There could be no reason why Britain, when there was nothing to be got out of him in exchange, should give to her prisoner a title which she had been perfectly ready to acknowledge when there was something to be gained." For she had accredited Lords Yarmouth and Lauderdale to negotiate with the Emperor in 1806; while the imperial title and its representatives are duly set forth in the protocols of the Congress of Châtillon to which both Napoleon and the Prince Regent sent plenipotentiaries, and when, but for the distrust or fatalism or madness of Napoleon, a treaty would have been signed by both. There is, then, something

[1] Forsyth, iii. 296, note; Didot, p. 232.   [2] Scott, ix. 114.

of the ostrich in the refusal of Great Britain to recognize the style of Emperor. And it seems, to say the least of it, in face of what occurred in 1806 and 1814, a strong statement of Scott's to assert that "on no occasion whatsoever, whether directly or by implication, had Great Britain recognized the title of her prisoner to be considered as a sovereign prince." Are, then, plenipotentiaries accredited to other than sovereign princes or republics, or are plenipotentiaries from any other source admitted to the congresses of nations? Are we to understand, then, that, when Yarmouth and Lauderdale went to Paris with their full powers, or when Castlereagh and Caulaincourt compared theirs at Châtillon, the British Government did not "by implication," though not "directly," recognize Napoleon as Emperor? With whom, then, were Yarmouth and Lauderdale dealing in 1806, or Castlereagh in 1814? [1] It is declared indeed, on good authority, that in the negotiations which led up to the Peace of Amiens the British plenipotentiaries hinted their readiness to recognize the First Consul as King of France. Napoleon turned a deaf ear.[2] Pasquier, a candid critic, points out that at Châtillon Britain, "which had so long and so perseveringly refused to recognize Napoleon as Emperor of the French, found herself the Power most anxious to treat with him, as she would with a sovereign whose rights had been most incontestably recognized." [3]

Again, in what capacity and to whom was Sir Neil Campbell accredited to Elba? By the protocol of April 27, 1814, Britain had recognized the sovereignty of Elba. Who, then, was the sovereign? Was it "General Bonaparte"? But Sir Neil officially signed documents in which he was called "S. M. l'Empereur Napoléon." [4]

It is true, however, that Britain, in view of the fact that the

[1] E.g., see Talleyrand to Louis XVIII, Nov. 25, 1814 (p. 142).
[2] Méneval, i. 99, 100. Cf. Las Cases, vii. 123.   [3] Pasquier, ii. 161.
[4] Napoleon at Fontainebleau and Elba, by Sir N. Campbell (1869), pp. 196–7.

whole Continent had bowed before Napoleon, had some reason to feel a just pride in that she, at any rate, had never bent the knee, had never formally and directly acknowledged him as Emperor. This was a successful point in her policy, and had caused the keenest annoyance to Napoleon. But is it not also true that this very fact gave her a matchless opportunity of displaying a magnanimity which would have cost her nothing, and raised her still higher, by allowing as an act of favour to a vanquished enemy, an honorary title which she had never conceded as a right to the triumphant sovereign of the West?

But "the real cause . . . lay a great deal deeper," says Scott. . . . "Once acknowledged as Emperor, it followed, of course, that he was to be treated as such in every particular, and thus it would have become impossible to enforce such regulations as were absolutely demanded for his safe custody." [1] Shallow indeed must the Government have been that deemed this reason "deep." For, to any such pretension on the part of Napoleon, it need only have opposed precedents, if indeed precedents were necessary, drawn from his own reign; though in our judgment it would have been true, as well as complimentary, to say that the circumstances were as unprecedented as the prisoner. Never before, indeed, has the peace and security of the universe itself required as its fundamental condition the imprisonment of a single individual.

But for a Government which loved precedents it would have been sufficient to allege the case of King Ferdinand of Spain, interned at Valençay in the strictest custody. Napoleon might indeed have rejoined that he did not recognize Ferdinand as King, though he was so by the abdication of his father, by the acknowledgment of the Spaniards, and by hereditary right. But Napoleon's rejoinder would only have assisted our Government, who would have pointed out that neither had they recognized him.

There was, however, a higher precedent yet. There is a

[1] Scott, ix. 137–8.

Sovereign whose pretensions soar far above Empire, who is as much above terrestrial thrones, dominations, and powers, as these in their turn are above their subjects. The Pope asserts an authority only, if it be short, of the Divine government of the world. He claims to be the Vicegerent and Representative of God on earth, the disposer and deposer of crowns. Napoleon boasted that he was an anointed Sovereign; it was the Pope who anointed him. Yet this very Superintendent and Source of Sovereignty was, without being deprived of his sublime character, put into captivity by Napoleon, not as Napoleon was confined, but almost as malefactors are imprisoned. There was no idle discussion then of "irreverence to the person of a crowned head," nor, on the other hand, of denial of the dignity of the Papacy. The wearer of the triple crown was placed under lock and key by Napoleon because it suited his purpose; just as Napoleon was kept in custody for the convenience and security of the Coalition.

We think, then, that Napoleon had given convincing proof that he did not hold that it was impossible to imprison a crowned head, or impossible to keep a crowned head in custody without sanctioning "his claim to the immunities belonging to that title," and that he could have opposed no argument on that point which even our Government could not have controverted with ease.

But, says Sir Walter, "if he was acknowledged as Emperor of France, of what country was Louis XVIII King?" [1] This, indeed, is Caleb's "hinder end of the mutton ham" with a vengeance.

In the first place, Napoleon never at any time was styled Emperor of France, nor did he now wish to be called anything but the Emperor Napoleon. No one could deem that that title would affect the actual occupant of the throne of France; there was no territorial designation implied; it might be as Emperor of Elba that the style was accorded.

[1] Scott, ix. 139.

But, secondly, no more preposterous argument could be used by a British Ministry. They represented the only Government that had really committed the offence which they now pretended to apprehend. For more than forty years their reigning Sovereign had indeed styled himself King of France, though the fifteenth and sixteenth Louis had been occupying the actual throne and kingdom of France for three-fourths of the time. For thirty-three years of this period—till 1793—there had been simultaneously two Kings of France, of whom the King of Britain was the groundless aggressor and pretender. The British title of King of France had been dropped under Napoleon's consulate (when the Union with Ireland necessitated a new style), possibly not without the desire of conciliating him. But the particular objection stated by Scott in the text came with a particularly bad grace from the Ministers of George III, or indeed from the Ministers of any English Sovereign since Edward III. All this is formal and trivial enough, but the whole argument concerns a formal triviality.

It is strange that Scott, the antiquary, should have forgotten all this. But it is at any rate fortunate for the British Government that they did not use Scott's belated argument to Napoleon himself, who would have pounced like a hawk on so suicidal a contention. And he would further have reminded them that he had punctiliously reserved and accorded to Charles IV full regal dignity, though he had placed his own brother Joseph on the throne of Spain.

But Sir Walter (and we quote him because his reasoning on this subject is the most pleasing and plausible) denies to Napoleon the title of Emperor not merely in respect of France, but in respect of Elba. Napoleon's "breach of the Treaty of Paris was in essence a renunciation of the Empire of Elba; and the reassumption of that of France was so far from being admitted by the Allies, that he was declared an outlaw by the Congress at Vienna." [1] We know of no renunciation in form or in es-

[1] *Ibid.* ix. 135.

sence of the title of Emperor of Elba. When Napoleon landed at Fréjus, he was, we suppose, in strict form the Emperor of Elba making war on the King of France. But either way this is a puerility unworthy of discussion.

It is, however, true that the Congress of Vienna had outlawed Napoleon. "In violating the Convention which had established him in the island of Elba, Bonaparte had destroyed the only title to which his existence was attached. . . . The Powers therefore declared that Napoleon Bonaparte has placed himself outside civil and social relations, and as the enemy and disturber of the tranquillity of the world has delivered himself 'à la vindicte publique.' " [1] Truly a compendious anathema. The curses of the mediæval Papacy or of the Jewry which condemned Spinoza were more detailed but not more effective. But, unluckily, the first breach in the Convention, which established him in the island of Elba, was not made by Napoleon but by the other side. The main obvious necessity for Napoleon in the island of Elba or elsewhere was that he should live.[2] With that object the signatories of that Treaty had stipulated that he should receive an income on the Great Book of France of two millions of francs, that his family should receive an income of two millions and a half of francs, that his son should have as his inheritance the Duchies of Parma, Piacenza, and Guastalla, and should at once assume the title of Prince of those states. Not one of these stipulations, which were the compensation for his abdication, had been observed when Napoleon left Elba. Neither he nor his relatives had ever received a franc. The Emperors of Russia and Austria, as well as Lord Castlereagh, urged on Talleyrand the execution of the Treaty. They insisted on it as a question of honour and good faith. To them Talleyrand could only answer confusedly that there was danger in supplying what

[1] See the declaration (printed in Forsyth, i. 433).
[2] *Sir Neil Campbell*, pp. 318, 343, 368.

might be used as the means of intrigue.[1] To his master he could only hint that the Powers seemed to be in earnest, and that possibly an arrangement might be made by which Britain might be jockeyed into furnishing the funds.[2]

It is a tale of ignominy and broken faith, but neither lies with Napoleon. The application on his behalf for the payment of the subsidy when due was not even answered by the French Government. Napoleon at St. Helena detailed no less than ten capital and obvious breaches of this treaty committed by the Allies. So fanatical an opponent of the Emperor as Lafayette declares that it seemed a fixed policy of the Bourbons to drive Napoleon to some act of despair. His family, says the Marquis, were plundered. Not merely was the stipulated income not paid to him, but the Ministry boasted of the breach of faith. His removal to St. Helena, as Lafayette, in spite of contradiction, insists, was demanded, and insidiously communicated to Napoleon as a plan on the point of execution. Projects for his assassination were favourably considered,[3] though these, as beyond the provisions of the Treaty, may be considered as outside our present argument. For under this head the contention is simply this, that it was the Allies and not Napoleon that broke the Treaty of Fontainebleau; that, on the contrary, he himself observed the Treaty until, on its non-fulfilment being flagrant, he quitted Elba and landed in France. In truth, he might well allege that by the non-fulfilment of the Treaty he was starved out of Elba[4]. We do not contend that this was his sole or even his main motive in leaving Elba. We only set it up as against the contention of the Allies that he was outlawed by breach of the Treaty. Were it internationally correct that he should be outlawed for the rupture of that Treaty, all the other signatory sovereigns should have been outlawed too.

---

[1] *Correspondance inédite de Talleyrand et de Louis XVIII*, pp. 42, 285–6, 307.
[2] *Ibid.* p. 288.
[3] *Mémoires de Lafayette*, v. 345.   [4] Houssaye, 1815, p. 168.

And, after this decree of outlawry was promulgated, the situation had materially changed in Napoleon's favour; for France by a plebiscite had consecrated what he had done. It is the fashion to sneer at plebiscites, and the suspicion under which they lie is not wholly undeserved. But this was the only possible expression of French opinion, the only possible form of French ratification. The will of the nation condoned or approved his return, just as it allowed the Bourbons to pass away in silence, without an arm raised to prevent or to defend them. We could perhaps scarcely expect the Coalition to take into consideration so trifling a matter as the will of the nation. But it is hard to see why the choice of the nation should be placed outside the pale of humanity, while the rejected of the nation and the deliberate violator of the Treaty of Fontainebleau should be replaced with great circumstance on the throne.

But, it may be said, if the British Government in this matter was mean and petty, was not Napoleon meaner and pettier? Should he not have been above any such contention? What did it matter to him? His name and fame were secure. Would Lord Bacon repine at not being known as Viscount St. Albans? No man will ever think of asking, as Pitt said, whether Nelson was a Baron, a Viscount, or an Earl.

With this view we have much sympathy. We may at once admit that Napoleon had risen to a historical height far above the region of titles, and that the name of General Bonaparte —the young eagle that tore the very heart out of glory—is to our mind superior to the title of First Consul or of Emperor. We may also remember that Charles V, on its being notified to him that the Diet had accepted his renunciation, said: "The name of Charles is now enough for me who henceforward am nothing;" that he at once desired that in future he was to be addressed not as Emperor but as a private person, had seals made for his use "without crown, eagle, fleece, or other device," and refused some flowers which had been sent to him because they were contained in a basket adorned with a crown.[1]

As against this we may point out that Napoleon was emphatically, as Napoleon III said of himself, a parvenu Emperor. To Charles V, the heir of half the world, the descendant of a hundred Kings, it could matter little what he was called after abdication, for nothing could divest him of his blood or his birth. Moreover, Charles's wish was to be a monk; he had quitted this earth; his gaze was fixed on heaven; he had lost the whole world to gain his own soul. But to the second son of a Corsican lawyer with a large family and slender means the same remark does not apply, and the same reflection would not occur. The habits and feelings of sovereignty were more essential and precious to him, who had acquired them by a gigantic effort, than to those who inherited them without question or trouble. He carried his idiosyncrasy to a degree which they would have thought absurd. The title of Emperor of Elba was in itself burlesque. The Grand Marshal in his hut at St. Helena transcends the characters who mum to Offenbach's music. Princes born in the purple would have seen this, and shrunk from the ridicule which such associations might cast on the sacred attributes of substantial sovereignty. But to Napoleon the title of Emperor represented the crown and summit of his dazzling career, and he declined to drop it at the bidding of a foreign enemy.

If this were all to be said for him it would be little. This, however, is but a small part of the argument. Napoleon took broader and higher ground. He considered, and, we think, justly, that the denial of the title Emperor was a slight on the French nation,[2] a contemptuous denial of their right to choose their own sovereign, an attempt to ignore many years of glorious French history, a resolve to obliterate the splendid decade of his reign.[3] If he were not Emperor, he said, no

[1] Stirling's *Charles V*, pp. 190–1.　　[2] Montholon, ii. 138.
[3] *Ibid.* ii. 137; Las Cases, v. 70–7.

more was he General Bonaparte; for the French nation had the same right to make him Sovereign that they had to make him General. If he had no right to the one title, he had no right to the other. We think that, in asserting the title as a question of the sovereign right and independence of the French people, he was standing on firm ground.

But, in truth, his position is not firm, it is impregnable. Scott devotes an ill-advised page to asking why Napoleon, who had wished to settle in England incognito, like Louis XVIII, who lived there as Count of Lille, did not condescend to live incognito at St. Helena. "It seems," says Sir Walter contemptuously, "that Napoleon . . . considered this veiling of his dignity as too great a concession on his part to be granted to the Governor of St. Helena." [1] This is an amazing sentence, when we remember Scott's advantages; "the correspondence of Sir Hudson Lowe with His Majesty's Government having been opened to our researches by the liberality of Lord Bathurst, late Secretary of State for the Colonial department." [2] The fact is, of course, that Napoleon deliberately and formally in September [3] or October 1816 [4] (when he referred to a similar offer made through Montholon to Cockburn eight months before) [5] proposed to assume the name of Colonel Muiron or of Baron Duroc. This was in reply to a note from Lowe to O'Meara of October 3, in which the Governor says: "If he (Napoleon) wishes to assume a feigned name why does he not propose one?" [6] Napoleon took him at his word, and so put him eternally in the wrong. [7] The negotiation was carried on through O'Meara, and lasted some weeks. Once or twice the high contracting parties appeared to be on the point of agreement, but we have no doubt that Sir Hudson wished to gain time to refer to his Government. Lowe, according to Mont-

---

[1] Scott, ix. 140.   [2] *Ibid.* ix. 129.   [3] Montholon, i. 392.
[4] Also in June 1816? Montholon, i. 307.
[5] Forsyth, i. 349; Montholon, i. 184, 421.
[6] *Ibid.* i. 319.   [7] *Voice*, ii. 277, 459.

holon, suggested the title of Count of Lyons, which Napoleon rejected. "I can," he said, "borrow the name of a friend, but I cannot disguise myself under a feudal title." [1] This seems sensible enough, but he had a better reason still. This very title had been discussed by the exiles on their first arrival at St. Helena, and Napoleon had appeared not averse to it; till Gourgaud had objected that it would be ridiculous, as the Canons of Lyons Cathedral were Counts of Lyons, and that the Emperor could not assume an ecclesiastical incognito.[2] This was thought to be conclusive. Meanwhile, the Governor was referring the question home. We do not know in what terms, for it is characteristic of Forsyth's murky compilation that he only prints Bathurst's reply. That reply is, indeed, amazing. Napoleon had offered a simple and innocent means of getting rid of what was not merely a perpetual irritation, but an absolute barrier to communication: for the Governor ignored all papers in which the imperial title occurred, and Napoleon ignored all others. "On the subject," says Bathurst, "of General Bonaparte's proposition I shall probably not give you any instruction. It appears harsh to refuse it, and there may arise much embarrassment in formally accepting it." [3]

We cannot conjecture the nature of the embarrassment apprehended by our Colonial Secretary. Forsyth, however, has been so fortunate, from the resources at his command, as to divine the Minister's meaning. The assumption of an incognito is, it appears, the privilege of monarchs, and not even thus indirectly could the British Government concede to Napoleon the privilege of a monarch. This particular privilege is shared by the travelling public, and even by the criminal population, who make most use of it. It would be as sagacious to refuse to a country squire the right to be addressed as "Sir" by his gamekeeper, because princes are so addressed, as to deny an assumed name to Napoleon because sovereigns and

[1] Forsyth, i. 42, 347, 353; ii. 63, etc. Montholon, i. 392; *Voice*, i. 155.
[2] Gourgaud, i. 97; Montholon, i. 184.   [3] Forsyth, ii. 122.

others use one when they voyage as private individuals. So we are still in the dark, more especially as it was Lowe who invited Napoleon to avail himself of this "privilege." But Napoleon had thus done his best: he could do no more: the blame and responsibility for all further embarrassment about title must remain not with him, not even with Lowe, but with the Ministers of George IV.

Lowe, by the by, had made a characteristically tactless suggestion of his own to solve the difficulty. He proposed to give Napoleon "the title of Excellency, as due to a Field Marshal." This judicious effort having failed, he himself cut the Gordian knot, dropped the "General," substituted "Napoleon," and called the Emperor "Napoleon Bonaparte," as it were "John Robinson." [1]

---

[1] Forsyth, ii. 211. Lowe in his letter attempts to father the idea on Bertrand! See Gourgaud, ii. 350. Cf. a composed note of Forsyth (iii. 439).

CHAPTER SEVEN
The Money Question

★

WE pass from the question of title on which we have been compelled to dilate, because it was the root of all evil, to the question of finance; which, fortunately—for it is the most squalid of the St. Helena questions—may be treated more briefly, as it is only incidental to others. The question of title has even its bearing on finance, for our Government may have held that if Napoleon was to be treated as an abdicated monarch, he might be held to require an expensive establishment. But the war had been costly, and the prisoner must be cheap. The most expensive luxury was Sir Hudson himself; his salary was £12,000 a year.[1] Napoleon and his household, fifty-one persons in all,[2] were to cost £8,000.[3] What more he required he might provide for himself. The real cost seems to have been £18,000 or £19,000 a year, though Lowe admits that Napoleon's own wants were very limited. But everything on the island was scarce and dear, "raised," as Lowe said, "to so extravagant a price," and Lowe pointed out that Bathurst's limit was impossible. The Governor magnanimously raised the captive to an equality with himself. He fixed the allowance at £12,000; and eventually there was rather more latitude. It is only fair to say that Lowe was, in this matter, less ungenerous than Bathurst, his official chief.

But, in the meantime, much had happened. Lowe was ordered by Bathurst to cut down the expenses of these fifty-one people, in the dearest place in the world, where, by all testimony, every article, even of food, was three or four times as costly as elsewhere, to £8,000 a year.[4] He writes to Montholon as to the household consumption of wine and meat. Napoleon seems to us to have treated the matter, at this stage,

[1] Forsyth, i. 119.
[2] *Ibid.* i. 151. Later on (p. 290) it is put at fifty-five.
[3] *Ibid.* i. 189, 190.   [4] *Ibid.* i. 189, 190, and note on 190, 211.

with perfect propriety. He said, "Let him do as he pleases so long as he does not speak to me about it, but leaves me alone." Even Sir Walter Scott regrets that Lowe's strict sense of duty impelled him to address the Emperor about such matters. "We could wish," he says, "that the Governor had avoided entering upon the subject of the expenses of his detention with Napoleon in person." [1] The Emperor put the point tersely enough. "Il marchande ignominieusement notre existence," he said.[2] And when Bertrand asks for a duplicate list of supplies to the Emperor, as a check on the servants, his master reproves him. "Why take the English into our confidence about our household affairs? Europe has its glasses fixed on us: the Governor will know it; the French nation will be altogether disgraced." At the same time Napoleon did not disdain, as he had not when on the throne disdained, to send for his steward and go into his accounts.[3] He tried to make and did make some reductions,[4] but he could not discuss these household details with his gaoler.

Then Lowe writes again, and Napoleon, visiting the table of his household, finds scarcely enough to eat.[5] This rests only on the authority of Las Cases, but it is not improbable that the authorities of the kitchen may have made a practical demonstration against the new economies. However that may be, Napoleon orders his silver to be broken up and sold. Montholon pleads in vain, and partially disobeys. Three lots of silver are sold at a tariff fixed by Lowe. Montholon has the Emperor's dinner served on common pottery. Napoleon is ashamed of himself—he cannot eat without disgust, and yet as a boy he always ate off such ware. "We are after all nothing but big babies." And his joy is almost infantine when Montholon next day confesses his disobedience, and restores uninjured the favourite pieces of plate.[6]

[1] Scott, ix. 178.   [2] Montholon, i. p. 385.
[3] Forsyth, i. 284, 293.   [4] *Ibid.* iii. 125.
[5] Las Cases, vi. 133; see, too, pp. 137, 158.   [6] Montholon, i, 430.

And indeed the last sale of silver had vanquished Lowe. He expressed lively regret, says Montholon; and was evidently afraid of the blame that this scandal might bring on him.[1] At any rate Napoleon remained master of the field, and there was no more trouble about money. The whole proceeding was of course a comedy. Napoleon had no need to sell a single spoon. He had ample funds in Paris, and ample funds even at St. Helena. And yet we cannot blame him. He was fighting the British Government in this matter, and we can scarcely hold that the Government was in the right. He had no weapons to fight with, and all that he could do was in some way or other to appeal to the world at large. This he did by breaking up his plate. It was a fact that must be known to every inhabitant of the island: it could not be suppressed by Lowe: thus it must soon be public property in Europe. Helpless as he was, he won the battle, and we cannot refrain from a kind of admiration, both at the result and at the meagreness of his means. Later on he attempted the same effect on a smaller scale. Fuel was short at Longwood, and Napoleon ordered Noverraz, his servant, to break up his bed and burn it.[2] This, we are told, produced a great effect among the "yamstocks" (for so were the inhabitants of St. Helena nicknamed),[3] "and the tyranny of the Governor," Gourgaud gravely adds, "is at its last gasp."[4]

Theatrical strokes were, of course, by no means unfamiliar to him. Like all great men, he was a man of high imagination, and this imagination made him keenly alive to scenic effect. While on the throne he had done much in this way, generally with success. He liked to date his victorious despatches from the palace of a vanquished monarch: he would fly into a histrionic passion before a sacred circle of ambassadors: he would play the bosom friend with a brother Emperor for weeks at a

[1] *Ibid.* i. 429. [2] Forsyth, ii. 419; *Voice*, ii. 191; Gourgaud, ii. 299.
[3] Forsyth, iii. 242, note, *Voice*, i. 91, note.
[4] Gourgaud, ii. 299; Forsyth, ii. 419.

time. He studied his costumes as carefully as any stage manager of these latter days. He would have placed in a particular part of the ranks veterans whose biographies had been supplied to him, and would delight them with the knowledge of their services. Metternich declares that the announcement of his victories was prepared with similar care. Rumours of defeat were sedulously spread: the Ministers appeared uneasy and depressed: then, in the midst of the general anxiety, the thunder of cannon announced a new triumph.[1] And his effects were generally happy. During the Russian campaign there are two more dubious instances: one of which was at least open to criticism, the other of which certainly caused disgust. In the midst of the terrible anxieties of his stay at Moscow, with fire and famine around him, with winter and disaster menacing his retreat, he dictated and sent home an elaborate plan for the reorganization of the Théâtre Français. This, of course, was to impress his staff with the ease and detachment of his mind, and France with the conviction that the administration of the Empire was carried on from Moscow with the same universal and detailed energy as in Paris. Later on, when he had to avow overwhelming calamities, he ended the ghastly record of the 29th bulletin by the announcement that the health of the Emperor had never been better. He calculated that this sentence would display him as the semi-divinity superior to misfortune, and maintain France in the faith that after all his well-being was the one thing that signified: that armies might pass and perish so long as he survived. It was inspired, perhaps, by a recollection of the sovereign sanctity with which Louis XIV had sought to encompass himself. It was at any rate the assertion of an overpowering individuality. We have something of the same nature in our own annals, though widely differing in degree and in conception. It is said that the order for the famous signal of Trafalgar, "England expects every man to do his duty," ran at first "Nelson expects

[1] Metternich, i. 56.

every man to do his duty." The sense of individuality, sublime in the admiral before the supreme victory, revolted mankind with the apparent selfishness of the general, who had led a nation to court and undergo disaster, in the very hour of catastrophe. And yet mankind perhaps was hardly just. The assertion of personality had been in Napoleon's case such a strength, that he could not afford to dispense with it even when it seemed inopportune. And we must remember that those who took part in the Russian campaign testify that the first question, the first anxiety of all was "How is the Emperor? Does he keep his health?"

On this question of expense, O'Meara represents Napoleon as making remarks so characterized by his excellent common sense, that we may believe them to be authentic. "Here through a mistaken and scandalous parsimony they (your Ministers) have counteracted their own views, which were that as little as possible should be said of me, that I should be forgotten. But their ill-treatment and that of this man have made all Europe speak of me. . . . There are still millions in the world who are interested in me. Had your Ministers acted wisely, they would have given a *carte blanche* for this house. This would have been making the best of a bad business, have silenced all complaints, and . . . would not have cost more than £15,000 or £16,000 a year." [1]

We might almost have forgiven the petty finance of the Government, had it not in one single instance overreached itself. Napoleon had asked for some books, mainly to enable him to write his memoirs. The Government supplied the books as "an indulgence" we presume not inconsistent "with the entire security of his person," [2] but they sent him in the bill or rather a demand for the sum. [3] Napoleon ordered Bertrand to refuse to pay this without a detailed account. So on his death

---

[1] *Voice*, ii. 140–1.   [2] Forsyth, i. 437.
[3] *Ibid.* i. 267, 300; ii. 355, note. Las Cases, vi. 311; Montholon, i. 315.

the books were impounded by Lowe, and sold in London for a few hundred pounds,[1] less than a quarter of what had been spent in procuring them. Their original cost had been fourteen hundred pounds, but Napoleon had added greatly to their value. Many of them, says Montholon, were covered with notes in the Emperor's handwriting; almost all bore traces of his study of them; [2] though this as usual is an exaggeration. Still, they would now be of great value and interest. Had this asset been preserved to the nation, we might have been inclined to shut our eyes as to its history and origin. The penny-unwise and pound-foolish policy of the Government lost both reputation and result.

[1] They fetched 9,986 frs. See Advielle, *La Bibliothèque de Napoléon à Ste-Hélène*, p. 31. Only nine books seem to have been annotated by the Emperor.
[2] Montholon, i. 316.

CHAPTER EIGHT
The Question of Custody

★

THE last group of grievances related to the question of custody. The main object of the coalesced Governments was, not unnaturally, that under no circumstances should Napoleon escape from confinement and trouble the world again. So they chose the most remote island that they could think of, and converted it laboriously into a great fortress. Strangers could scarcely conceal their mirth, as they saw Lowe adding sentry to sentry, and battery to battery, to render more inaccessible what was already impregnable;[1] although, before leaving England, he had avowed to Castlereagh that he saw no possible prospect of escape for Napoleon but by a mutiny of the garrison.[2] Nevertheless he increased the precautions at compound interest. Las Cases in his intercepted letter to Lucien described them with some humour, and declared that the posts established on the peaks were usually lost in the clouds.[3] Montchenu, the French Commissioner, declared that if a dog were seen to pass anywhere, at least one sentinel was placed on the spot.[4] He is indeed copious on the subject, though he considered his interest and responsibility in the matter second only to those of Lowe himself. He details with pathetic exactitude the precautions taken. The plain of Longwood, where Napoleon lived, is, he tells us, separated from the rest of the island by a frightful gully which completely surrounds it and is only crossed by a narrow tongue of land not twenty feet broad, so steep that if 10,000 men were masters of the island fifty could prevent their arriving at Longwood. One can only arrive at Longwood by this pathway, and, in spite of these difficulties, the 53rd Regiment, a park of artillery, and a company of the 66th are encamped at the gate—farther on, nearer the town, there is another post of twenty men, and the whole

[1] Balmain, Feb. 18, 1818.　　[2] Forsyth, i. 118
[3] *Ibid*. i. 483.　　[4] Didot, p. 59.

enclosure is guarded day and night, by little detachments in view of each other. At night the chain of sentries is so close that they almost touch each other. Add to this a telegraph station on the top of every hill, by which the Governor receives news of his prisoner in one minute, or at most two, wherever he may be. It is thus evident that escape is impossible, and even if the Governor were to permit it, the guardianship of the sea would prevent it. For, from the signal stations a vessel can generally be descried at a distance of sixty miles.[1] Whenever one is perceived a signal cannon is fired. Two brigs of war patrol round the island day and night: a frigate is placed at the only two places where it is possible to land.[2] (No foreign vessel, it may be added, and only a few privileged British vessels, such as men-of-war, or ships bringing necessary provisions, appear to have been allowed under any pretext to communicate with the shore.[3])

Surely, then, the agonized [4] apprehensions of the Governor were misplaced: his custody might have been less strict; and Napoleon might have then been allowed to keep himself in health by riding over this barren rock without the accompaniment of a British officer. A boyish practical joke of his, seen after reaching the island, and Cockburn's remark on it, make this more clear. Napoleon, Bertrand, and Gourgaud are out riding, followed by Captain Poppleton. Bertrand begs Poppleton not to follow so close; Napoleon sets off at a gallop with Gourgaud; they soon lose Poppleton, who, it appears, was not a dashing horseman. Poppleton, disconsolate, returns and reports to the Admiral. Cockburn laughs at the affair as a boyish joke, "une espièglerie de sous-lieutenant," and says, "It is a good lesson for you, but, as to danger of escape, there is none. My cruisers are so well posted round the island that the devil himself could not get out of it;" [5] the same conviction that Lowe had expressed to Castlereagh.

---

[1] Cf. Henry, ii. 7.   [2] Didot, pp. 60–1, 154.   [3] Gourgaud, i. 117.
[4] See *Memoir of Hugh Elliot*, p. 413.   [5] Montholon, i. 205.

Later on, when Napoleon was confined to the house by illness, the Governor became alarmed. Was the prisoner in the house at all, or was he sliding down some steep ravine to a submarine boat? He determined on a firm and unmistakable policy. He sent (August 29, 1819) a letter to "Napoleon Bonaparte" giving that personage notice that the orderly officer must see him daily, come what may, and may use any means he may see fit to surmount any obstacle or opposition; that any of Napoleon's suite who may resist the officer in obtaining this access would be at once removed from Longwood and held responsible for any results that might occur; and if the officer has not seen Napoleon by ten o'clock in the morning he is to enter the hall and force his way to Napoleon's room.[1] Brave words indeed! Napoleon replies through Montholon that there is no question for him of any choice between death and an ignominious life, and that he will welcome the first [2] —implying, of course, what he had often said,[3] that he would resist the officer by force. What happens? On September 4, Lowe comes to withdraw his instructions.[4] Forsyth omits all mention of this incident, but Montholon gives the documents, which can scarcely be fabricated. And we know that there was no result except that the unhappy officer at Longwood is stimulated to fresh exertions, and leads a miserable life. To such straits is he reduced for a sight of the prisoner that he is recommended to betake himself to the keyhole.[5] Sometimes he is more fortunate, and sees a hat, which may contain Napoleon's head.[6] Sometimes he peeps through a window and sees the prisoner in his bath. On one of these occasions Napoleon perceived him, and, issuing forth, advanced towards the captain's hiding-place in appalling nudity.[7] But, as a rule, the existence of this hapless officer is one of what hunting men would call blank days.[8]

[1] Montholon. ii. 353–5.   [2] *Ibid*. ii. 357.   [3] *Voice*, i. 44.
[4] Montholon, ii. 359.   [5] Forsyth, iii. 169.   [6] *Ibid*. iii. 182.
[7] Balmain, Aug. 19, 1819.   [8] Forsyth, iii. 172.

"April 3rd. Napoleon still keeps himself concealed. I have not been able to see him since the 25th ult. . . . April 19th. I again waited on Montholon, and told him I could not see Napoleon. He appeared surprised, and said they had seen me. . . . I was nearly twelve hours on my legs this day endeavouring to see Napoleon Bonaparte before I succeeded, and I have experienced many such days since I have been stationed at Longwood. . . . April 23rd. I believe that I saw Napoleon Bonaparte to-day in the act of stropping his razor in his dressing-room."[1] Again the hapless Captain Nicholls reports: "I must here beg leave to state that in the execution of my duty yesterday I was upon my feet upwards of ten hours, endeavouring to procure a sight of Napoleon Bonaparte, either in his little garden, or at one of his windows, but could not succeed; that during the whole of this time I was exposed to the observation and remarks of not only the French servants, but also of the gardeners and other persons employed about Longwood House; and that I have *very frequently* experienced days of this kind since I have been employed on this duty."[2]

To such a pitch had mismanagement reduced the peremptory Governor and his ministerial chiefs. Instead of "You must do this and you must do that," his officer has to lead the life of a tout, and an unsuccessful tout, exposed to the derision of the gardeners and household as well as the ironical survey of the invisible prisoner. Napoleon had won the day, mainly through the wooden clumsiness of his opponents.

So invisible indeed did the captive at last become that we learn from an officer on the island that on the arrival of newspapers from England the first inquiry of the inhabitants of St. Helena was, "What news of Bonaparte?"[3] This corroborates the statement of Antommarchi that Napoleon's death was only known in Jamestown by an order coming down for a large quantity of black cloth. This excited the curiosity of the inhabitants, which was at length set at rest by a Chinaman.

[1] Forsyth, iii. 157.   [2] *Ibid.* iii. 160–1.   [3] *Ibid.* ii. 180.

They were astonished to know that Napoleon was dead. They had no idea that he was ill.

Were there any real attempts to get Napoleon away from St. Helena? We doubt it. On one occasion, after receiving despatches from Rio Janeiro, Lowe doubled and even tripled the sentries described by Montchenu! The French Government had indeed discovered a "vast and complicated plan" to seize Pernambuco, where there were said to be 2,000 exiles, and with this force to do something unexplained to remove Napoleon. A Colonel Latapie seems to have had the credit of this vast and complicated mare's nest.[1] A "submarine vessel" —the constant bugbear of British Governments—capable of being at the bottom of the sea all day and of unnatural activity at night, was being constructed by "a smuggler of an uncommonly resolute character," called Johnstone, apparently a friend of O'Meara. But the structure of the vessel excited suspicion, and she was confiscated before completion by the British Government. Our great Scottish master of fiction narrates all this without a vestige of a smile.[2] Another submarine vessel was being constructed on, it appears, the "Sommariva system," at Pernambuco, whence most of these legends are launched.

If Maceroni can be believed, which is at the least doubtful, O'Meara, on his return from St. Helena, made preparations on a large scale for the rescue of Napoleon. "The mighty powers of steam," says Maceroni, "were mustered to our assistance. British officers volunteered to exchange out of their regiments in Europe in order to contrive being put on duty at St. Helena. But I cannot enter into particulars." This, for obvious reasons, we regret. Maceroni, however, does inform us more specifically that this great enterprise split on the money difficulty: which resolved itself into a vicious circle. The mother of Napoleon was willing to hand over her whole

[1] St. Cère, p. 263; Didot, p. 282; Balmain, Jan. 15, 1818; Scott, ix. 284; Forsyth, iii. 42–4.
[2] Scott, ix. 284.

fortune in return for the accomplished rescue of her son: O'Meara wanted money at once for the inception of the scheme. The plan, he said, could not proceed without money: the money, she said, could only be given in payment for its success. So the conspiracy, if it ever existed, came to an end.[1] The family of Bonaparte were by this time somewhat wary as to projects of rescue, and the inseparable incident of a demand for cash.

Forsyth happily preserves some of the indications of plots for escape which alarmed our Government and their agent at St. Helena. Two silly and unintelligible anonymous letters addressed to some merchants in London; another with "an obscure allusion to St. Helena, Cracow, and Philadelphia," addressed to a gentleman at Cracow; [2] news of a fast-sailing vessel being equipped by a person named Carpenter in Hudson's River; [3] these were the tidings that kept our Ministers in an agony of precaution. But even Forsyth breaks down in the narrative of a ghostly vessel which harassed our Government, and intimates that it must have been the *Flying Dutchman*.[4] And at last the shadow of tragedy comes to darken the farce; for a few months before the end, Bathurst expresses the belief that Napoleon is meditating escape.[5] The supreme escape was indeed imminent, for death was at hand.

On the other hand, Montholon's testimony on this subject is direct and simple enough. A ship captain offered, according to Montholon, on two occasions, to get Napoleon off in a boat. A million francs was the price—to be paid on the Emperor's reaching American soil. Napoleon at once refused to entertain the proposal.[6] And Montholon believes that under no circumstances would he have entertained it, even had a boat been able to reach the only possible point, and, what was also necessary, had the Emperor been able to conceal himself all day in

---

[1] Maceroni, ii. 428.   [2] Forsyth, i. 310.
[3] *Ibid*. i. 311, 455.   [4] *Ibid*. iii. 151.
[5] *Ibid*. iii. 250.   [6] Montholon, i. 348.

a ravine, and descend at night to the coast, with the risk of breaking his neck a hundred times over in the process.[1]

Again, Las Cases has a plan, and Gourgaud thinks it practicable. Napoleon "discusses the chances of success, but distinctly declares that were they all favourable he would, none the less, refuse to have anything to do with a project of escape."[2]

Montholon after this makes an entry which is significant enough. "A plan of escape," he says, "is submitted to the Emperor. He listens without interest, and calls for the *Historical Dictionary*." [3]

Nor, as we have said, do we think that Napoleon ever entertained the idea of escaping in the garb of a waiter, or in a basket of dirty linen. The Russian Government, in its memorial to the Congress of Aix-la-Chapelle in 1816, says that a feasible project of escape was laid before the Emperor. It was to have taken place on the evacuation of France by the allied armies. But the Emperor postponed it.[4] This, however, is given on the authority of Gourgaud, and is probably one of the fantastic legends with which that officer after his departure from Longwood loved to tickle the irritable credulity of Sir Hudson Lowe. Bertrand says that the actual conditions made escape impossible, and explicitly states that Napoleon never formed any such plan.

Did he indeed wish to escape? On that point we have the strongest doubts; [5] though Malcolm, it is fair to add, told Scott that escape was never out of his thoughts. How Malcolm ascertained this, however, he omitted to state.

Whither indeed could Napoleon fly? The United States of North America, his original choice of a destination, seemed the only possible refuge; and yet he firmly believed that he would

[1] Montholon, ii. 433. Cf., too, Bertrand's *Preface*, x. (the short preface to the dictated *Campagnes d'Égypte*).
[2] Montholon, i. 278. Cf. Forsyth, iii. 232; Ségur, *Mélanges*, pp. 280–2; Montholon, ii. 100–1.
[3] Montholon, i. 427.   [4] Didot, p. 302.
[5] Ségur, *Mélanges*, p. 281.

soon be assassinated there by the emissaries of the restored Government in France. To all proposals of escape he always made, according to Montholon, this reply: "I should not," he said, "be six months in America without being murdered by the assassins of the Comte d'Artois. Remember Elba—was not my assassination concerted there? But for that brave Corsican, who had accidentally been placed as quartermaster of gendarmerie at Bastia, and who warned me of the departure for Porto Ferrajo of the garde-du-corps who afterwards confessed all to Drouot, I was a dead man. Besides, one must always obey one's destiny, for all is written above. Only my martyrdom can restore the crown to my dynasty. In America I shall only be murdered or forgotten. I prefer St. Helena." [1] When another plan is presented to him, he again lays stress on the dynastic argument. "It is best for my son that I should remain here. If he lives, my martyrdom will restore his crown to him." [2]

For a man in middle life, corpulent and listless, to attempt, under any circumstances, to leave a lonely rock, garrisoned by a large military force and surrounded by vigilant cruisers, in order to reach, after a long and perilous passage by ocean, a country where he believed he would be murdered, seems preposterous. And yet these are the facts of the case. But in one respect they are understated, as they omit the most material fact of all.

For Napoleon was no longer what he had been. This is not remarkable; it would have been strange had it been otherwise. It was impossible for the human frame to stand the constant strain on body, mind, and nerve which he had imposed upon himself. In his cooler moments he was quite aware of this, and had himself laid down the law tersely, and peremptorily, for himself and others, on this subject. "Ordener is worn out," he had said at Austerlitz of one of his generals. "One has but a short time for war. I am good for another six years, and then I shall have to stop." [3] Strangely enough, his

[1] Montholon, ii. 434–5.   [2] *Ibid.* i. 286; ii. 164.
[3] Ségur, *Histoire et Mémoires*, iv. 400.

judgment was exactly verified. Six years and a month from Austerlitz would have brought him to 1812, to the Russian campaign, which, had he observed his own rule, he would have avoided. It is noteworthy that throughout 1812, and notably at the Battle of Borodino, when he was prostrate, those attached to his person, like Ségur, observed a remarkable change in his health and energy.[1] Ségur, indeed, seems to attribute the morbid and feverish activity which drove him into that fatal expedition to constitutional disease.[2] Some vivid scraps of the notebook of Duroc, his closest attendant and friend, relating to the beginning of this war, have been preserved, which confirm this view: "Aug. 7. The Emperor in great physical pain: he took opium prepared by Méthivier. 'Duroc, one must march or die. An Emperor dies standing, and so does not die. . . . *We must bring this fever of doubt to an end.*" [3] Strange stories were afloat of his signing documents as "Pompey," of his miscalling Kaluga sometimes Caligula, sometimes Salamanca. No one perhaps can estimate the shock of this Russian catastrophe. On his return the change was more marked. Chaptal, a scientific observer of his master, says that it was remarkable. Napoleon had become stout in 1809 [4] and had then to some extent degenerated. But after Moscow Chaptal observed a much greater transformation. There was a notable failure in the sequence of his ideas. His conversation consisted mainly of incoherent and imaginative bursts. There was no longer the same force of character; not the same passion or power of work. Riding fatigued him. Somnolence and the pleasures of the table gained on him.[5] It is true that with his back to the wall he fought an unrivalled campaign of defence and despair. But this was the last flash

[1] *Ibid.* iv. 83, 182–3, 381–2, 386; vi. 1, 9, 18. Hobhouse, ii. 73.

[2] Ségur, iv. 82. [3] Villemain, i. 203.

[4] He became indeed stouter after Austerlitz, for which he gives a curious reason. Miot, ii. 280.

[5] Chaptal, pp. 330–2. Cf. Ségur, iii. 476, iv. 83, v. 93; Méneval, iii. 184.

of the Conqueror. He did not, indeed, cease to be a great Captain. He could still plan in the cabinet. But he was no longer so formidable or so active in the field. The matchless supremacy of his youth had passed away.

At Elba, again, he physically degenerated. A terrible activity had become necessary to his life. The suppressed energy, the necessary change of habits, injured his health.[1] He became enormously fat; this was the great change that struck his adherents on his return to the Tuileries in the following March.[2] He indeed used this circumstance as an argument to prove his change of character, in a manner that suggests a reminiscence of Shakespeare. Striking his stomach with both hands, "Is one ambitious when one is as fat as I am?" He had no longer that "lean and hungry look," that denotes the "dangerous" man who "thinks too much." It was, moreover, soon clear that his health was broken. Jérôme found him ill, and assured M. Thiers that his brother was then suffering from a bladder complaint.[3] Another brother, Lucien, says emphatically that his health was bad—in a critical condition indeed—and gives details which have not been published. Thiers had other evidence to the same effect, though he holds, and Houssaye with him, that Napoleon's energy disproves the probability of serious ailment.[4] Savary testifies that he could scarcely sit his horse on the battlefield.[5] Lavallette, who saw him the night he left Paris for Flanders, says that he was then suffering severely from his chest.[6] In any case, it was abundantly evident that the Napoleon who returned in March 1815 was very different from the Napoleon who had left in April 1814.[7]

[1] *Sir Neil Campbell*, p. 305.

[2] Pétiet, *Souvenirs Militaires*, p. 195.

[3] Thiers, xx. 594; see, too, p. 47. As to Lucien, see Jung's *Lucien Bonaparte*, pp. 263, 285.

[4] Thiers, xx. 55, note; H. Houssaye.   [5] Rovigo, iv. Part ii. 60.

[6] Lavallette, ii. 155.

[7] Ségur, *Mélanges*, p. 271; Pasquier, iii. 275-6; Pétiet, *Souvenirs*, p. 214; Hobhouse, ii. 76.

We will go so far as to risk an opinion that when he returned from Elba he had realized that his career as a conqueror was over.[1] In Elba he had had leisure, for the first time
since he attained power, to take stock calmly and coldly of his
situation, and to remember his own maxim as to the limited
period of life during which war can be carried on with success. We think, then, that he understood that his period of
conquest was past. But this was not to say that his headstrong
and imperious temperament could ever have been shaped into
anything like a constitutional ruler, or that he could have
restrained himself or his army into permanent pacification.
With his Marshals he would, we think, have had no difficulty. But his prætorians would hardly have been so easy
to satisfy.[2] The limitation of his frontier, too, would have been
a goad as well as an eyesore. Against these we balance the
partial exhaustion of his people and of himself; [3] facts to
which he could scarcely have been permanently blind.

During the Hundred Days, though he displayed what in another man would have been energy, he had ceased to be Napoleon. He was a changed, doomed man. "I cannot resist the
conviction," says Pasquier, who was in constant contact with
the men who surrounded him, "that his genius and his physical powers were alike in a profound decline." [4] He allowed
himself to be bullied by his new legislature, and displayed a
certain helplessness which was a new and ominous sign. We
are told, on the authority of Sismondi, that his Ministers, to
their astonishment, would constantly find him asleep over a
book.[5] Another of the strange features of that period was a
tendency to hold endless conversations, which must have occu-

[1] Las Cases, ii. 324; cf. vii. 134–5.
[2] And yet see Montholon, i. 71.
[3] See Las Cases, *Report on Napoleon's bodily health and strength,*
i. 388–9.
[4] Pasquier, iii. 276. Cf. Caulaincourt in *Vie Militaire du G^{l.} Foy,*
p. 258.
[5] *Memoirs of John Murray,* i. 276.

pied much precious time, and which betrayed a secret perplexity, very unusual with him.[1] Even on the eve of Waterloo,
on the battlefield, to the amazement of Gérard and Grouchy,
he wastes precious time in discoursing to them about politics
in Paris, the Chamber and the Jacobins.[2] This discursiveness
was partly due, says Mollien, to a lassitude which would overcome him after a few hours' work.[3] When this novel sensation
came over him he sought rest and distraction in talk. But the
salient proof of the change lay in his dealings with Fouché.
He had not the energy to deal with Fouché. His main regret in
reviewing that period at St. Helena was that he had not hanged
or shot Fouché. But during the Hundred Days, nay, from the
moment he arrives in Paris to the moment he boards the
Bellerophon, he is fooled by Fouché, betrayed by Fouché, and
probably delivered over to the British by Fouché.[4] Napoleon
suffers all this patiently, though not ignorantly.[5] He took a
course, indeed, which combined the errors of all possible
courses. He told Fouché that his intrigues were discovered,
and kept Fouché as Minister of Police.[6]

At last he shakes off the dust of Paris, its Parliament and its
traitors, and joins his army. It might be thought that in the air
of battle he would regain his strength. But it was not so. The
strategy by which he silently and swiftly launched his army
into Flanders was indeed a combination worthy of his best
days. But on his arrival at the scene of war, his vigilant vitality, once superhuman, had forsaken him. He, formerly so keen
for exact news of the enemy, seemed scarcely to care to know
or inquire about the movements of the Allied Armies. He,
once so electrically rapid, had ceased to value time. His celer-
ity of movement had been of the essence of his earlier victories. But on the morning of Ligny,[7] and on the succeeding

[1] Lavallette, ii. 139.   [2] Grouchy, v. 116.   [3] Mollien, iv. 198.
[4] *Castlereagh Correspondence*, x. 339; Lavallette, ii. 163; Las
Cases, iii. 19, etc.
[5] Lavallette, ii. 149.   [6] *Ibid*. ii. 149.   [7] Lamarque, i. 95.

day, he lost many precious hours—and so perhaps the campaign. He himself acknowledges that had he not been so tired he should have been on horseback all the night before Waterloo: [1] though, as it was, he mounted his horse an hour after midnight and rode till dawn.

Then comes the supreme battle. Napoleon appears to have watched it with some apathy,[2] and on seeing the catastrophe, to have calmly remarked, "Il paraît qu'ils sont mêlés," and walked his horse off the field.

He flies to Paris, and there he is the same. He arrives at the Élysée early on the morning of June 21.[3] He is received on the steps by Caulaincourt, whose tender and faithful arm supports him into the palace. The army, he says, had done wonders, but had been seized by a panic. Ney, like a madman, had sacrificed his cavalry.[4] He himself is suffocated, exhausted; he throws himself into a hot bath, and convokes his Ministers for early next morning.[5] Lavallette saw him soon afterwards, and gives, in a few words, a ghastly, speaking picture of his appearance: "As soon as he saw me he came to me with a fearful epileptic laugh. 'Ah, my God! my God!' he said, raising his eyes to heaven, and paced two or three times round the room. This emotion was only temporary: he soon recovered his self-command, and asked what was happening at the Chambers." [6] He recognized afterwards that he should have gone that day, as it was urged on him, booted and muddy, to the Chambers, have harangued them, have tried the effect of his magnetic individuality, and, had they remained insensible, have ended their sitting in Cromwellian fashion. He should

---

[1] Gourgaud, ii. 159.   [2] Ségur, *Mélanges*, p. 272.

[3] I give this date with no confidence, for I know of no recent event as to which the testimonies are so conflicting. Thiers, Norwins, Montholon, and others say six o'clock, or some time in the early morning of June 21; others, such as Maret, and the *Journal de l'Empire*, say nine o'clock the previous evening.

[4] Villemain, ii. 257; *Souvenirs de Vicence*, ii. 192.

[5] Gourgaud, ii. 553.   [6] Lavallette, ii. 156.

too, he acknowledges, have had Fouché shot at once. Instead of this, he holds a council, from which Fouché, by his side, sends notes to rally the Opposition in Parliament.[1] As the council proceeds, the results of the traitor's manipulation become manifest. There is distress and there is despair: the loyal adherents, the princes of his house,[2] implore the Emperor to show energy: Napoleon sits numb.[3] His carriage stands horsed in the courtyard ready to take him to the Chambers; it is sent away.[4] In the face of treachery and opposition and intrigue he remains passive and resourceless. At last, at a second council, he mechanically signs his abdication, his antechambers empty at once, and his palace becomes a desert.[5]

But, outside, the soldiers and the multitude clamour for him, they adjure him not to desert them, but to organize and head a national resistance.[6] A word from him, says his brother, would have put an end to his domestic foes. This is an exaggeration, for Lafayette had utilized the time which the Emperor had lost, and secured the National Guard. But the enthusiasm was formidable. It might have been the precursor of a successful revolution, had the Emperor cared to utilize it in that way. At any rate, it alarms Fouché and his satellites; they send the Emperor a hint; [7] and he at once retires from his capital and his friends, sending his own carriage empty through the crowd of his adherents, as if they were his enemies, and hurrying off in another.[8]

He retreats to Malmaison, where he is practically a prisoner.[9] He will not move, he will not give an order, he sits reading novels.[10] He will arrange neither for resistance nor for flight. One day decides both. He is induced to offer his services as general to the Provisional Government. The reply he re-

---

[1] Villemain, ii. 276, 270. Cf. Lamarque, i. 138-9.

[2] Jung, *Lucien Bonaparte*, iii. 308-10; Thiers, xx. 345.

[3] Miot, iii. 438.   [4] Montholon, i. 4.   [5] Rovigo, iv. Part ii. 103.

[6] Montholon, i. 16-8; Pasquier, iii. 264.   [7] Pasquier, iii. 265.

[8] Gourgaud, ii. 554; Montholon, i. 23-4.

[9] Montholon, i. 29-36.   [10] *Madame de Montholon*, p. 5.

ceives is a direction to leave the country. He obeys without a
word, and leaves in a quarter of an hour.[1]

Arrived at Rochefort he shows the same apathy, the same
indecision, the same unconsciousness of the value of every moment.[2] It seems clear that had he acted with promptitude, he
had reasonable chances of escaping to America.[3] His brother
Joseph had offered him one opportunity. Joseph, who bore a
strong resemblance to the Emperor, proposed to change places
with him, and let Napoleon embark in the American vessel
in which he himself afterwards escaped.[4] But Napoleon declared that anything in the nature of disguise was beneath his
dignity,[5] though he had certainly not held this opinion on his
way to Elba. Again he might have attempted flight in a neutral (Danish) ship,[6] or in a chassemarée (a swift, masted,
coasting vessel),[7] or in a frigate. He had indeed agreed to set
sail in the Danish ship with Savary, Bertrand, and Marchand.
Their effects were on board, and the four were on the point
of starting, when Napoleon changed his mind. Then some
young naval officers offered themselves as the crew either of a
chassemarée or a rowing-boat which should steal through the
blockade.[8] But the frigate offered the best chances of success,
and Maitland in his narrative admits that these were not
slight.[9] There were at the Île d'Aix at that moment two
French frigates besides smaller vessels. One of the captains was
doubtful if not hostile: but the other implored Napoleon to take
the chance. He would attack the British ship, while the Emperor escaped in the other frigate.[10] In former days the Em-

---

[1] Montholon, i. 53.
[2] *Ibid.* i. 70; *Madame de Montholon*, pp. 12–13; Las Cases, i. 27;
Croker, i. 68.
[3] Pasquier, iii. 195.   [4] Montholon, i. 30.   [5] Las Cases, iii. 339.
[6] Gourgaud, i. 34; Las Cases, i. 27; Montholon, i. 81; Bertrand,
pp. xxx. 111.
[7] Las Cases, i. 30.
[8] Montholon, i. 81; Las Cases, i. 43.   [9] Maitland, p. 100.
[10] *Madame de Montholon*, p. 11.

peror would not have hesitated to entrust Cæsar and his fortunes to such a hazard. But now he seemed under some maleficent charm or blight. He dawdled about, summoned councils of his suite [1] to ask their advice as to what he had better do, displayed his every movement to the watchful enemy, did, in fact, everything that a few years before he would have despised anyone for doing.[2] At last he surrenders himself helplessly to the *Bellerophon,* where he sits dozing over Ossian on the deck.[3] His suite confess to Maitland that much of his bodily activity and mental energy has disappeared.

Once only in that voyage did his apathy forsake him. At dawn, one morning, when the ship was making Ushant, the watch, to their surprise, saw the Emperor issue from his cabin and clamber up to the poop. There he asked the officer on duty if the coast were indeed Ushant, and then taking a telescope he gazed fixedly at the land. From seven till near noon he remained thus motionless. Neither the officers of the ship, nor his staff as they watched him, durst disturb that agony. At last, as the outline faded from his sight, he turned his ghastly face, and clutched at the arm of Bertrand, who supported him back to his cabin. It was his last sight of France.[4]

At St. Helena his lethargy becomes naturally more marked; it amazed himself. He spends hours in his bed, and hours in his bath.[5] He soon ceases to dress till late in the afternoon.[6] He is surprised to find that he is happiest in bed, he for whom the whole day had once been all too short.

And this is the man who, in the opinion of the British Government and Sir Hudson Lowe, was likely to glide down an inaccessible rock, unperceived by ubiquitous sentries, and

[1] *E.g. Gourgaud,* i. 38; Montholon, i. 85; Las Cases, i. 33.
[2] *Madame de Montholon,* pp. 12, 13.　[3] Maitland, pp. 139, 210.
[4] *Memoirs of an Aristocrat,* p. 233.
[5] Forsyth, iii. 72, 67; Gourgaud, ii. 66; Las Cases, iv. 100, 121; v. 21.
[6] Las Cases, i. 292.

in some unexplained manner, pass vigilant vessels of war, in order once more to disturb the world. It is safe to say that had he effected the impossible and escaped, he could never have seriously disturbed the world again, except as a tradition.[1] But it was impossible for him to escape. Even had he been allowed to range over the whole island, had all the sentries been removed, it was out of the question for him, in his physical condition, given a reasonable police and watchful cruisers, to leave the island without the connivance of the Governor. Napoleon himself, though he sometimes hoped to leave St. Helena, never, we are convinced, even thought of escape, though Gourgaud records a jesting scheme for this purpose, launched by the Emperor amidst laughter after dinner.[2] He based such meagre hopes as he entertained on the Opposition party in Parliament, or on Princess Charlotte's succession to the Crown. And so he desires Malcolm and Gourgaud to set forth all his grievances to that Princess.[3]

Napoleon had the faculty, when he chose, of creating a fool's paradise for himself. In the Russian campaign he had, for example, ordered his marshals to operate with armies which he knew had ceased to exist. When they remonstrated he simply replied, "Why rob me of my calm?"[4] When the Allies invaded France he professed to rely greatly on the army of Marshal Macdonald. "Would you like," said the Marshal to Beugnot, "to review my army? It will not take you long. It consists of myself and my chief of the staff. Our supplies are four straw chairs and a plank table."[5] Again, during the campaign of 1814 the Emperor was detailing his plans to Marmont.

[1] Scott, indeed, disputes this view by telling an anecdote which had greatly amused Napoleon himself. A grenadier, who saw him as he landed at St. Helena, exclaimed: "They told us he was growing old; he has forty good campaigns in his belly yet, damn him." Las Cases, iii. 171.

[2] Gourgaud, ii. 207.

[3] Lady Malcolm does not record this, but see Gourgaud, ii. 148,470.

[4] Ségur, v. 348; cf., too, v. 180.   [5] Beugnot, ii. 52.

Marmont was to do this and that with his corps of ten thousand men. At each repetition of this figure Marmont interrupted to say that he had only three. Yet Napoleon persisted to the end: "Marmont with his ten thousand men."[1] But the strangest instance of this is detailed by Méneval, who tells us that when the Emperor added up numbers of his soldiers he always added them up wrong, and always swelled the total.[2] So at St. Helena he really, we think, brought himself to believe that he would be released when Lord Holland became Prime Minister,[3] or when Princess Charlotte ascended the throne.[4] He sometimes even professed to be persuaded that the expense of his detention would induce the British Government to agree to his liberation.[5] Reports of the most amazing character were occasionally brought to Longwood, the invention, we should imagine, of the Jamestown gossips.[6] O'Meara informs Napoleon one day, for example, that the Imperial Guard has retired into the Cévennes and that all France is in insurrection. All that we are told of the effect of this sensational news is that the Emperor plays reversi.[7] Another day Montholon returns from Jamestown, where he has read the newspapers, and declares that all France demands the Emperor, that there is a universal rising in his favour, and that Britain is at the last gasp.[8] We doubt if he put the slightest faith in this sort of report. He had, we suspect, very little hope of any kind. But such hope as he had rested on Princess Charlotte and Lord Holland. Lord Holland because he and, what was more important, Lady Holland, had enthusiastically espoused his cause; Princess Charlotte, partly because she was supposed to have expressed sympathy for him, partly, perhaps, because she had married Prince Leopold, who had wished to be his aide-

---

[1] Stanhope's *Wellington*, p. 129.
[2] Méneval, i. 421.   [3] Gourgaud, ii. 330, 153.
[4] *Ibid.* i. 143, ii. 153, i. 82; Montholon, ii. 14.   [5] *Ibid.* i. 412, 456.
[6] Gourgaud, i. 94, 133, 444, 561; ii. 389, 433, 326.
[7] *Ibid.* i. 121.   [8] *Ibid.* i. 94.

de-camp. "That," said the Emperor, "is a lucky fellow not to have been named my aide-de-camp when he asked for it; for had he been appointed he would not now be on the steps of the English throne." [1]

There was indeed one source of peril, of which both Lowe and the French Commissioner were well aware, against which it was difficult to guard: the personal fascination exercised by the captive. Montchenu constantly deplores this ominous fact. Every one, he says, leaves Napoleon's presence in a state of the greatest enthusiasm.[2] "Were I you," said the Marquis to the Governor, "I would not allow a single stranger to visit Long-wood, for they all leave it in a transport of devotion, which they take back with them to Europe." [3] "What is most astonishing," says the Russian Commissioner, "is the ascendancy that this man, dethroned, a prisoner, surrounded by guards and keepers, exercises on all who come near him. Everything at St. Helena bears the impress of his superiority. The French tremble at his aspect, and think themselves too happy to serve him.[4] . . . The English no longer approach him but with awe. Even his guardians seek anxiously for a word or a look from him. No one dares to treat him as an equal." [5] These alarming facts were coupled with the not less alarming good-nature of the captive. He would go into a cottage, sit down and chat with the people, who would receive "Sir Emperor" with awful joy.[6] He would talk to slaves and give them money.[7] He threatened indeed to become beloved. The Governor was frightened out of his wits at this new and indefinable menace to the security of the island, so he at once retrenched the boundaries so that no cottages should be within them.[8]

---

[1] Montholon, i. 433; Las Cases, vii. 116.
[2] Didot, p. 85.   [3] *Ibid.* p. 114.
[4] Balmain, Sept. 8, 1816. Sturmer uses almost the same words.
[5] See St. Cère, p. 88. See, too, Didot, p. 58.
[6] Warden, p. 124; Montholon, i. 204.
[7] Gourgaud, i. 115, 117; Las Cases, i. 400; Forsyth, ii. 178.
[8] Scott, ix. 266; Forsyth, ii. 463; *ibid.* i. 309, 344.

CHAPTER NINE

Lord Bathurst

★

"NOTHING," wrote the Russian Commissioner to his Government after nearly three years' experience at St. Helena, "can be more absurd, more impolite, less generous, and less delicate than the conduct of the English to Napoleon." [1] It would not be fair or just, however, to debit Lowe or Cockburn with the responsibility for these ignominies, or for the general principle of the Emperor's treatment. They were only the somewhat narrow and coarse agents of a sordid and brutal policy. It was the British Ministry which was answerable jointly and severally for the treatment of Napoleon; and which, strangely enough, was equally condemned by the partisans of Lowe. "Worst of all," says the Governor's most efficient advocate, . . . "was the conduct of the British Government, which, viewed in itself, was utterly undignified: viewed from Sir Hudson Lowe's standpoint, was unfair and treacherous." [2] When, however, we remember who and what these Ministers were we cease to marvel. Vandal, in one of the most eloquent passages of his noble history, points out that the eventual victory of Great Britain over Napoleon was the victory of persistency over genius. "The men who governed in London, flung by the illness of George III into a chaos of difficulties, placed between a mad King and a discredited Regent, exposed to the virulent attacks of the Opposition, to the revolt of injured interest, to the complaints of the city, face to face with a people without bread and with an almost ruined commerce . . . sometimes despair of even maintaining Wellington at Lisbon. But in their extreme peril none of them think of yielding—of asking or even accepting peace—or of sacrificing the British cause or British pride." Rarely, he continues, have men displayed more admirable proofs of cool and obstinate courage. "Yet, who are

[1] Balmain, April 22, 1819.
[2] Seaton, *Sir Hudson Lowe and Napoleon*, p. 113.

these men? Among them there is not a single Minister of great renown, of a glorious past, of a superior intelligence. The successors of Pitt . . . have only inherited his constancy, his tenacity, his hatred. But knowing that they bear the destinies of their country and of the world, they derive from that consciousness a virtue of energy and patience which makes them equal to the greatest." [1] Liverpool, Eldon, Bathurst, Castlereagh, and Sidmouth were men whose names can scarcely be said to glow in history. They had, however, felt doggedly that they must fight it out to the bitter end; and, supported throughout by the victories of their navy and the grim patience of their people, as well as, latterly, by military success, had pulled through and emerged victorious. But victory had not taught them magnanimity. They had caught their great enemy: their first wish was to get somebody else to shoot him or hang him: failing which, they were determined to lock him up like a pickpocket. All that they saw clearly was that he had cost them a great deal of trouble and a great deal of money, so that he must cost them as little more as possible. They were honest men acting up to their lights: we can only regret that the men were dull and the lights were dim.

The Minister charged with carrying out this policy was Lord Bathurst, Secretary of State for the joint department of War and the Colonies.

Who was Bathurst?

It is difficult to say. He was, we know, grandson of that secular Lord Bathurst who, sixty years after his first elevation to the peerage, was created an Earl, and who, in the last months of his life, in his ninety-first year, was the subject of a famous apostrophe by Burke. He was, we know, son of that second Lord Bathurst who was the least capable of Chancellors. He himself was one of those strange children of our political system who fill the most dazzling offices with the most complete obscurity. He had presided over the Foreign Office. He was at

[1] Vandal, ii. 535–6.

this time, and was for a term of fifteen years, a Secretary of State. Yet even our most microscopic Biographical Dictionary may be searched in vain for more than a dry recital of the offices that he filled, the date of his birth, and the date of his death.

In virtue of his office he was now in charge of Napoleon. He tersely instructed Lowe that the Emperor was to be treated till further orders as a prisoner of war, but that he was to be allowed "every indulgence which may be consistent with the entire security of his person." [1] He then passed through Parliament an Act of Draconian but perhaps necessary severity. Any British subject who should assist in Napoleon's escape, or, after his escape, assist him on the high seas, was to be punished with death without benefit of clergy. Lowe, by the by, used to allude to this Act in delicate raillery of the Commissioners. "After all, I cannot hang *you*," he would say. Meanwhile Bathurst was tightening the screw. £8,000 was to be the limit of Napoleon's expenditure on table and household; he was to pay all his own followers and servants, and the household was at once to be reduced by the magical number of four: no names or degrees were specified, except Piontkowski —lots were to be drawn for the other three—so that it was clearly an economy of four mouths that was aimed at. [2] The remainder were to be persuaded to leave him, as their residence in the island added greatly to the expense. [3] It may be presumed, therefore, that the "indulgence, consistent," after all, "with the entire security of his person"—of intercourse with a few fellow-countrymen and of the attendance of his old servants—was to be, if practicable, withdrawn. Lowe, moreover, was to draw the bonds more straitly than Cockburn. No communication was to reach Napoleon except through Lowe.

[1] Forsyth, i. 437.
[2] *Ibid.* i. 298. Piontkowski was to be one of them, it is not explained why. The others might draw lots. Bathurst hints that too large a household might aid in Napoleon's escape, but this is obviously not the reason.
[3] *Ibid.* i. 190.

The faculty accorded to Bertrand by the Admiral of giving
cards of admission which would enable visitors to Napoleon
to pass the sentries was withdrawn. A declaration was to be
signed by all the French courtiers and servants of the Emperor
that they would submit to all regulations imposed on their
master, and so forth. He attached great importance to enclos-
ing Napoleon in a sort of area railing which he despatched
from England, and which should add the final precaution to
security. "We consider it," he writes, "a very essential point,
particularly until the iron railing shall arrive, to ascertain, late
in the evening and early in the morning, that he is safe." [1]

But it seems to have been found inexpedient to carry constraint too far. For the interest in the captive was intense.
Every scrap of news from St. Helena was eagerly devoured by
the public. The craving for each fragment of intelligence was
so great, that it was scarcely possible to preserve from the
avidity of the press the most private letters written from St.
Helena. A lady who came from there in 1817 narrates how,
on landing at Portsmouth, persons of all ranks seemed ready
to tear the passengers in pieces for information about the
captive. And, as soon as they reached the hotel, strangers
brought portraits of Napoleon to have the likeness attested. [2]
Warden's worthless book was for the same reason extremely
popular. Santini's not less worthless book was not less popular.
It went through seven editions in a fortnight. So, at least, its
author declares. [3]

Lord Holland, too, raised in the House of Lords a debate
on the treatment of Napoleon. And from this time forth there
reigns a blander tone in the regulations of Bathurst. His next
letter to Lowe, written a month after the debate, is couched
in a spirit that may almost be deemed urbane. "You may

[1] *Ibid.* i. 313; cf. p. 151. Cf. Lady Malcolm, p. 163; Gourgaud,
i. 510, 511. It was, perhaps, first suggested by Lowe. Forsyth, i. 151.
[2] *Blackwood's Magazine*, Jan. 1834, p. 48. I think that these
recollections must be by Mrs. Skelton.
[3] Maceroni, ii. 425.

assure him of your disposition to make his situation more comfortable by a supply of the publications of the day. . . . I think it right also to add that there exists in this country no indisposition to allow him the gratifications of the table—more especially of wine." [1] And later on in the same year he expands the limit of even £12,000 a year, if that sum be inadequate for "such an establishment as would be requisite for a general officer of distinction." [2] (Napoleon, it will be observed, has gradually risen from a "general not in employ" to "a general officer of distinction.")

Bathurst seems to have been in all respects as worthy of Lowe as Lowe of Bathurst, and to both there was a common standard of tact and taste. Take the following specimen. Rats are the curse of St. Helena, and on this subject the Secretary of State writes to the Governor: "You will also receive a private letter from Mr. Goulburn on the great inconvenience to which he (Napoleon) is said to be exposed by the quantity of rats with which his house is infested. There is something so ludicrous in a fallen leader's complaint on such a subject, *and is one so little in unison with the animals' sagacity,* that it is not a topic likely from choice to be brought forward as a grievance; but the number of these animals may amount to be a real one; and though I have reason to believe that the increase is owing to the negligence of his servants, *in which he is very willing to encourage them,* yet it is fit on every account that the subject should be examined and a proper remedy applied." [3] We cannot call to mind any complaint of Napoleon's on the subject, though his house was overrun with these disgusting vermin. But the graceful allusions of the Secretary of State which we have italicized lose none of their point from this circumstance; though he may be held to be going a little far when he hints that the Emperor, always scrupulously dainty in such things, wilfully encouraged the negligence of his servants in order to promote the increase of rats.

[1] Forsyth, ii. 382.   [2] *Ibid.* ii. 443.   [3] *Ibid.* ii. 413.

When Napoleon is dying Bathurst touches a note which is almost sublime. "If he be really ill," writes the Secretary of State, "he may derive some consolation by knowing that the reported accounts which have of late been transmitted of his declining health have not been received with indifference. You will therefore communicate to General Buonaparte the great interest which His Majesty has taken in the recent accounts of his indisposition, and the anxiety which His Majesty feels to afford him every relief of which his situation admits. You will assure General Buonaparte that there is no alleviation which can be derived from additional medical assistance, nor any arrangement consistent with the safe custody of his person at St. Helena (and His Majesty cannot now hold out any expectation of his removal) which His Majesty is not most anxious to afford," [1] and so forth. The force of Bathurst could no further go. Fortunately before this precious effusion was received at St. Helena, its prisoner was where the sympathy of George IV, strained through Bathurst, could not reach him. Scott thinks that it would have been a solace to him.[2] Comment on such an opinion seems unnecessary.

The whole correspondence, so far as we know it, is sordid and pitiful enough. Making all allowances for the cost and exhaustion of the war and for the natural anxiety that the great disturber of peace should not escape, it appears, to us, at the end of the century in which it passed, a humiliating compound of meanness and panic. But the responsibility for this ignominious episode, this policy of petty cheeseparing and petty police, must rest not with the instruments but with the principals; with the Liverpools and Bathursts at home, not with the Cockburns and Lowes at St. Helena: although the Ministers, as we have seen, tried to dissociate themselves from the sinister reputation of Lowe by extending a conspicuously cold shoulder to him on his return.

[1] Forsyth, ii. 495.   [2] Scott, ix. 292.

CHAPTER TEN

The *Dramatis Personæ*

★

THE *dramatis personæ* of this long tragedy are few in number, and some even of these, the Poppletons and the like, flit like ghosts across the stage, without voice or substance. Of Poppleton,[1] for example, whose name occurs so frequently, we only know that he was long the orderly officer at Longwood, that he was not much of a horseman, that he sometimes dug potatoes,[2] and that, on leaving, he surreptitiously accepted a snuff-box as a present from the Emperor, one of the most heinous crimes in Lowe's criminal calendar.[3] We have, indeed, occasional vivid glimpses, such as Napoleon's description of the Admiral who succeeded Malcolm: He "reminds me of one of those drunken little Dutch skippers that I have seen in Holland, sitting at a table with a pipe in his mouth, a cheese and a bottle of Geneva before him." [4] But there are other names which occur in every page of the various narratives, notably those of the Emperor's little suite. Of the characters not already noticed the Grand Marshal, Count Bertrand, and his wife take, of course, the first place.

Bertrand has one agreeable singularity, he published no book, which is in itself a pleasant contrast to the copious self-revelation of Gourgaud and Las Cases; though there is a posthumous preface [5] of his which contains some curious facts, and it is believed that he left some manuscript records behind him. He seems to have been an excellent officer—Napoleon repeatedly said that he was the best engineer officer in existence,[6] but this may possibly have been alleged for the purpose of teasing Gourgaud. He was, moreover, devoted to his master,

---

[1] Balmain, Sept. 8, 1816.   [2] *Voice*, i. 430.

[3] Forsyth, iii. 320, note.   [4] *Voice*, ii. 113.

[5] To the *Campagnes d'Égypte et de Syrie*, dictated to him by Napoleon and published in 1847.

[6] Gourgaud, ii. 373, 377, 378, 381.

but not less devoted to his wife.[1] This double allegiance, which had already caused inconvenience at Elba,[2] plunged him into constant difficulties with the Emperor,[3] who resented it even on his death-bed. But Bertrand resisted his wife's entreaties that he would not accompany the Emperor to St. Helena, stayed till the end, though not without thoughts of going,[4] for a time at any rate, and remains in his loyal silence the most sympathetic figure of the Emperor's surroundings. For some reason or another he was an object of Lowe's special hatred.[5] But Henry, the friend of Lowe, and almost every other impartial authority commend him.[6] After Napoleon's death Admiral Lambert patched up a truce between Bertrand and the Governor, which the Emperor when dying is said to have enjoined.[7]

Madame Bertrand was said to be an English creole by birth; on the English side a niece of Lord Dillon, and on the creole side a connection of the Empress Josephine.[8] Her English origin had indeed caused her to be suspected at Elba of English sympathies,[9] but of this not the slightest trace is discoverable. Her appearance seems to have possessed a singular charm. She was, says an English lady on the island, "a most engaging, fascinating woman. She spoke our language with perfect fluency, but with a slight French accent. Her figure was extremely tall and commanding; but a slight, elegant bend took from her height, and added to her interesting appearance; her eyes black, sparkling, soft, and animated; her deportment that of a young queen, accustomed to *command* admiration,

---

[1] Montholon, i. 162; Maitland, p. 226.   [2] Pons, p. 215.
[3] *E.g.*, Gourgaud, ii. 51, 437; Las Cases, iii. 26–8.
[4] Bertrand, pp. xxxvii–xl.   [5] Forsyth, iii. 156.   [6] *Ibid.* iii. 303–4.
[7] *Ibid.* iii. 299; Henry. ii. 86. But Bertrand (p. xlii) says nothing of this, and declares that Admiral Lambert patched up the reconciliation.
[8] *Madame de Montholon*, p. 23; Gourgaud, i. 37, note; *Blackwood's Magazine*, Jan. 1834, p. 55.
[9] Pons, p. 215.

yet *winning* to preserve it." [1] Her character was, however, liable to tumults of creole passion, and on the announcement that Napoleon was to be sent to St. Helena she flung herself into his cabin, made a scene, and then attempted to drown herself. [2] The result, and even the attempt, had, fortunately, no element of tragedy. For while her body was half out of the cabin window, her husband restrained her from within, while Savary, with whom she had a feud, was shouting in fits of laughter, "Let her go, let her go." [3] Maitland had constant struggles with her while she was on board the *Bellerophon*, culminating in a scene when "the little self-possession that still remained gave way," and he called her "a very foolish woman," desiring her not to speak to him again. Nevertheless when, a little later in the day, she left the ship, she came up to the captain "in a conciliatory and friendly manner that did her the highest honour," reminded him that he had called her a very foolish woman that morning, but asked him to shake hands, "as God knows," added the poor lady, "if we shall ever meet again." [4] Maitland sums her up as a kind mother and affectionate wife, with many excellent qualities, "though perhaps a little warm." [5] Forsyth says that she seems to have won the goodwill and regard of all who knew her. [6] One trait of humour is recorded of her. A child was born to her at St. Helena, whom she presented to the Emperor as the first French visitor that had entered Longwood without Lord Bathurst's permission. Madame de Montholon records that she lived through their long and dreary captivity in complete harmony with this seductive creature. [7] After Madame de Montholon's departure she was left for two years without the society of a countrywoman, and she had to beg Lowe for the relief of a little company. [8] No

[1] *Blackwood*, Jan. 1834, p. 55. See, too, Henry, ii. 10; Maitland, p. 226.
[2] Gourgaud, i. 47; Las Cases, i. 61; Maitland, pp. 152-3, 156-7.
[3] *Madame de Montholon*, p. 23.   [4] Maitland, p. 196.
[5] *Ibid.* p. 226.   [6] Forsyth, iii. 184.
[7] P. 24. But see Gourgaud, i. 487, and Forsyth, i. 231, note.
[8] Forsyth, iii. 183.

one made greater sacrifices in order to accompany Napoleon and her husband than Madame Bertrand. She was fond of luxury and of society; she was accustomed to play a leading part in a splendid court; she had, indeed, at Trieste, held a vice-regal court of her own; [1] her exquisitely beautiful children [2] were approaching an age when their education would have to be her first object: but after the first paroxysm she went uncomplainingly to her tropical Siberia, and seems to have been a peace-maker in a community which, though small, afforded an unbounded field for that blessed calling.

Of the personality of M. and Madame de Montholon we catch but a faint view, though their names are written large in the chronicles of the captivity. Montholon [3] was of ancient family, and claimed, indeed, to be by inheritance an English or Irish peer. One of his ancestors, it is alleged, had saved the life of Richard Cœur de Lion, and had been created in consequence Earl of Lee and Baron O'Brien: [4] titles of a fairy texture which Montholon claimed to inherit, but which diligent research fails to identify. He also claimed to have been created Duke of Castel Volturno by Napoleon, and to have been Hereditary First Huntsman under Louis XVI. No corroboration is offered for any of these glowing statements, which are obviously part of the Montholon romance. However that may be, he had been known to Napoleon ever since he was a child of ten years old, when, being in Corsica with his mother and step-father, M. de Sémonville, he had received mathematical lessons from the young Napoleon, then a captain of artillery. Afterwards he was at school with Lucien and Jérôme, and with Eugène de Beauharnais.[5] Hence he was, as may be supposed, closely identified with the career of Napoleon, and he was still further connected with the imperial interest through

---

[1] *Blackwood's Magazine*, Jan. 1834, p. 55.
[2] *Ibid.* p. 55; Henry, ii. 10, 90.
[3] Balmain, Sept. 8, 1816; Henry, ii. 91.
[4] Montholon, i. lxxxii, note. [5] *Madame de Montholon*, pp. 2, 3.

the marriage of his sister with the pure and chivalrous Mac-donald.[1] It was the strange fate of Montholon to know Napo-leon in the obscurity of his early days, to be associated with the magnificence of his Empire, to follow him into exile, to watch by his death-bed with the tenderness of a son, to live to assist reluctantly in the fantastic attempt on Boulogne,[2] and so to be partaker of the third Napoleon's captivity for exactly the term of the captivity of the first. Six years of his life were spent in sharing the imprisonment of the first, and six years in sharing that of the third, Napoleon. During this latter period he found himself compelled to write that that which grieved him most in the Castle of Ham was to think that the Emperor at St. Helena was better treated by the English than his nephew by the French. He lived to see the re-establishment of the Empire, which Gourgaud missed by a few months: but Gourgaud, characteristically enough, was in opposition to the Prince President.

Montholon was, happily, a blind devotee; happily, for a blind devotee was required in the little court. After the depar-ture of Las Cases, therefore, it was not difficult for Montholon to succeed to the vacant place, for the conjugal devotion of Bertrand, and the moroseness of Gourgaud, disabled them for competition; and so Montholon became the most familiar and necessary of the Emperor's staff. But even he wished to go. Bathurst, in February 1820, was writing caustically enough of Bertrand and Montholon: "They are both in fact upon the wing, but watching each other." [3] As to Bertrand, his own statement is that it was necessary at the end of 1820 that his children should go to France with their mother for their edu-cation. Napoleon gave his consent. But when the vessel had arrived that was to take them he suddenly declared that the wife could not go safely without the husband, and that the

[1] *Madame de Montholon*, p. 2, note.
[2] Unwillingly, says Montholon, i. xcv.
[3] Holland's *Foreign Reminiscences*, p. 335.

husband must obtain a substitute from France before he could leave. This, as Bertrand represents it, was a device of the Emperor, then in failing health, to keep them all. It was consequently arranged that if in a year there was no change in the situation he should go on leave for nine months. Montholon wished to accompany his wife when she left in 1819, and had, as he states, and we do not doubt, his daily struggles with Napoleon, who besought him to remain.[1] Nine weeks indeed before the Emperor's death we find him discussing with Lowe who should succeed Bertrand and himself as attendants on the exile,[2] and Planat, as we have seen, was on the point of starting to replace him.

Of Albinie Hélène de Vassal, Madame de Montholon,[3] but for the insane jealousy of Gourgaud, we should know nothing or next to nothing,[4] though she left behind her some vivid notes of her exile. We learn incidentally from Méneval that her marriage with Montholon encountered some difficulties, for she had two divorced husbands living. The Emperor forbade the banns, but afterwards gave Montholon permission to marry "the niece of the President Séguier." Montholon had tricked his sovereign, for his bride was the forbidden lady under another description.[5] "A quiet unassuming woman," says Maitland, "who gave no trouble, and seemed perfectly satisfied, provided she were allowed to accompany her husband." [6] She provided the music of the Emperor's drawing-room, singing Italian songs, with little voice; and strumming on the piano.

Emmanuel, Marquis [7] of Las Cases, had had a somewhat chequered career. At an early age he entered the French Navy and took part in the siege of Gibraltar. Before he was twenty-one he had passed as a lieutenant, and soon afterwards was

---

[1] Forsyth, iii. 157–8, 162–4.   [2] *Ibid.* iii. 256–7.
[3] *Ibid.* iii. 394.   [4] Masson takes a harsh view of her.
[5] Méneval, iii. 19.   [6] Maitland, p. 229.
[7] He was born a marquis under the old monarchy, but was made a Count of the Empire, and styles himself Count.

placed in command of a brig. Then came the Revolution, and the young officer was one of the first to emigrate. This was ultimately fortunate, for his recollections of Coblentz and of the Emigration had always a particular savour for Napoleon. From Coblentz he was despatched on a secret mission to Gustavus III of Sweden. Then Las Cases drifted to England, formed a part of the disastrous expedition to Quiberon, and on his escape thence gave lessons in London, where he published a *Historical Atlas*, which proved remunerative. After the Eighteenth of Brumaire he returned to France, served under Bernadotte, and became a Chamberlain and Councillor of State. On Napoleon's first abdication he refused to adhere to the resolution of the Council of State deposing the Emperor (although he accepted from Louis XVIII a commission as Captain in the French Navy),[1] and retired to England. During the Hundred Days he returned, of course, to Paris, and, after Waterloo, besought Napoleon to take him to St. Helena. Born three years before his master, Las Cases survived him twenty-one, dying in 1842.[2]

We give these facts in detail, because they explain the preference which causes such jealousy. Las Cases belonged to the old nobility, he had served in the Navy before the Revolution, he had been involved in the Emigration,[3] he had seen much of England, and was thus able to satisfy Napoleon's insatiable curiosity on phases of life with which he had no personal contact.[4] Moreover, Las Cases was a man of the world. He had fought, gambled,[5] and travelled, had seen life in the hundred-sided character of a needy and ingenious exile, and had observed the Empire and its Court from a much more independent situation than Napoleon's. Besides, he adored his

[1] Las Cases, i. 386.
[2] *Nouvelle Biographie Générale*, Art. "Las Cases"; *Correspondance de Napoléon*, xxxii. 249.
[3] Las Cases, v. 85, etc.; vii. 65.
[4] *Ibid.* v. 281.　　　　　　　　　　[5] Gourgaud, i. 232.

master, had no secrets from him, regarded him as superhuman and divine. We have seen indeed that he had no scruples in the Emperor's service. "Napoleon is my God," he would say, or, "I do not regret my exile since it places me close to the noblest of created beings." [1] He had even the complaisance to be much shorter than the Emperor.[2] There were, of course, drawbacks. He humiliated his master by being violently sea-sick on a British man-of-war, in spite of a new naval uniform, and of the great bound in naval rank which he had achieved after a quarter of a century spent on shore.[3] Then, too, his colleagues hated him. Their usual name for him was "The Jesuit." [4] His favour with Napoleon, though perfectly explicable to us from his experience and his contrast with the too domestic Bertrand, the less cultured Montholon, and the impracticable Gourgaud, was a constant irritation to them. Then again his departure is not easily explained. He might have returned but would not,[5] imbedding himself in vapid phrases, which even now we cannot exactly interpret, but which we translate into a conviction that his colleagues had rendered his life at Longwood impossible.

In spite of all, in spite of his unblushing fabrications, his want of veracity, the irrepressible suspicion that he may after all have been only an enthusiastic Boswell seeking biographical material for publication, we confess to a sneaking kindness for the devoted rhetorical little man; and we cannot forget that he insisted on handing over to Napoleon four thousand pounds, which was probably his entire fortune. With him was his son, then a boy, who afterwards assaulted Sir Hudson Lowe in the streets of London, and tried to bring about a duel with the ex-Governor. Nineteen years after Napoleon's death, the young man returned to St. Helena with the expedition to fetch

---

[1] Forsyth, i. 238; St. Cère, p. 88.
[2] Las Cases, ii. 133.   [3] Montholon, i. 96.
[4] Gourgaud, i. 265; Forsyth, i. 239, ii. 93.
[5] See Gourgaud, ii. 2; Montholon, i. 467, 470.

back the Emperor's remains; and became a senator under Napoleon III.

Piontkowski remains a figure of mystery. He was a trooper in the Polish Lancers, who had followed Napoleon to Elba, and had been given a commission in consequence of his fidelity. At a time when the British Government would not allow Gourgaud to take with him his old servant, or Las Cases to be rejoined by his wife, they sent Piontkowski, unbidden and unwelcome,[1] to join the Emperor. If we may trust the others, Gourgaud found him out at once to be untruthful and to have made false statements about his campaigns.[2] Napoleon knew nothing of him,[3] disliked him, and, not unnaturally, distrusted him. After his departure, indeed, Napoleon openly suspected him of being a spy;[4] Las Cases disdainfully mentions him as "the Pole." He vanished, as suddenly as he came, nine months afterwards,[5] with, apparently, plenty of money.[6] We do not believe him to have been a spy, but his appearance and career at Longwood still require elucidation.

"The young ladies born in that island are extremely pretty," [7] says a witness who lived at St. Helena during the Emperor's residence, and our various chronicles are full of them. There were the two Balcombes, Miss Wilks, Miss Robinson, who was known as "the Nymph," and Miss Kneipps, who was known as "the Rosebud."

With Miss Wilks Gourgaud was desperately in love. "There is a woman!" he exclaims during their first acquaintance.[8] He lost his heart at once, and asked himself, "Alas! Why am I a prisoner?" [9] It was no comfort to him to be assured by Bertrand

[1] Montholon, i. 202; Maitland, p. 231; Gourgaud, i. 108-9, 113; Las Cases, ii. 259.

[2] Gourgaud, i. 120, 108-9.

[3] Las Cases, ii. 259-60; Forsyth, i. 320; Gourgaud, i. 113, 189.

[4] Gourgaud, ii. 335.

[5] See, as to the cause, Montholon, i. 410.   [6] Gourgaud, ii. 95.

[7] *Blackwood's Magazine*, Jan. 1834, p. 52.

[8] Gourgaud, i. 104.   [9] *Ibid.* i. 87.

that he was preferred to the other suitors,[1] or by Napoleon that he should be provided with a better marriage in France.[2] He sees the ship that bears her away, and heaves a despairing "Adieu, Laure!"[3]

All testimony is unanimous that Gourgaud in this instance placed his affections well. "Miss Wilks was then in the first bloom of youth, and her whole demeanour, affability, and elegant, modest appearance conspired to render her the most charming and admirable young person I ever beheld, or have since met with, in all my peregrinations in Europe, Asia, and Africa for the space of thirty years."[4] This is the high testimony of a lady who accompanied her on her first visit to Napoleon. The Emperor was scarcely less fascinated. He had long heard, he said, with a bow, of the elegance and beauty of Miss Wilks, but was now convinced that report had scarcely done her justice.[5]

She was the daughter of Colonel Wilks, the East Indian Governor of the island, whose conversations with the Emperor have been published. She eventually married General Sir John Buchan, and lived to be ninety-one. She died in 1888, and used to tell how Napoleon, at parting, had given her a bracelet, and, when she had said she was sorry to leave the island, had replied: "Ah! Mademoiselle, I only wish I could change places with you."[6]

Napoleon gave fanciful names to people and to places. One quiet glen he had named the Valley of Silence, but, when he found that a pretty girl lived in it, he renamed it the Valley of the Nymph. The Nymph was a farmer's daughter, "a very pretty girl of about seventeen,"[7] named Marianne Robinson, whose sister had married a Captain Jordan of the 66th Regiment,[8] quartered at St. Helena. Warden devoted a page of

[1] Ibid. i. 129.   [2] Ibid. i. 124.   [3] Ibid. i. 166.
[4] Blackwood's Magazine, Jan. 1834, p. 53.
[5] Ibid., Jan. 1834, p. 54.   [6] Times, May 4, 1888.
[7] Warden, p. 126.   [8] Henry, ii. 18, note.

his book to her, and states that the visits of Napoleon became so frequent to the little farm that the gossips of Jamestown warned the father, who afterwards forbade his daughter to appear when the Emperor called.[1] This silly scandal Napoleon thought it worth his while to contradict in the *Letters from the Cape,* stating that he only once spoke to her, in broken English, without alighting from his horse.[2] Montchenu, however, who had an eminently prurient mind, repeats the statement, and avers that Napoleon made her a declaration, that he talked much of her beauty, and thus aroused the jealousy of Miss Balcombe.[3] Napoleon did, no doubt, visit the Nymph more than once,[4] and Gourgaud declares that she hinted to the Emperor that she was in the habit of taking early and solitary walks.[5] But, so far from taking up the challenge, he rallies Gourgaud on having made a new conquest—an impeachment to which that gallant officer was always prepared to plead guilty. Finally, the Nymph marries, and so puts an end to this vulgar gossip. Her husband is a merchant captain, a "M. Édouard" (Edwards),[6] who has been attracted to her, according to the complacent belief of Longwood, by the reported admiration of the illustrious prisoner. "It is enough for me to have said that she is pretty," said the Emperor, "for this captain to fall in love with her and marry her."[7] Napoleon also makes the mysterious comment, that the marriage proves that the English have more decision than the French,[8] a remark which appears to indicate some hesitating aspirations on the part of some member of the Household, probably Captain Piontkowski. She brings the husband to Longwood, when Napoleon says that she has the air of a nun, and that her husband resembles Eugène Beauharnais. Napoleon, as is his wont, asks him some crude and tactless questions; the mariner blushes, the Emperor pledges him in a toast, and, after an

---

[1] Warden, p. 126.   [2] *Letters, etc.,* p. 88.   [3] Didot, p. 56.
[4] Gourgaud, i. 113, 115.   [5] *Ibid.* i. 131.
[6] Henry, ii. 18, note.   [7] Gourgaud, ii. 225.   [8] *Ibid.* ii. 227.

hour and a half of this sort of thing, the couple take their leave.[1] After a while Napoleon follows them, and insists on embracing not the Nymph but her husband, on the ground, says Mr. Robinson, that he is so like Joseph Bonaparte: probably a mistake for Eugène.[2] And so, with this unexpected exit, the Nymph vanishes into space.

Then there was another beauty, whom they called "the Rosebud." The editors of Gourgaud tell us that she was a Miss Kneipps.[3] She makes transient appearances, but we know nothing of her, or of some still more shadowy Miss Churchills,[4] except that the large heart of Gourgaud found nooks for them all.

Miss Betsy Balcombe, however, is the girl whose name occurs most frequently in the St. Helena records. Twenty-three years after the Emperor's death, under her married name of Mrs. Abell, she published her recollections of his exile. Her father, Mr. Balcombe, was a sort of general purveyor, sometimes called by courtesy a banker; and the traditions of the island declare him to be a son of George IV.[5] As a matter of fact, his father was the landlord of the New Ship Inn at Brighton. Napoleon lived at this gentleman's villa while Longwood was being prepared for his reception, and there made acquaintance with his two daughters. Betsy was about fifteen and the younger of the two. They both talked French, but Betsy was the prettier and the favourite,[6] for she represented a type which was new to the Emperor, a high-spirited hoyden, who said and did whatever occurred to her on the spur of the moment.[7] The pranks that she played she records in her book: they must certainly have been in the nature of a piquant novelty to Napoleon. She boxed his ears, she attacked him

---

[1] *Ibid.* ii. 229; Montholon, ii. 158–9.

[2] Forsyth, ii. 466.

[3] Gourgaud, i. 87; *Madame de Montholon*, p. 38; *Voice*, i. 116.

[4] Montholon, ii. 105.

[5] Cf. *Brighton in the Olden Time*, by Bishop, pp. 193–4.

[6] Didot, p. 51.   [7] *Madame de Montholon*, pp. 41–2.

with his own sword. But the suite were not unnaturally disgusted at the familiarity with which she treated their master, and Napoleon himself wearied of her, denounced the whole family as "canaille" and as "misérables."[1] One flirtation kept the whole island alive: Would Major Ferzen marry Betsy or not? Napoleon said, "No, the Major would not so degrade himself."[2] Still, at rare intervals, she amused him to the last. The Emperor, a few weeks before she left, sent the sisters two plates of bonbons.[3] Lowe ordered them to be returned.[4] And, with this last characteristic memory of St. Helena and its ruler, the Balcombe family sailed from the island on the same ship with Gourgaud.

But though the mosquitoes were harassing, the dominant population of St. Helena was the rats;[5] more formidable than regiments, or cannon, or Lowe. On this subject there is an almost hysterical unanimity. "The rats," says O'Meara, "are in numbers almost incredible at Longwood. I have frequently seen them assemble like broods of chickens round the offal thrown out of the kitchen. The floors and wooden partitions that separated the rooms were perforated with holes in every direction. . . . It is difficult for any person, who has not actually heard it, to form an idea of the noise caused by these animals running up and down between the partitions and galloping in flocks in the garrets." Frequently O'Meara has to defend himself against them with his boots and his bootjack.[6] They run round the table while the Emperor is at dinner without taking heed of anyone.[7] As Napoleon takes his hat from the sideboard, a large rat springs out of it and runs between his legs.[8] The curse of the isle, says Sturmer, is the rats; the curse of locusts was not to be mentioned beside it.[9]

[1] Gourgaud, ii. 364   [2] Ibid. ii. 364; cf. ii, 193, 225.

[3] Ibid. ii. 428.   [4] Ibid. ii. 455.

[5] *Madame de Montholon*, p. 52; Forsyth, i. 215; Las Cases, iv. 306-7, ii. 383.

[6] *Voice*, i. 494.   [7] Montholon, i. 153.

[8] *Voice*, i. 312.   [9] St. Cère, p. 66.

The inhabitants are powerless against them. A slave sleeping in a passage had part of his leg eaten off by them.[1] So had one of the Emperor's horses. Bertrand, while asleep, was bitten seriously in the hand.[2] The children had to be protected from them at night.[3] Trifling, and indeed diverting, as this pest seemed to the distant Bathurst, it must have been an odious addition to the petty miseries of Longwood. Nor was Bathurst alone in his merriment. Among the squalid caricatures, with which the French Press attempted to besmirch the memory of their fallen Sovereign, there are several devoted to this topic. Napoleon received by the population of St. Helena— the rats; Napoleon granting a constitution to the rats; Napoleon sleeping at peace because guarded by a cat-sentry; and so forth. One need not dilate on these pleasantries.

[1] St. Cère p. 66.   [2] Montholon, i. 153.   [3] *Ibid.* ii. 376.

CHAPTER ELEVEN
The Commissioners

★

IN this dreary drama, as in most human transactions, the element of comedy is not absent, nor even the salt of farce. The comedy is supplied by Sir Hudson Lowe, his beans and his counters. The farce is the career of the Commissioners.

By the Treaty of August 2, 1815,[1] it was provided, at the instance of Castlereagh, which he afterwards regretted, that Austria, Prussia, and Russia were "to appoint Commissioners to proceed to and abide at the place which the Government of His Britannic Majesty shall have assigned for the residence of Napoleon Buonaparte, and who without being responsible for his custody will assure themselves of his presence." And by the next article His Most Christian Majesty of France was to be invited by the signatory Courts to send a similar functionary. Prussia, combining a judicious foresight with a wise economy, declined to avail herself of this privilege. But the other Courts hastened to nominate their representatives. These had, it will be observed, one sole and single duty, to "assure themselves of his presence." It is sufficient to observe that none of them ever once saw him face to face, except one who beheld his corpse.

The Russian once from the racecourse thought he saw him standing on the steps of his house.[2] On the same occasion the Austrian, concealed in a trench, perceived through a telescope a man in a three-cornered hat whom he judged to be the Emperor.[3] The Frenchman had the same telescopic glimpse,[4] but, remaining till Napoleon's death, was privileged to see his remains.[5] That is the whole record of their mission, to "assure themselves of his presence."

---

[1] Forsyth, i. 435.
[2] Balmain, Oct. 1, 1817. But Sturmer, who was with him, gives a much less positive account.
[3] St. Cère, p. 155. Cf. Gourgaud, ii. 297-8.
[4] Didot, p. 25.   [5] *Ibid.* p. 34.

They had, therefore, a large balance of time to spend in interviewing and abusing the Governor, to whom they were a torment, as implying a rival authority, and who treated them accordingly. He characteristically assured the Austrian that he had searched through Puffendorf, Vattel, and Grotius in vain to find a parallel to their position,[1] or, he might have added, to his own. But this in no degree comforted those who wanted to see Napoleon if only for a moment, and to whom that satisfaction was denied. The slightest contact between the Commissioners and Longwood was vigilantly watched and instantly reported to Lowe. But they continued to prowl round Longwood, the Emperor maliciously observing them from behind his perforated shutters or venetian blinds, and sometimes sending out his suite to pick up news from them. But this again was by no means what the Commissioners came for.

Once, indeed, Napoleon asked them, as private individuals, to luncheon; for he did not doubt that their curiosity would prevail over their etiquette and the constraint of the Governor. This was a pathetic incident. The meal, indeed, would not have been a pleasant one, as he spent all the morning in preparing an elaborate appeal to them. But they never came. He waited till five o'clock, when an orderly brought a cavalier refusal from the Russian and the Austrian on the ground of "les convenances."[2] Montchenu sent no answer, though this must have been the occasion on which he is supposed to have sent the heroic reply: "Tell your master that I am here to guard him and not to dine with him."[3] On no other occasion was the option open to Montchenu or the Commissioners. It was their last and only chance.

Montchenu, the French Commissioner, took himself the most seriously, and therefore, in this absurd commission, was by much the most absurd. His appointment is said to have been the revenge of Talleyrand for all that he had endured

---

[1] St. Cère, p. 49. [2] Montholon, ii. 210, 211; Gourgaud, ii. 347-8.
[3] Didot, p. 103, note; Sturmer, p. 251; *Voice*, i. 431.

at the hands of Napoleon. "It is my only revenge, but it is terrible," he said. "What torture for a man like Napoleon to be obliged to live with an ignorant and pedantic chatterbox. I know him, he cannot endure such a boredom, he will become ill and die as before a slow fire."[1] As we have seen, however, this subtle vengeance failed in its object, for Montchenu never once succeeded in inflicting himself on the captive. In early life he had known the Emperor, when Napoleon was a subaltern at Valence in a regiment of which Montchenu was lieutenant-colonel, and when both were rivals for the affections of Mademoiselle de Saint-Germain, who, however, preferred M. de Montalivet, whom she married, to either.[2] He seems to have retained this amorous complexion at St. Helena, and his conversation, as reported by Gourgaud, appears to consist entirely of indecorous observations and immoral advice.[3] He endeavoured to "embrace Mrs. Martin," whoever she may have been.[4] He sent Lady Lowe a declaration of love in eight pages, which Lady Lowe offered to show Gourgaud.[5] His fatuity was only equalled by his vanity. He boasted at large about his success with English ladies. Some 4,000 he has known: he intimates that "they were not cruel."[6]

Montchenu appeared to have pleasant recollections of Valence;[7] he questioned Gourgaud as to the later loves of Napoleon;[8] he showed the Emperor little attentions, sent him newspapers and the like.[9] Napoleon's memories of Montchenu do not seem to have been so favourable. "I know this Montchenu," he says. "He is an old fool, a chatterbox, a carriage general who has never smelt powder.[10] I will not see him."[11] The worst of this description, says the Russian Commissioner, is that it is accurate.[12] Again, "Poor fool, poor old fool, old booby," Napo-

---

[1] *Mémoires de Rochechouart*, p. 405.   [2] Montholon, i. 310, 311.
[3] *Voice*, i. 508; Gourgaud, ii. 4, 5, 308.   [4] Forsyth, i. 240.
[5] Gourgaud, ii. 480.   [6] *Ibid.* ii. 480–1.
[7] Montholon, i. 311.   [8] *Ibid.* ii. 477.   [9] *Ibid.* i. 335.
[10] St. Cère, p. 61.   [11] Balmain, Sept. 10, 1816.
[12] *Ibid.*, Sept. 10, 1816; Forsyth, i. 235; *Voice*, i. 102.

leon calls him.[1] And again, "He is one of those men who support the ancient prejudice that Frenchmen are born mountebanks."[2] Later on the Emperor threatens to kick the old Marquis out of doors should he appear at Longwood; not because he is the French Commissioner, but because of some papers that he has signed.[3] He is an object of ridicule to all. He had been the laughing-stock of Paris. One eminent compatriot described him as "bavard insupportable, complètement nul." Even Lowe cuts jokes at him.[4] From his willingness to accept and his reluctance to extend hospitality, he was known as M. de Monter-chez-nous.[5] Henry, who attended him medically, had, however, the laugh against himself. He had reckoned up a long tale of fees; the Marquis rewarded him with an obliging note.[6]

This nobleman was now past sixty. He had been a page of Louis XV. Having entered the army before the Revolution, and followed the princes into exile, he made at the Restoration the same astonishing bound in military promotion that Las Cases had accomplished in the naval service.[7] In December 1815 he was nominated as French Commissioner at St. Helena, an appointment which had the negative advantage of securing him from his creditors.[8] His positive duties "were to assure himself habitually by his own eyes of the existence of Bonaparte." His own eyes, as we have seen, never enabled him to do more than assure himself of the end of that existence. Nevertheless, he set off in a serious and indeed heroic spirit. He began his despatches from Teneriffe on the voyage out. "I have the honour to warn you," he says to his chief, "that I am quite decided never to separate myself from my prisoner so long as he lives."[9] He arrives on the anniversary of Waterloo, lands precipitately, and demands at once to be conducted to

[1] *Voice*, i. 64; Forsyth, i. 235.
[2] Didot, p. 5.
[3] Gourgaud, ii. 364.
[4] Forsyth, i. 192.
[5] Seaton, p. 111; Jackson, p. 139.
[6] Henry, ii. 70–1.
[7] Didot, pp. 4, 5.
[8] St. Cère, p. 15.
[9] Didot, p. 38.

Longwood, that he may send his Government a certificate of the existence of Napoleon by the ship leaving next day.[1] He is with difficulty appeased, but tells Lowe that it is essential that he should be in a position to say that he has seen the captive.[2] Two days afterwards (June 20), the Governor asks Count Bertrand if the Emperor will receive the Commissioners. "Have they brought any letters for the Emperor from their sovereigns?" asks Bertrand. "No; they have come under the Convention of August 2, 1815, to assure themselves of his presence." Bertrand will take the Emperor's orders. Have they got the Convention? There is a terrible doubt. No one had thought of bringing a copy; no copy can be found; and yet it is from this instrument that they derive their authority and their official existence. The Commissioners are at their wits' end. At last, by a freak of fortune, after a search of three weeks, Sturmer finds in his trunk some loose sheets of the *Journal des Débats*, which he had brought in due course of packing, and which happened to contain the precious treaty.[3] In this undignified form it was forwarded to Napoleon,[4] who answers through Montholon on August 23 by a protest against it. Lowe communicates to the Commissioners an extract from this letter, which amounted to a refusal to see them officially.[5] In the meantime, says Lowe, "they are sick with their desire of seeing him."[6] Soon they become mad with the same desire. Montchenu wants to break into the house with a company of grenadiers.[7] He is reminded that Napoleon has sworn to shoot the first man who enters his room without his leave.[8] Then the impatient Marquis attempts the entry alone and is turned back by a sergeant.[9] He made his final and not less fruitless attempt to penetrate into Longwood as late

[1] St. Cère, p. 17; Forsyth, i. 196–7; Didot, p. 12.
[2] Forsyth, i. 197.   [3] Didot, p. 68; St. Cère, pp. 9, 10, 11.
[4] July 23; Forsyth, i. 256.   [5] St. Cère, p. 12.   [6] Forsyth, i. 233.
[7] St. Cère, p. 18. See, too, his renewed activity in Sept. 1820; Forsyth, iii. 239–40.
[8] St. Cère, p. 13.   [9] Montholon, i. 333–4.

as September 1820, and was then repulsed by Lowe, though Montchenu declared that he would force his way in even should the sentry "fire at him a shot which would soon re-echo through the whole of Europe." Eventually he has to subside into an attitude of watchfulness, in ambush for the subordinate members of the French colony, in hopes of inveigling them to meals,[1] and ultimately to gossip. In this last effort he to some extent succeeded, and he became on such terms with Gourgaud as to bid him a tender farewell, strictly enjoining him to make known to whom it might concern the terrible dreariness of life at St. Helena, and the consequent necessity that the Commissioner's salary should be not less than £4,000 a year.[2]

Montchenu was distinguished from the other Commissioners by the possession of a secretary; a distinction which was not altogether an advantage. We have an impression that the secretary, M. de Gors,[3] was entrusted with the duty of supervising his chief. At any rate he reported upon him with startling candour. After, we presume, copying Montchenu's despatches, de Gors accompanies them with a scathing commentary. "I am sorry to have to say it, on account of M. de Montchenu, but I am bound to declare that his criticisms on his colleagues are unfounded, and are too much coloured by his own personality. He should have been more just to M. de Balmain, the only one who has really taken to heart the common interests of the commission, to which by excess of zeal he has sacrificed his health and repose. M. de Montchenu should not have forgotten that it is to Balmain that the mission owes any degree of interest that it possesses. But he has never been able to make up his mind to join Balmain in a simple visit to the inhabitants of Longwood. He has chattered a good deal, always blamed what he did not do himself, and has himself never done anything when the opportunity offered. He has occupied himself with disputes of precedence; and things have

[1] *Ibid.* i. 335; Gourgaud, ii. 446.
[2] Gourgaud, i. 484. [3] Didot, p. 7; Montholon, ii. 221.

now taken such a turn that the post of Longwood will not be captured without a thousand difficulties."[1]

It is unnecessary to add anything to the description of Montchenu by Montchenu's secretary. We may pass to the Commissioner who, in the secretary's opinion, shone so much in comparison with his own chief.

The Count of Balmain,[2] the Russian Commissioner, was one of the Ramsays of Balmain, or rather of a branch settled in Russia for a century and a quarter.[3] He began inauspiciously by proposing to bring a young Parisian seamstress with him in an unofficial capacity, but this scandal appears to have been averted by the horror of the other Commissioners.[4] Not that such a proceeding would have conspicuously jarred with the morals of St. Helena, for, if we may credit our French chroniclers, the naval chiefs there lived with mistresses;[5] and the loves of Gourgaud himself, if we may judge from his innuendoes, were neither limited nor refined.[6]

Balmain seemes to have been the Commissioner of the coolest judgment and most agreeable manner; and Longwood, so to speak, set its cap at him, but without much success.[7] Balmain, says Sturmer, has acquired general esteem. He is extremely modest and extremely prudent, avoiding carefully anything that could give umbrage to the Governor. He is, besides, accomplished, and writes well. Obliging, amiable, and unpretentious, he is beloved by all who know him. He is thus a striking contrast with M. de Montchenu, for whom he has a scarcely veiled contempt.[8] His instructions were not identical with those of his colleagues, for he was thus enjoined: "Dans vos relations avec Bonaparte, vous garderez les ménagements

[1] Didot, pp. 29, 30.   [2] Forsyth, i. 192. Cf. Jackson, p. 138.
[3] Balmain, preface to his report (*Revue Bleue*).
[4] St. Cère, p. 3.
[5] Gourgaud, i. 207, ii. 145, 151; Balmain, July 8, 1817; *Voice*, ii. 211, cf. note. Cf., too, *Voice*, ii. 224, 335 note, 434 note.
[6] *E.g.* Gourgaud, i. 103, 131, 414; ii. 80.
[7] *E.g. Ibid.* ii. 349, 352, 353, 356.   [8] St. Cère, p. 20.

et la mesure qu'exige une situation aussi delicate, *et les égards personnels qu'on lui doit!*[1]—a sentence which is neither found nor implied in the instructions of the others. But what was infinitely more effective than the sentence was the fact that the italics represent a line drawn under those words by the Emperor Alexander himself. So grave an emphasis was not lost on Balmain, who declared that his Emperor desired him to use a courtesy and reserve in regard to Napoleon which compelled him to dissociate himself from some of Montchenu's more startling proceedings.[2] But the underscoring by the Emperor does not seem to have long guided the policy of the Russian Government, for it presented to the Congress of Aix-la-Chapelle a memorial which might have been written by Bathurst himself, and which embodied the undying rancour of Pozzo di Borgo. It demanded rigorous treatment of Napoleon; more especially that he should be compelled to show himself twice a day, by force if necessary, to the Commissioners and the Governor. But all the thunders and all the menaces of all the Powers of Europe failed to exact this simple condition. Napoleon never showed himself, and remained master of the field.

Balmain commenced his career at St. Helena by falling in love with a Miss Bruck (or Brook), by whom he was refused:[3] he ended it by marrying Miss Johnson, the step-daughter of Sir Hudson, who seems afterwards to have amused the Court of St. Petersburg by her eccentricities and her accent. This courtship, which was carried on during his last two years at St. Helena, complicated his relations with the Governor, for it hampered him in the expression of his opinions, though it did not prevent constant conflicts with that official. But it makes his testimony as to Lowe all the more valuable and impartial.

With all his circumspection, however, Balmain does not

---

[1] Instructions prefixed to Balmain's reports.
[2] See this memorial in Didot, p. 293.   [3] Didot, p. 190.

escape the mist of unveracity that befogged St. Helena.[1] On November 2, 1817, Montholon records that the Emperor sends Gourgaud to pump (if so expressive a vulgarism be permitted) the Commssioners, who have, he knows, received despatches from their Governments. Gourgaud returns, according to Montholon's narrative, bringing an immaterial falsehood, supposed to come from Sturmer, and the statement from Balmain that his Emperor has charged him with certain communications for Napoleon.[2] Gourgaud's record, it should be noted, in no respect confirms this. Montholon continues by narrating that for two days afterwards there are constant communications with the Russian.[3] A paper of explanations is dictated by the Emperor.[4] On December 17, Montholon states that Napoleon is determined to send Gourgaud to Europe, for he is possessed by recollections of Tilsit and Erfurt, and is therefore anxious to make overtures to the Emperor Alexander, "though I see nothing in the communications to Balmain to warrant these hopes." [5] On January 11, 1818, he has this entry: "An important communication from Count Balmain is transmitted through General Gourgaud. Dreams of a return to Europe, and of princely hospitality in Russia." [6] We turn to Gourgaud, and find that on that day he tried, as the Emperor desired, to meet Balmain, but failed to do so.[7] Neither there, nor elsewhere, does he hint at any communication such as that described by Montholon. In vain, too, we search Balmain's despatches, published or manuscript, which are indeed in a very different vein.[8] What this communication, conveyed from some one through some one, neither of whom knew anything about it, purported to be, we also learn from Montholon. On February 10, 1818, he has a vague entry about hopes from the fraternal friendship of

[1] Montholon, ii. 9.   [2] *Ibid*. ii. 221–2.
[3] *Ibid*. ii. 222.   [4] *Ibid*. ii. 226.   [5] *Ibid*. ii. 237.
[6] *Ibid*. ii. 246.   [7] Gourgaud, ii. 437–8.
[8] Not a trace in Balmain's MS. despatches which I have seen.

Alexander, and as to the acceptability of Gourgaud at the Russian court. Under these influences Napoleon dictates an elaborate reply to the mysterious message, which had never been sent or received. In this paper he thanks the Emperor Alexander, as a brother, for the assurances received from him through Balmain and for the hospitality offered by him in Russia, proceeds to answer three questions which the Emperor Alexander had ordered Balmain to put, as to the occupation of the Duchy of Oldenburg in 1812, as to the war with Russia, and as to the failure in the negotiations for a Russian marriage: and concludes by offering the Emperor Alexander his alliance should that sovereign throw over the Bourbons, and by declaring himself even willing to conclude a treaty of commerce with Britain should that be the necessary condition of a good understanding.[1] This paper was doubtless given to Gourgaud for his guidance; and it was in all probability substantially the same document as that which Bertrand attempted to hand to Balmain two months afterwards, and which Balmain declined to receive.[2]

What is the meaning of it all? It is clear that there was no communication from Balmain to Napoleon. Putting aside the improbability of it, and the absolute silence of Balmain the reputed author, as well as of Gourgaud the reputed channel, the Emperor Alexander was at that time in no mood for inviting Napoleon to Russia, or asking him retrospective historical questions. On the contrary, this was the year of the Congress of Aix-la-Chapelle, where the Russian Government demanded more stringent custody for Napoleon. It is true that Fain in his *Manuscrit de 1812* says that Alexander through Balmain sent to ask Napoleon why he had not made peace at Toulon and to express his regret that the fallen emperor had not taken refuge in Russia, where he would have been treated as Louis XVIII was at Mittau. Fain, who fixes this message at nine years after 1812, does not seem to know that Balmain

[1] Montholon, ii. 251, 260.   [2] Balmain, April 10, 1818.

left St. Helena in 1820. But it is clear from the context that Montholon is the sole authority for the statement, which also gives Montholon and not Gourgaud as the channel of the interrogation. We may dismiss with absolute confidence the story of the communication. But why, then, did Napoleon found a State paper on a message which he never received, and answer questions which never were asked? The explanation would appear to be this. Montholon tells us, two months before Gourgaud's departure, that the Emperor is determined to send Gourgaud to Europe to appeal to the Emperor Alexander.[1] It seems to us, then, that in view of Gourgaud's departure he wished to give this officer a paper, a kind of credential which could be shown; that he had faint hopes of winning the sympathy of the Russian Emperor, partly from the recollection of the ascendancy that he had once exercised over Alexander, partly because he was no doubt aware that Balmain's instructions had a shade of favour in them, partly because he must have been aware that Alexander had no love for the Bourbons, and that circumstances might make it necessary to make new arrangements for filling their unstable throne; that he therefore desired especially to clear himself on the points which had alienated Alexander from him; that the supposititious message from Alexander furnished a ground on which to base his explanations; that many who saw the paper would not know that this ground was fictitious; and that if the document or its purport ever reached Alexander, the message and the questions could be explained away as misunderstood conversation. It is even possible, though by no means probable, that Balmain may in conversation have asked such questions of the suite out of pure curiosity. At any rate, if the paper ever reached Alexander at all, matters would have gone so far that this flaw would seem insignificant. Strange were the workings of that astute and unscrupulous mind: we do not profess to follow them: we can only ascertain the facts,

[1] Montholon, ii. 237.

and speculate. For one thing, Napoleon in those days never liked to neglect a chance, even if it seemed remote. And the interests of his son, which were ever before him, must be kept in mind. It might some day be useful for the dynasty that an attempt should be made to clear away the misunderstanding with Russia. Meanwhile Balmain, innocent and honourable gentleman as he appears to have been, and as the tone of his despatches indicates, was going on his blameless way, unconscious of these wiles, and resolute as would appear only on one course—that of keeping Longwood and its intrigues at arm's length.

On Balmain's departure Montchenu (aware perhaps of his secretary's preference for the Russian) summed up his character with vindictive severity. "You have no idea," he writes, "of M. de Balmain's extravagances, of his ineptitude, of his weakness and eccentricity." And he proceeds to compare himself with his colleague. Often did Sir Hudson say to the other Commissioners, "Ah, gentlemen, why do you not behave like the Marquis?" [1]—at least so the Marquis complacently records.

Bartholomew, Baron Sturmer, was the Austrian Commissioner.[2] He was only twenty-eight when he reached St. Helena, and he had not long been married to a pretty and agreeable Frenchwoman,[3] who kept Las Cases, to his extreme indignation, at a distance, although he claimed that she had received the greatest kindnesses in Paris from Madame de Las Cases and himself.[4] His position was the most difficult of all, for his Government constantly enjoined him to work harmoniously with Lowe, which was in effect impossible.[5]

Napoleon tried to open relations with the representative of his father-in-law. He once sent to ask if, in case of grave

[1] Didot, p. 190; St. Cère, pp. xi–xii.
[2] Forsyth, i. 191. See as to Sturmer, Ambassador at Constantinople in 1845, Layard's *Autobiography*, ii. 60.
[3] Montholon, i. 310; Gourgaud, i. 208, note; *Voice*, ii. 191, 245; Jackson, p. 139.
[4] Las Cases, v. 277–9; St. Cère, p. 53.   [5] *Voice*, ii. 401, note.

illness, he might entrust Sturmer with a message to the
Austrian Emperor which should reach that monarch and no
one else. Sturmer could only reply, helplessly, that he would
ask his Government for instructions, which of course never
arrived.[1]

Sturmer was withdrawn in 1818, on the suggestion of the
British Government, made at the instance of Lowe. Layard
found him in 1845 ambassador at Constantinople,[2] and describes him and his wife. To Montchenu, on Sturmer's departure, was awarded the cumulative sinecure of representing
Austria as well as France. The Marquis saw his opportunity. He at once demanded of his Government a commission as lieutenant-general, a high decoration, and £500
a year increase of salary from them, as well as a salary of
£1,200 a year from the Austrian Government.[3] How these
modest requests were received history may guess but does not
record.

Whether from the diversity of their instructions, or the ma-
lignity of the climate, or the humours of their courts, the Commissioners could scarcely be called an harmonious body. On
only three points did they show any agreement. One was contempt for Sir Hudson Lowe, on which they were bitterly
unanimous.[4] Another was the dearness of St. Helena and the
consequent inadequacy of their salaries, on which they con-
curred to the pitch of enthusiasm.[5] The third was the effect of
their stay on their nerves. "Far from acclimatizing myself to
this horrible rock," writes Balmain, "I suffer constantly from
my nerves; my health is already ruined by the climate." [6]
Three months later fresh nerve attacks drive him to Brazil.[7]
But this is as nothing to the nerves of Sturmer. Sturmer for six

[1] St. Cère, p. xxiv, see also pp. 129-30.
[2] See *Autobiography*, ii. 60.
[3] Balmain, July 27, 1818.   [4] *Ibid*, June 5, 1818.
[5] Forsyth, i. 192; Montholon, ii. 264; St. Cère, pp. 115-6.
[6] Balmain, May 28, 1818.   [7] *Ibid*., Aug. 18, 1818.

or eight months before he left was seized with a sort of hysteria. He wept without knowing why, and laughed without knowing why. At last his nervous attacks became so violent that he had to be held by four men when the fit seized him, and could only be calmed by opium.[1] The climate or Lowe or both were too much for the systems of these unlucky diplomatists.

[1] St. Cère, pp. 215–6.

CHAPTER TWELVE

The Emperor at Home

★

No picture of St. Helena at this time can be complete without at least a sketch of the central figure: all the more as it is the last of the many portraits of Napoleon that we can obtain. Of his physical appearance from the time of his passing into British hands there are various accounts, too long and minute to be inserted here. These, therefore, or the most graphic of them, we relegate to an appendix.

As to his habitation, Longwood itself was a collection of huts which had been constructed as a cattle-shed.[1] It was swept by an eternal wind, it was shadeless, and it was damp.[2] Lowe himself can say no good of it,[3] and may have felt the strange play of fortune by which he was allotted the one delightful residence on the island [4] with twelve thousand a year while Napoleon was living in an old cow-house on eight.

The lord of so many palaces, who had slept as a conqueror in so many palaces not his own, was now confined to two small rooms of equal size—about fourteen feet by twelve, and ten or eleven high.[5] To this little measure had shrunk all his conquests, glories, triumphs, spoils. Each of these rooms was lit by two small windows looking towards the regimental camp. In one corner was the little camp bed with green silk curtains, which the Emperor had used at Marengo and Austerlitz. To hide the back door there was a screen, and between this screen and the fireplace an old sofa, on which Napoleon passed most of his day, though it was so covered with books that there was scarcely space for comfort. The walls were covered with brown nankeen, and amid the general squalor a magnificent wash-hand-stand with silver ewers and basins displayed an uncongenial splendour. But the ornaments of the room were other

---

[1] Montholon, i. 159, 160, 186. [2] *Voice*, ii. 431-4.
[3] Forsyth, i. 214, 215. [4] *Voice*, ii. 430.
[5] Cf. Las Cases, iii. 2.

than this; they were the salvage of the wreck of his family and his empire. There was, of course, a portrait (by Isabey) of Marie Louise, then living in careless beatitude with Neipperg at Parma. There were the portraits of the King of Rome, riding a lamb, and putting on a slipper, both by Thibault: there was also a bust of the child. There was a miniature of Josephine. There hung also the alarum clock of Frederick the Great taken from Potsdam, and the watch of the First Consul when in Italy, suspended by a chain of the plaited hair of Marie Louise.[1]

In the second room there were a writing-table, some bookshelves, and another bed, on which the Emperor would rest in the daytime, or to which he would change from the other, when he was, as was generally the case, restless and sleepless at night.[2]

O'Meara gives a graphic picture of Napoleon in his bedroom. He sat on the sofa, which was covered with a long white cloth. On this "reclined Napoleon, clothed in his white morning gown, white loose trowsers and stockings all in one. A chequered red Madras (handkerchief) upon his head, and his shirt collar open without cravat. His air was melancholy and troubled. Before him stood a little round table with some books, at the foot of which lay in confusion upon the carpet, a heap of those he had already perused."[3]

His usual costume was, however, more formal than this. He wore a hunting uniform, a green coat with sporting buttons, and, when the cloth grew shabby, had it turned rather than wear English cloth.[4] With these he wore white kerseymere breeches and stockings. He gave up wearing his uniform of the Chasseurs of the Guard six weeks after he arrived in the island.[5] He retained, however, the famous little cocked hat —several of which by the by were stolen as relics in the first

[1] *Voice*, i. 40–2; Las Cases, iii. 2, 4.
[2] Las Cases, iii. 3–4.
[3] *Voice*, i. 41–2.
[4] Gourgaud, ii. 256.
[5] Montholon, i. 181.

months of his exile—but the tricoloured cockade he laid aside
with some ceremony two years after Waterloo, telling his
valet to keep it as a relic, or in view of better days.[1] These
details are not wholly vapid, because he had method and
meaning even in such trifles. Moreover, if we would picture
to ourselves Napoleon in his final phase, we must know them.

What was his manner of life?

He breakfasted alone at eleven, dressed for the day about
two, and dined, at first, at seven, though he afterwards
changed the hour to four. Just before Gourgaud left there was
a new arrangement; the midday breakfast was abolished, there
was dinner at three, and supper at ten; then a few days afterwards dinner is to be at two—changes suspected by Gourgaud
as intended to suit the health and convenience of Madame
de Montholon,[2] but which were probably devised to beguile
the long weariness of the day or to cheat the long wakefulness
of the night. For he practically passed all his days in his hut,
reading, writing, talking, but withal bored to death.

The world saw nothing of this shabby interior: what it
did see was totally different, for Napoleon kept up, as part of
his contention about title, the utmost state consistent with his
position. He drove out with six horses to his carriage, and an
equerry in full uniform riding at each door.[3] But the six
horses, sometimes a source of danger from the sharpness of
the turns and the pace at which he chose to be driven, were
not a mere luxury.[4] The roads at St. Helena were such that
the ladies of his party when they went out to dinner or to a
ball had to be conveyed in a Merovingian equipage drawn by
several yoke of oxen.[5]

The etiquette was not less severe indoors. Gourgaud and
Bertrand and Montholon were kept standing for hours, till
they nearly dropped from fatigue.[6] On one occasion Napoleon

---

[1] Montholon, ii. 135.   [2] Gourgaud, ii. 440, 441, 443.
[3] Didot, p. 58; *Madame de Montholon*, p. 54.
[4] Didot, p. 47.   [5] Las Cases, i. 393; ii. 99.   [6] Forsyth, iii. 394.

is annoyed by an irrepressible yawn from Bertrand. The Grand Marshal excuses himself by stating that he has been standing more than three hours. Gourgaud, pale and almost ill with fatigue, would lean against the door.[1] Antommarchi, who, by the by, had to put on a court dress when he visited his patient,[2] had to stand in his presence till he nearly fainted.[3] On the other hand, if one of them was seated by the Emperor and rose when Madame Bertrand or Madame de Montholon entered the room, he was rebuked.[4] The Emperor had always been keenly alive to this ritual.[5] He discourses on it diffusely to Las Cases.[6] He noticed at once in the Hundred Days the advance of democracy when one of his Ministers rose to leave him without permission.[7] Even in the agony of Rochefort he observed a small breach of etiquette of the same kind.[8] Indeed, when Gourgaud mentions to him that in China the sovereign is worshipped as a god, he gravely replies that that is as it should be.[9]

At St. Helena the small court that remained was chivalrously sedulous to observe the strictest forms to their dethroned Emperor. None of them came to his room without being summoned.[10] If they had something of importance to communicate, they asked for an audience.[11] None uninvited joined him in a walk;[12] and all in his presence remained bare-headed, until he became aware that the English were ordered to remain covered in speaking to him, when he desired his followers to do the same.[13] None spoke to him first, unless when conversation was in flow.[14] But Bertrand once or twice contradicted his master so abruptly that the Emperor at once remarked it,

[1] *Madame de Montholon*, pp. 56–7.
[2] Forsyth, iii. 226.   [3] Henry, ii. 77.
[4] Gourgaud, i. 141.   [5] See, *e.g.*, Gourgaud, i. 157–8, 383.
[6] Las Cases, ii. 283.   [7] Lavallette, ii. 139.
[8] *Madame de Montholon*, p. 9.
[9] Gourgaud, ii. 61. Cf. a trait narrated by Las Cases, vii. 245.
[10] Las Cases, v. 27.   [11] *Ibid.* v. 27.   [12] Warden, p. 178.
[13] Las Cases, v. 27.   [14] *Ibid.*

and observed that he would not have dared to behave so at the Tuileries.[1] Bertrand, too, incurred the imperial displeasure by not dining as Grand Marshal regularly at the imperial table; for sometimes his wife wished him to dine with her.[2] Anything of this kind that savoured of shortcoming and neglect seriously annoyed Napoleon. Little things that might have escaped his notice in the bustle of Paris weighed on him at St. Helena; [3] they brought home to him, too, the change in his position. Then there was the question of the title. But Bertrand, though he might sometimes flag in observance, always sent out the letters on behalf of his master sealed with the seal and styled with the pomp of the Grand Marshal of the Palace and of the Emperor,[4] though there was little at St. Helena to recall either the one or the other. At dinner Napoleon was served with great state, on gold and silver plate, and waited on by his French servants in a rich livery of green and gold.[5] Twelve English sailors, chosen from the squadron, were at first allotted to him and dressed in the same costume,[6] but they disappeared with the *Northumberland*, to which ship they belonged; and Napoleon declined Lowe's offer to replace them with soldiers. A vacant place was reserved next him for the Empress, but this was sometimes given to some favoured lady.[7] There was a vast variety of dishes, of which the Emperor ate heartily; on an honoured guest he would press particular dainties.[8] As always, his dinner occupied but a short time. At the Tuileries it was an affair of twenty minues; at St. Helena five minutes more was allowed to enable Bertrand to have his fill of bonbons. And in the earlier days at Longwood he would

---

[1] Gourgaud, i. 80; Montholon, i. 173. Cf. Maitland, p. 214.
[2] Gourgaud, i. 152; Montholon, i. 195–6.
[3] Las Cases, iii. 26–7.   [4] Didot, p. 47.
[5] *Blackwood's Magazine*, Jan. 1834, p. 51; Montholon, i. 195.
[6] *Madame de Montholon*, p. 52; Montholon, i. 194.
[7] *Blackwood's Magazine*, Jan. 1834, p. 51; Warden, p. 114.
[8] Gourgaud, i. 536.

send at dessert for some volume of French tragedy, which he would read aloud.[1]

To many this petty pomp may seem absurd, but with the suite we cannot help feeling a melancholy sympathy; as we see these gallant gentlemen determined to prove that whatever Napoleon might be to others, to them he was always their sovereign.

And we must here notice the strange composition of the party. Montholon, as we are informed by his biographer, held an hereditary office under the old dynasty to which Louis XVIII offered to restore him on the first Restoration;[2] a statement of which we should like some confirmation. Las Cases was a Royalist emigrant. Gourgaud was the foster-brother of the Duc de Berry, and was one of Louis XVIII's Guard during the first Restoration. Of the four, Bertrand was the only one who could be described as free from all connection with Royalism. And Napoleon on one occasion describes himself gaily as the only one of the party who had ever been a Republican.

The one pleasure of the captive's life was an arrival of books. Then he would shut himself up with them for days together—bathing in them, revelling in them, feasting on them.[3] But indeed he was always inclined to remain in the house. He hated the signs of prison, the sentries, the orderly officer, the chance of meeting Lowe. By remaining at home, he tells Gourgaud, he preserves his dignity: there he is always Emperor, and that is the only way in which he can live.[4] So he tries to obtain exercise indoors. Lowe reports on one occasion that the Emperor had constructed a sort of hobby-horse made of cross beams. He sat at one end of the beam with a heavy weight at the other and played a sort of see-saw.[5] But these specifics

[1] Montholon, i. 196; *Madame de Montholon*, p. 57.
[2] Montholon, i. lxxxvii; ii. 511, note.
[3] Las Cases, iv. 289; Montholon. i. 315, 317; *Voice*, i. 67.
[4] Gourgaud, ii. 374.   [5] Forsyth, iii. 269.

would fail, and in his deprivation of exercise he would become ill, he would be touched with scurvy, his legs would swell, and he would derive a morbid satisfaction from the reflection that he was suffering from the Governor's restrictions.[1] Then in the last year of his life he determined to live again. He rode a little,[2] but his main interest was his garden. Surrounded by a gang of Chinese labourers, he would plan and swelter and dig.[3] A great painter, says Montholon, would have found a worthy subject in the mighty conqueror wearing red slippers and a vast straw hat, with his spade in his hand, working away at dawn, directing the exertions of his impressed household, and, what Montholon confesses were more efficacious, the labours of the Chinese gardeners.[4] Horace Vernet painted a portrait of him in this costume, resting from his labours with a somewhat flabby expression and countenance. So strenuously did he move earth to make a shelter that Lowe became alarmed. He feared that his sentinels might find their supervision limited; he gave a solemn warning that the work should not proceed; he took credit to himself that he did not demolish it. Little or no heed seems to have been taken of this futile fussiness, for Lowe was now practically ignored. Napoleon threw himself into the operations with his usual ardour: spent much time and money on them: bought large trees and moved them, with the aid of the artillery regiment and some hundreds of Chinese. All this distracted him for a time, and gave him exercise.

His unlucky suite had to delve whether they liked or not. But this was perhaps a not unwelcome change of labour. For indoors their work was hard. Napoleon hated writing, and had almost lost the art, for what he did write was illegible.[5] It is recorded that on his marriage he with incredible difficulty

[1] Gourgaud, ii. 328, 334.
[2] May 1820–for the first time for four years. Forsyth, iii. 227, 235.
[3] Ibid. iii 196.
[4] Montholon, ii. 371; Forsyth, iii. 195–6, 198–9.
[5] Chaptal, p. 353. Nor could he write without inking his hands. Méneval, i. 421; Montholon, ii. 10.

managed to write a short note to his father-in-law. With infinite pains his secretaries contrived to make it presentable.[1] He could only dictate; and this he did with a vengeance;[2] on one occasion at Longwood he is stated to have dictated for fourteen hours at a stretch, with only short intervals from time to time to read over what had been written.[3] Shorthand was unknown to his household, so the operation was severe; though Las Cases did invent for himself some sort of hieroglyphic system.[4] Moreover, he sometimes dictated all night. Gourgaud would be sent for at four in the morning to take the place of the exhausted Montholon.[5] He would cheer his secretaries by telling them that they should have the copyright of what they wrote, which would bring them in vast sums.[6] But this illusion did not quench their groans, and indeed in bitterer moments he told them that if they were under the impression that their work belonged to them they made a great mistake.[7] What was the result of all these labours we do not know—some of it perhaps is yet unpublished.[8] But there is a great bulk in print, and some material may have been utilized in other ways, as in the *Letters from the Cape*. Gourgaud, indeed, suspected the Emperor of several compositions, of the *Manuscrit de Ste Hélène*,[9] for example, which he certainly did not write, and of an article in the *Edinburgh Review*,[10] which was composed by Allen at Holland House, from information supplied by Cardinal Fesch and Louis Bonaparte.[11] It is probable that there was a good deal of dictated inspiration constantly proceeding from St. Helena to Europe; and Gourgaud blames the Emperor for producing so many pamphlets.[12] Some of these manuscripts

[1] Méneval, ii. 313.   [2] Jackson, p. 144; Bertrand, p. xii.
[3] Montholon, i. 296. See, too, ii. 10.   [4] Las Cases, i. 201.
[5] Gourgaud, ii. 133; Las Cases, iv. 289.
[6] Las Cases, ii. 263; Gourgaud, ii. 163, i. 544.
[7] Gourgaud, ii. 296.   [8] Scott, ix. 226; Las Cases, vi. 220–1.
[9] Gourgaud, ii. 296; Scott, ix. 168.   [10] Gourgaud, ii. 314
[11] Holland's *Foreign Reminiscences*, p. 307; *Voice*, ii. 206, note.
[12] Gourgaud, ii. 232. Cf. Montholon, ii. 437.

NAPOLEON: THE LAST PHASE

were buried in a corner of the garden, and did not, apparently, see the light.[1]

Besides gardening, riding, reading, and composition he had few distractions. At one time he took to buying lambs and making pets of them, but this innocent whim soon passed.[2] Polo was played on the island, but not by him.[3] Sport strictly so called was difficult and indifferent. Gourgaud, who was indefatigable, would sometimes shoot turtle-doves,[4] sometimes a pheasant or a partridge,[5] and sometimes a sow.[6] Sir Hudson Lowe turned out some rabbits for Napoleon to shoot,[7] but with his unlucky inopportuneness chose the moment when the Emperor had been planting some young trees.[8] However, the rats killed the rabbits, and so saved the trees; at any rate, the rabbits disappeared. Napoleon only began to shoot in his last days, and then performed feats which would make a sportsman weep. It had always been so. At Malmaison in old days he had kept a gun in his room and fired at Josephine's tame birds.[9] And now he began, during his gardening enthusiasm, in defence of his enclosure, by shooting Madame Bertrand's pet kids, to her infinite distress,[10] and any other vagrant animals that strayed within his boundary.[11] Finding a bullock there, he slew that beast also.[12] Then he sent for some goats and shot them.[13] This shooting, it need scarcely be said, caused uneasiness to the Governor, and to Montchenu his colleague, as well as a remote pang to Forsyth his biographer. What would happen, asked Lowe, if Napoleon killed some one by mistake? Could Napoleon be tried and punished for manslaughter? Such was the perturbation, that these questions were actually submitted to the Law Officers of the Crown.[14]

[1] Gourgaud, ii. 240, 343.   [2] Balmain, Jan. 30, 1819.
[3] Gourgaud, i. 221.   [4] *Ibid.* i. 109.   [5] *Ibid.* i. 108.
[6] *Ibid.* i. 217; Forsyth, i. 237.   [7] Montholon, i. 376.
[8] Gourgaud, i. 242.   [9] Chaptal, p. 334.   [10] Henry, ii. 55.
[11] Didot, p. 187; Forsyth, iii. 206, 210.
[12] Forsyth, iii. 217.   [13] *Ibid.* iii. 207, 235.
[14] *Ibid.* iii. 210-1, 489; Didot, pp. 187-8.

At first he rode, but the close attendance of an English officer was intolerable,[1] and for four years he did not get on a horse.[2] During this long repose he said comically of his horse that if ever there were a canon it was he, for he lived well and never worked.[3] He had never been nervous on horseback, he said, for he had never learned to ride. It may interest some to know that he considered the finest and best horse that ever he owned to be, not the famous Marengo, but one named Mourad Bey.[4]

He played a few games—billiards, in a careless fashion; [5] and reversi,[6] to which he had been used as a child; and chess.[7] At chess he was eminently unskilful, and it taxed all the courtliness of his suite to avoid defeating him; a simple trickery which he sometimes perceived.[8] On the *Northumberland* he had played vingt-et-un, but prohibited it when he found that it produced gambling.[9] Gourgaud gives an amusing account of a game in which he stakes four turtle-doves, while the Emperor on his side stakes a promise to receive some young ladies in whom Gourgaud is interested, and give them his autograph. Napoleon loses but does not pay. At all games he liked to cheat, flagrantly and undisguisedly, as a joke; but refused, of course, to take the money thus won, saying, with a laugh, "What simpletons you are. It is thus that young fellows of good family are ruined." [10]

It was apparently a solace to him to read aloud, though he did not read remarkably well, and had no ear for the cadences of poetry.[11] But one of the difficulties of those who like reading aloud is to find an appreciative audience, and so it was in the present case. Montholon tells us of one at least who slum-

[1] Montholon, i. 206. [2] Forsyth, iii. 227.
[3] Las Cases, vi. 207. [4] Gourgaud, ii. 70.
[5] Las Cases, vi. 63. [6] *Ibid.* ii. 52. [7] *Ibid.* ii. 235.
[8] *Madame de Montholon*, pp. 32, 57; Warden, p. 99; Cockburn, p. 12; Las Cases, i. 123.
[9] Las Cases, i. 103, 123. [10] Montholon, i. 194. Cf. Chaptal, p. 326.
[11] *Madame de Montholon*. p. 59.

bered (we suspect Gourgaud at once), a circumstance which the Emperor did not forget.[1] On another occasion Gourgaud remarks of a French play: "The 'Awakened Sleeper' sends us to sleep." [2] When the Emperor reads aloud his own memoirs the same genial companion criticizes them with such severity that Napoleon declines to read them aloud any more.[3] At one reading, however (of *Paul and Virginia*), Gourgaud weeps outright, while Madame de Montholon complains that recitals so harrowing disturb digestion.[4]

He was supposed to declaim like Talma, and prolonged declamation of French tragedy in a warm climate may sometimes invite repose. Tragedy was his favourite reading, and Corneille his favourite author in that department of literature.[5] There is on record a discourse on Corneille's tragedies, pronounced by the Emperor in the hazardous salons of the Kremlin. "Above all, I love tragedy," he said: "sublime and lofty, as Corneille wrote it. His great men are more true to life than those in history, for one only sees them in the real crisis, in the supreme moments; and one is not overloaded with the preparatory labour of detail and conjecture which historians, often erroneously, supply. So much the better for human glory, for there is much that is unworthy which should be omitted, much of doubt and vacillation: and all this should disappear in the representation of the hero. We should see him as a statue, in which the weakness and tremors of the flesh are no longer perceptible." [6] Next to Corneille he seems to have loved Racine.[7] But he was catholic in his tastes, and would readily turn to Beaumarchais,[8] Molière, and the *Arabian Nights*,[9] though these may have been concessions to the frailty of his audience. Like Pitt, his great adversary, he relished *Gil Blas*,

[1] See Gourgaud, i. 405, 421; Holland's *Foreign Reminiscences*, p. 305.
[2] Gourgaud, ii. 116. [3] *Ibid.* ii. 197. [4] *Ibid.* ii. 63.
[5] Rémusat, i. 279; *Voice*, ii. 391.
[6] Villemain, i. 226. Cf., too, Ségur, ii. 457 (the eve of Austerlitz).
[7] Montholon, i. 201. [8] *Ibid.* ii. 57.
[9] Gourgaud, ii. 116, 118, 119.

but thought it a bad book for the young, as "Gil Blas sees only the dark side of human nature, and the youthful think that that is a true picture of the world, which it is not." [1] He frequently read the Bible; [2] sometimes, in translations, Homer [3] and Virgil, [4] Æschylus [5] or Euripides. [6] From English literature he would take *Paradise Lost*, [7] Hume's *History of England*, and *Clarissa Harlowe*. [8] With Ossian, to whatever literature that poet may belong, he would commune as with an old friend. For Voltaire's *Zaïre* he had a positive passion. He had once asked Madame de Montholon to choose a tragedy for the evening's entertainment: she had chosen *Zaïre*, and thereafter they had *Zaïre* till they groaned in spirit at the very name. [9]

It might seem strange at first sight that we see little or no mention of Bossuet. For the great Bishop had been the writer who, at the critical moment, had "touched his trembling ears." The *Discourse of Universal History* had awakened his mind as Lodi awoke his ambition. On the fortunate day when he happened on the discourse, and read of Cæsar, Alexander, and the successions of empires, the veil of the temple, he tells us, was rent, and he beheld the movements of the gods. From that time in all his campaigns, in Egypt, in Syria, in Germany, on his greatest days, that vision never quitted him. [10] At St. Helena it forsook him for ever, and so we need not marvel that he avoids Bossuet.

He had always been a great reader, [11] though he declared that in his public life he only read what was of direct use for his purposes. [12] When he was a scholar at Brienne the frequency of his demands for books was the torment of the College librarian. When he was a lieutenant in garrison at Valence he

[1] *Ibid.* ii. 193.   [2] Las Cases, iii. 321; iv. 142.
[3] *Ibid.* vi. 137, 163; Montholon, i. 198.
[4] Gourgaud, i. 215.   [5] Las Cases, vii. 108.
[6] Gourgaud, i. 256.   [7] *Ibid.* i. 437.
[8] *Ibid.* i. 548.   [9] *Madame de Montholon*, p. 59.
[10] Villemain, i. 158.   [11] Chaptal, p. 174, but see p. 348.
[12] *Madame de Montholon*, p. 61.

read ravenously and indiscriminately everything he could lay
his hands on. "When I was a lieutenant of artillery," he said
before the collected princes at Erfurt, "I was for three years in
garrison at Valence. I spent that time in reading and reread-
ing the library there." [1] Later, we read of his tearing along to
join his armies, his coach full of volumes and pamphlets which
would be flung out of the window when he had run through
them.[2] When he travelled with Josephine, all the newest
books were put into the carriage for her to read to him.[3] And
though he declared that his reading was purely practical, he
always had a travelling library of general literature, with
which he took great pains. He had planned a portable collection of three thousand choice volumes which should be printed
for him. But when he found it would take six years and a quarter of a million sterling to complete, he wisely abandoned the
project.[4] Even to Waterloo he was accompanied by a travelling library of 800 volumes in six cases—the Bible, Homer,
Ossian, Bossuet, and all the seventy volumes of Voltaire.[5]
Three days after his final abdication we find him writing for
a library from Malmaison, books on America, his chosen destination, books on himself and his campaigns, a collection
of the *Moniteur*, the best dictionaries and encyclopædias.[6]
Now, in his solitude, he devoured them—history, philosophy,
strategy, and memoirs. Of these last alone he read seventy-
two volumes in twelve months.[7] Nor was he by any means a
passive reader: he would scribble on margins, he would dictate notes or criticisms. But the reading aloud was almost
entirely of works of imagination, and the selection does not
inspire one with any passionate wish to have been present.

[1] Beausset, i. 323–4.   [2] Odeleben, i. 156–7.
[3] Chaptal, p. 348. Cf. Méneval, ii. 41.
[4] Barbier, *Dict. des Ouvrages Anonymes*, i. xi, etc.; Méneval, 41–2
[5] *Porte-feuille de Buonaparte*, p. 33.
[6] *Corresp. de Napoléon*, i, xxviii, 300. Cf. Las Cases, i. 318.
[7] Gourgaud, i. 560.

Nor, as we have seen, did the actual audience greatly appreciate the privilege.

What strikes one most in his habits is the weariness and futility of it all. One is irresistibly reminded of a caged animal walking restlessly and aimlessly up and down his confined den, and watching the outside world with the fierce despair of his wild eye. If Gourgaud was bored to death, what must the Emperor have been!

He is, as a rule, calm and stoical. Sometimes, indeed, he consoles himself with a sort of abstract grandeur; sometimes he gives a sublime groan. "Adversity was wanting to my career," [1] he says. He takes up one of the official year-books of his reign. "It was a fine empire. I ruled eighty-three millions of human beings, more than half the population of Europe." He attempts to control his emotion, as he turns over the book, even to hum a tune, but is too visibly affected. [2] Another time he sits in silence, his head resting on his hands. At last he rises. "After all, what a romance my life has been!" he exclaims, and walks out of the room. [3] Nor does fame console him, for he doubts it. "All the institutions that I founded are being destroyed, such as the University and the Legion of Honour, and I shall soon be forgotten." [4] And again: "History will scarcely mention me, for I was overthrown. Had I been able to maintain my dynasty, it had been different." [5] Misgiving of the future, self-reproach for the past, [6] the monotony of a suppressed life, these were the daily torments that corroded his soul. For six years he supped the bitterness of slow, remorseful, desolate death.

Moreover, with his restless energy thrown back on himself, he was devoured by his inverted activities. He could not exist except in a stress of work. Work, he said, was his element; he was born and made for work. [7] He had known, he would

---

[1] Las Cases, i. 408. [2] Gourgaud, i. 415. Cf. Montholon, ii. 246.
[3] Las Cases, iv. 342. [4] Gourgaud, ii. 13. [5] *Ibid*. ii. 96.
[6] *Ibid*. ii. 57-8. [7] Las Cases, vi. 208.

say, the limits of his powers of walking or of seeing, but had never been able to ascertain the limits of his power of work.[1] His mind and body, says Chaptal, were incapable of fatigue. How was employment to be found at Longwood for this formidable machine? The powers of brain and nerve and body which had grappled with the world now turned on him and rent him. To learn enough English to read in the news-papers what was going on in the Europe which he had con-trolled, to dictate memoirs giving his point of view of what interested him at the moment, to gossip about his custodians, to preserve order and harmony in his little household, these were the crumbs of existence which he was left to mumble. There is no parallel to his position. The world has usually made short work of its Cæsars when it has done with them. Napoleon had sought death in battle, and by suicide, in vain. The constant efforts of assassination had been fruitless. The hope of our Ministers that the French Government would shoot or hang him had been disappointed. So Europe buckled itself to the unprecedented task of gagging and paralyzing an intelligence and a force which were too gigantic for the wel-fare and security of the world. That is the strange, unique, hideous problem which makes the records of St. Helena so profoundly painful and fascinating.

[1] Montholon, i. 401; Gourgaud, ii. 450.

CHAPTER THIRTEEN
The Conversations of Napoleon

★

IT is not wise to record every word that falls from a great man in retirement. The mind which is accustomed to constant activity and which is suddenly deprived of employment is an engine without guidance; the tongue without a purpose is not always under control. The great man is apt to soliloquize aloud, and then the suppressed volume of passion, of resentment, of scorn, bursts all dams. Napoleon was aware of this danger. "You are right to check me: I always say more than I wish when I allow myself to talk of subjects which so thrill with interest." [1] There is not so much of this as might be expected in the conversation of the Emperor at St. Helena. He sometimes lashes himself into a rage over the Governor and the restrictions and the rock itself, but as a rule he is calm and meditative, thinking aloud, often with contradictory results. This detachment of mind had been noticed on his return from Elba by Lavallette. "Never did I see him more imperturbably calm: not a word of bitterness with anyone, no impatience; listening to everything, and discussing everything, with that rare sagacity and that elevation of mind which were so remarkable in him; avowing his faults with a touching ingenuousness, or discussing his position with a penetration which his enemies could not equal." [2]

The recorded conversations of Napoleon present a certain difficulty. After the first two years of the Consulate he rarely unbuttoned himself in talk. And those with whom he may have done so most frequently, such as Duroc, or Berthier, or Bertrand, are mute. He was no doubt a great talker in public, but when he talked in public he said not what he thought, but what he wished to be considered as his ideas. At St. Helena we have a great mass of these disquisitions,[3] for he was always

[1] Montholon, ii. 151.   [2] Lavallette, ii. 140.
[3] As to his constant repetitions, see Las Cases, v. 167.

in the presence of diarists, and knew it.[1] Las Cases and
Montholon record nothing else. But all through his reign
there are abundant notes of the clear, eloquent, pungent discourse which he affected in public. Villemain gives some
admirable specimens on the authority of Narbonne. These are
almost too elaborate to be exact. There is, however, scarcely
one of the innumerable memoirs published on the Napoleonic
era which does not attempt to give specimens of Napoleon's
talk.

But to get at the man, or what little is accessible of the man,
we must go elsewhere. In our judgment Roederer is the author who renders most faithfully the conversation of Napoleon. He gives us specimens of the earlier consular style when
Napoleon was still a Republican in manner and surroundings,
when he was still a learner in civil government, before he
eyed a crown: specimens of his discourse at the Council of
State: chats at the Malmaison or St. Cloud: and also long conversations of the later period, reported verbatim; with lifelike
accuracy, so far as one can now judge. Read, for example, Roederer's report of his conversations with Napoleon in January
and February 1809, in 1811, and especially in 1813.[2] They
form in our judgment the most vivid representations of the
Emperor that exist. Concise, frank, sometimes brutal, but always interesting—such seems to have been the real talk of Napoleon. The secret of the charm is that he can bring his whole
mind instantaneously into play on a subject, and so he lights
it up in a moment with reminiscence, historical parallel, native shrewdness, knowledge of mankind in general and of
the men with whom he has had dealings in particular.

It is not possible to give a digest of Napoleon's conversation
at St. Helena. It is set forth in a score of volumes of very unequal merit and trustworthiness: it is not always easy to separate the wheat from the chaff. Some of these are filled with

[1] Las Cases, i. 11, note; vi. 240-1.
[2] Roederer, iii. 533-9, 540-8, 562-7, 580-3.

dictations by Napoleon, which have, of course, an interest and distinction of their own, but which are not conversations. For talk as revealing the man, we feel convinced that Gourgaud's is the most faithful transcript, and far superior to the other records. Montholon is not so trustworthy, or so intelligent. Las Cases pads and concocts. O'Meara's book is a translation into English of conversation carried on in Italian. It is both spirited and interesting, but does not inspire any confidence. But Gourgaud gives, we believe, an honest narrative and, wiping off the bilious hues of jealousy and boredom, an accurate picture. His are, indeed, reminiscences of high interest. But what is really remarkable is the air of rough truth about all that he records. They are not full-dress reminiscences:[1] they are, as it were, the sketch of the moment on the wrist-band and the thumb-nail. Where he differs from Las Cases and Montholon we have no doubt which to believe. On state occasions they hasten to drape their hero in the toga or the dalmatic: Gourgaud takes him as he is, in his bath, in his bed, with a Panama hat or a red Madras handkerchief round his head, in a bad temper or in a good. We will give two instances of what we mean: the executions of Ney and Murat.

Montholon records the Emperor as saying, on February 21, that "the death of Ney is a crime. The blood of Ney was sacred for France. His conduct in the Russian campaign was unequalled. It should have covered with a holy ægis the crime of high treason, if indeed Ney had really committed it. But Ney did not betray the King,"[2] and so forth. This expression of feeling is what the public would expect Napoleon to have

[1] As specimens of full-dress conversations, take those of Colonel Wilks, published by Mr. Julian Corbett in the *Monthly Review*. They are majestic dialogues, something in the style of Dr. Johnson's Parliamentary Debates. Wilks, for all we know, may have talked in this style, but he must have taken great pains in polishing the Emperor's share; for nothing can be conceived more unlike the conversations of Napoleon.

[2] Montholon, i. 227. Cf. *Voice*, i. 24.

uttered, though hardly on February 21, as he did not receive the news of Ney's execution till the middle of March.[1] Gourgaud records no such language: he reports Napoleon as varying in his view. Once he says that they have assassinated Ney: at another time he declares that he only got his deserts.[2] "No one should break his word; I despise traitors":[3] "Ney has dishonoured himself."[4] "He was precious on the field of battle, but too immoral and too stupid to succeed."[5] Napoleon even goes so far as to say that he ought never to have made Ney a marshal of France; that he should have left him a general of division; for he had, as Caffarelli had said of him, just the courage and honesty of a hussar.[6] He says that in 1814 he was a mere traitor, that he behaved, as always, like a rascal. Contrast this with the Duchesse d'Angoulême's remorse on reading Ségur's *History of the Russian Campaign*. Had we known in 1815, she says, what Ney did in Russia, he would never have been executed.[7] Contrast this with Napoleon himself when in Russia. "What a man! What a soldier; Ney is lost! I have 300 millions in the cellars of the Tuileries. I would give them all to get him back."[8] So too at Friedland: "He is not a man, he is a lion."[9] We can only conclude from this cruel change that Napoleon never forgot or forgave the terrible interview with Ney at Fontainebleau in April 1814,[10] nor the vaunt of Ney in 1815 to bring him back in a cage.[11] He only summoned him to the army, indeed, at the last moment, just before Ligny.[12] At the end there was in truth no love lost between the two heroes.

Again there comes the news of the death of Murat. As in

---

[1] Las Cases, ii. 341. Bertrand, it is true, told Gourgaud on Jan. 23 that Ney and Davoust were dead (Gourgaud, i. 130), but this was evidently a Jamestown rumour of which half was false. Ney was only shot on the previous December 7.

[2] Gourgaud, i. 498.   [3] *Ibid.* i. 77.   [4] *Ibid.* i. 316.
[5] *Ibid.* i. 498.   [6] *Ibid.* ii. 458.   [7] Ségur, vii. 284–5.
[8] *Ibid.* v. 287.   [9] *Ibid.* viii. 133.   [10] *Ibid.* vii. 153.
[11] Gourgaud, i. 490–1.   [12] *Porte-feuille de Buonaparte*, p. 39.

the case of Napoleon's discourse to Montholon about Ney's death, there is a strange particularity in this event, in that it is first announced to Napoleon by three separate people. Las Cases reads him the news. "At these unexpected words the Emperor seizes me by the arm, and cries, 'The Calabrians were more humane, more generous than those who sent me here.' This was all. After a few moments of silence, as he said no more, I continued reading."[1] This, perhaps, is the authorized version, as it is that given in the *Letters from the Cape*.

O'Meara also brought the first news. "He heard it with calmness, and immediately demanded if Murat had perished on the field of battle. At first I hesitated to tell him that his brother-in-law had been executed like a criminal. On his repeating the question, I informed him of the manner in which Murat had been put to death, which he listened to without any change of countenance."[2]

Then Gourgaud brings the first tidings. "I announce the fatal news to His Majesty, who keeps the same countenance, and remarks that Murat must have been mad to risk such an enterprise. I say that it grieves me to think of a brave man like Murat, who had so often faced death, dying by the hands of such people. The Emperor cries out that it is horrible. I urge that Ferdinand should not have allowed him to be killed. 'That is your way of thinking, young people, but one does not trifle with a throne. Could he be considered as a French General? He was one no longer. As a King? But he had never been recognized (by the Bourbons?) as one. Ferdinand had him shot, just as he has had a number of people hanged.' " But Gourgaud watches him, as they read the newspapers to him, and says that he suffers.[3]

We cannot tell which of the three chroniclers really first reported the news to Napoleon, but we feel that Gourgaud's narrative is vivid and true. Long afterwards Napoleon says to

---

[1] Las Cases, ii. 236. [2] *Voice*, i. 23–4.
[3] Gourgaud, i. 134–5. Cf. *Voice*, ii. 104.

Gourgaud, "Murat only got what he deserved. But it is all my fault, for I should have left him a marshal, and never have made him King of Naples, or even Grand Duke of Berg." [1]

So in the few specimens that we propose to give of Napoleon's conversation at St. Helena we shall mainly confine ourselves to the notes taken by Gourgaud. Napoleon, however, repeated himself constantly, and so we obtain corroborative versions of many sayings in all the chronicles of the exile.

One of the chief topics was Religion, and one of the books that Napoleon most loved to read aloud was the Bible.[2] The reading was not always for the highest motive, for on one occasion he reads up the books of Samuel and Kings to see what is their testimony in favour of legitimate monarchy.[3] But on other occasions the Bible is read with no such object; and he was, we are told, a great admirer of St. Paul.[4] His thoughts, indeed, in this dark hour turn much to questions of faith, not altogether to edification. But here again, as always in matters of fact, we are confronted with an obstacle. Bertrand states solemnly that never in France or in camp or at Elba or at St. Helena did he hear Napoleon dissert on the existence of God or the divinity of Christ. He always stopped such discussions by saying that he believed whatever his parish priest believed. The world, however, will not accept this view; it is determined to have Napoleon's views on these subjects. And it seems impossible that Gourgaud could have invented what he professes to report. However that may be, we have in his book endless records of religious conversations full of verisimilitude. We have, of course, often read anecdotes in which the Emperor is represented as pointing to the firmament and declaiming a vague Deism. Newman, too, in a noble passage, has given from tradition the final judgment passed

---

[1] Gourgaud, i. 263.
[2] *E.g.* Gourgaud, i. 195; *Madame de Montholon*, p. 65.
[3] Gourgaud, i. 550. Cf. Lady Malcolm, p. 160.
[4] *Madame de Montholon*, p. 65.

on Christianity by Napoleon at St. Helena: wherein he is reported to have compared the shadowy fame of Cæsar and Alexander with the living force of Christ, and to have summed up with, "Can He be less than divine?" [1] But the real Napoleon talked in a very different fashion. Gourgaud talks of the stars and their Creator in the way attributed to Napoleon, but the latter snubs him. Briefly, Napoleon's real leaning seems to be to Mahometanism; his objection to Christianity is that it is not sufficiently ancient. Had it existed, he says, since the beginning of the world, he could believe it. [2] But it had not; nor could it have sustained itself till now without the Crucifixion and the Crown of Thorns, for mankind is thus constituted. [3] Nor can he accept that form of religion which would damn Socrates, Plato, and, he courteously adds, the English. [4] Why in any case should punishment be eternal? Moreover, he avers that he was much disturbed by the arguments of the Sheiks in Egypt, who contended that those who worshipped three deities must necessarily be Pagans. [5]

But, as he proceeds, he becomes more hostile to Christianity. "As for me," he breaks out on one occasion, "my opinion is formed that Christ never existed. He was put to death like any other fanatic who professed to be a prophet or a Messiah. There were constantly people of this kind. When I look back from the New Testament to the Old I find one able man— Moses, but the Jews are cowardly and cruel." And he ends by returning to the Bible with a map and declaring that he will write the campaigns of Moses. [6]

So slight is his belief in the Saviour, that he mentions as an extraordinary fact that Pope Pius VII did actually believe in Christ. [7]

Mahometanism, on the other hand, is more simple; and, he

[1] *Sermons on Various Occasions*, pp. 43–5.   [2] Gourgaud, i. 441.
[3] *Ibid.* ii. 226.   [4] *Ibid.* ii. 270; cf. i. 546.
[5] *Ibid.* i. 454.   [6] *Ibid.* ii. 270–2.   [7] *Ibid.* i. 441.

characteristically adds, is superior to Christianity in that it conquered half the world in ten years, while Christianity took three hundred years to establish itself.[1] Another time he declares Mahometanism to be the most beautiful of all religions.[2] And once he even says "We Mahometans."[3]

Although he prefers Mahometanism to Christianity, he prefers the Roman to the Anglican communion, or, at any rate, the Roman to the Anglican ritual. He gives as the reason for his preference, that in the Roman Church the people do not understand the prayers, and that it is not wise to try and make such matters too clear.[4] And yet he thinks that the clergy should marry, though he should hesitate to confess himself to a married priest, who would repeat everything to his wife.[5] He declares that he himself, having been anointed, is capable of shriving a penitent.[6] He is not so favourable to the hierarchy as to the ritual of Rome. He is hostile to the Papacy. Britain and Northern Europe have wisely, he says, emancipated themselves from this yoke, for it is ridiculous that the chief of the State should not be chief of the Church of the State.[7] For this reason he regrets that Francis I did not, as he nearly did, emancipate himself and his people by adhering to the Reformation.[8] He himself had regretted in old days when wearied with his disastrous struggle against the Papacy, that, instead of concluding the Concordat, he had not declared himself a Protestant. The nation would have followed him, and would have thus freed itself from the yoke of Rome.[9]

As to man, he proclaims himself a materialist. Sometimes he thinks that man was created in some particular temperature of the air, sometimes that he was produced from clay, "as Herodotus narrates that Nile mud was transformed into rats,"[10]

[1] Gourgaud ii. 78. [2] Ibid. i. 454.
[3] Ibid. ii. 152. Cf. Madame de Montholon, pp. 65–6; Las Cases, iii. 90–1.
[4] Gourgaud, i. 441. [5] Ibid. i. 450. [6] Ibid. i. 143.
[7] Ibid. ii. 68–9. [8] Ibid. ii. 78; Las Cases, v. 253.
[9] Las Cases, v. 253; Chaptal, p. 243. [10] Gourgaud, ii. 271.

that he was warmed by the sun, and combined with electric fluids.[1] "Say what you like, everything is matter, more or less organized. When out hunting I had the deer cut open, and saw that their interior was the same as that of man. When I see that a pig has a stomach like mine, and digests like me, I say to myself, 'If I have a soul, so has he.' A man is only a more perfect being than a dog or a tree, and living better. The plant is the first link in a chain of which man is the last. I know that this is all contrary to religion, but it is my opinion that we are all matter." [2] Again: "What are electricity, galvanism, magnetism? In these lies the great secret of nature. Galvanism works in silence. I think myself that man is the product of these fluids and of the atmosphere, that the brain pumps up these fluids and imparts life, and that the soul is composed of these fluids, which after death return into the atmosphere, whence they are pumped into other brains." [3]

Again: "When we are dead, my dear Gourgaud, we are altogether dead.[4] What is a soul? where is the soul of a sleeper or of a madman or of a babe?" [5]

Another time he breaks out: "Were I obliged to have a religion, I would worship the sun—the source of all life— the real God of the earth." [6]

The editors think that Napoleon talked in this way in a spirit of opposition to Gourgaud, who was a believer—more or less orthodox.[7] He did, we think, often argue thus to bring out the strength of the orthodox position. But often he is only thinking aloud in the bitterness of his heart—as when he says that he cannot believe in a just God punishing and rewarding, for good people are always unfortunate and scoundrels are always lucky: "Look at Talleyrand, he is sure to die in his bed." [8]

Bertrand thinks, says Gourgaud, that the Emperor "has

[1] *Ibid.* i. 64, 440.   [2] *Ibid.* ii. 311. Cf. Montholon, ii. 198.
[3] Gourgaud, i. 386.   [4] *Ibid.* ii. 437.   [5] *Ibid.* i. 440.
[6] *Ibid.* i. 434.   [7] *Ibid.* ii. 270, note; cf. ii. 548.
[8] *Ibid.* ii. 408; Montholon, ii. 234.

religion," [1] and we certainly think that Napoleon was more religious than these conversations represent. But he had much leeway to make up. He was the child of a Revolution which abjured religion. And yet there was strength in him to perform the most courageous acts of his life, the restoration of the French Church,[2] the conclusion of the Concordat, and the compelling his scoffing companions in arms to follow him to church.

Whatever may have been his motives, they must have been potent to make him break with the traditions of his manhood. For the religious faith and observance which still lurked timidly in the civic life of France had disappeared from among its soldiers. "The French army at this time," says Count Lavallette of the army of Egypt, "was remarkably free from any feeling of religion." [3]

And the same author tells a curious anecdote of a French officer who was with him on a boat which was nearly wrecked. The officer says the Lord's Prayer from beginning to end. When the danger is over he is much ashamed and apologizes thus: "I am thirty-eight years old, and I have never uttered a prayer since I was six. I cannot understand how it came into my head just then, for I declare that at this moment it would be impossible for me to remember a word of it." [4] And this hostility to religion seems to have continued, in spite of Concordats, to the end of Napoleon's reign; for, as we are told on the same authority, when mass was celebrated in the Emperor's presence at the great function of the Champ de Mai during the Hundred Days, thirteen years after the Concordat, every one turned his back to the altar.[5]

His life of camps, his revolutionary associations, his conflict with the Papacy, kept Napoleon aloof from the faith in which he was born. Talleyrand told Henry Greville that Louis XVIII

---

[1] Gourgaud, i. 387. [2] Chaptal, pp. 236-7.
[3] Lavallette, i. Part ii. 111. [4] *Ibid.* i. Part ii. 78.
[5] *Ibid.* ii. 155.

was surprised, on arriving in Paris, to find that the library of his predecessor's cabinet consisted principally of books on theological subjects, and that these were his favourite study. Greville asked in reply if Talleyrand thought that Napoleon was a believer. "Je suis porté a croire qu'il était croyant, mais il avait le goût de ces sujets," said Talleyrand.[1] We can only offer the commentary that the religious faith of Napoleon was at least equal to that of his successor on the throne or to that of his prince of Benevento.

All that we can safely gather from his conversation at St. Helena is that his mind turns greatly on these questions of religion. He ponders and struggles. A remark which he lets fall at St. Helena explains probably his normal state of mind. "Only a madman," he says one day, "declares that he will die without a confessor. There is so much that one does not know, that one cannot explain." [2] And as he spoke of the mysteries of religion, we may speak of his frame of mind with regard to them. "There is so much that one does not know, that one cannot explain."

Besides this high and engrossing topic, Napoleon ranges over a hundred others, characteristic of the man, and interesting to us, besides his discursive reminiscences and his acute views of the future. These last, as recorded by Las Cases and Montholon, give one the idea rather of political programmes, destined for external consumption, than of his own inner thoughts. Some are professedly so. Montholon, as it were, suddenly produces from his portfolio a constitution dictated by Napoleon for the empire of France under his son.[3] We do not know if it be authentic, but we observe that the editors of the Emperor's works coldly ignore it. We ourselves incline to the belief that it was composed in the seclusion of Ham with an eye to the Bonaparte restoration which soon afterwards took place. The official editors print, however, Montholon's record

[1] *Diary of Henry Greville*, i. 30–1.
[2] Gourgaud, ii. 43; cf. i. 474.   [3] Montholon, ii. 380.

of the instructions dictated by the dying man for his son on April 17, 1821, which seems to be a genuine manifesto.[1]

To us, of course, what he says of the English is of rare interest. He had all his life been waging war against Britain in some form or another, and yet he had always been strangely ignorant with regard to us. Metternich, who had been in England, noticed when Napoleon was on the throne, that as regards England he believed only what he chose to believe, and that these ideas were totally false.[2] This is the more strange, for the cause of his victories lay largely in the care with which he studied his adversaries. And, throughout his reign, he had kept a keen eye on British journalism and British politics. His sensitiveness to the criticism of English newspapers, which, after all, was the only newspaper criticism that he had to face, was no secret to his household.[3] He insisted on every abusive phrase being translated to him, and was furious at the result. In spite of this painful education he never at St. Helena touched on the English without betraying the strangest ignorance of their character and habits of mind. "Had I," he says, "been allowed to go to London in 1815, I should have been carried in triumph. All the populace would have been on my side, and my reasoning would have convinced the Greys and the Grevilles." [4] Even had he entered London as a conqueror, he seems to have persuaded himself that the result would have been the same. He told Las Cases that four days after landing in England he would have been in London. "I should have entered it not as a conqueror, but as a liberator. I should have been William III over again, but more generous and more disinterested. The discipline of my army would have been perfect, and the troops would have behaved as if they were in Paris. No sacrifices, not even an indemnity, would have been exacted from the English. We should have presented ourselves,

[1] Montholon, ii. 517; *Corresp. de Napoléon*, xxxii. 373.
[2] *Mémoires*, i. 107.   [3] Rémusat, i. 222; iii. 227.
[4] Gourgaud, i. 105, 122,

not as conquerors, but as brothers who came to restore to them
their liberties and their rights. I should have bade the English
work out their own regeneration themselves; for, as they were
our elders in political legislation, we wished to have nothing
to do with it except to enjoy their happiness and prosperity;
and I should have acted in good faith. So that in a few months,
the two nations, so long hostile, would have become identical
by their principles, their maxims, and their interests." [1] It is
scarcely necessary to suggest that he did not believe a word of
this ridiculous rhodomontade; but that he should have
launched it at all indicates an amazing ignorance of the people whom he proposed to assimilate.

He liked to listen to the stories of Las Cases' residence in
England, the scandals of the court, and of Carlton House,[2]
where Las Cases had been presented. ("And what the devil
were you doing there?" the Emperor not unnaturally asks at
this point.[3]) Otherwise he derived but little assistance from
his suite in the elucidation of the British character and institutions. Gourgaud for example, thought that the Riots, of
which so much was being said in England, were a political
sect; or, as his editors explain it, the advance guard of the
Whig party.[4]

What did he think of the English? Though he sometimes
broke out against them, not unnaturally, he seems to have held
them in a certain unspoken respect. "The British nation would
be very incapable of contending with us if we had only half
their national spirit," he said on one occasion.[5] When he is
most bitter he quotes Paoli, the real author of the famous
phrase "They are a nation of shopkeepers." "Sono mercanti,
as Paoli used to say." [6]

Sometimes he gibed, not unreasonably, at the nation which
had been his most persistent enemy, and which had accepted

---

[1] Las Cases, ii. 277–8. Cf. *Voice*, i. 349; ii. 378, etc.
[2] Las Cases, iv. 315, etc.   [3] *Ibid*. iv. 338.
[4] Gourgaud, ii. 123, and note.   [5] *Ibid*. i. 434.   [6] *Ibid*. i. 69.

the invidious charge of his custody. But once he paid them a noble tribute. He begins quaintly enough: "The English character is superior to ours. Conceive Romilly, one of the leaders of a great party, committing suicide at fifty because he had lost his wife. They are in everything more practical than we are: they emigrate, they marry, they kill themselves, with less indecision, than we display in going to the opera. They are also braver than we are. I think one can say that in courage they are to us what we are to the Russians, what the Russians are to the Germans, what the Germans are to the Italians." And then he proceeds: "Had I had an English army I would have conquered the universe, for I could have gone all over the world without demoralizing my troops. Had I been in 1815 the choice of the English as I was of the French, I might have lost the battle of Waterloo without losing a vote in the Legislature or a soldier from my ranks. I should have won the game." Has there been, considering the speaker and the circumstances, more signal praise of our national character? [1]

On two other occasions, when on the throne, he had, in confidential talk, paid rare compliments to Britain. To Auguste de Staël, who had declared that he could not serve under the French Government, for it had persecuted his mother, Napoleon said, "Then you must go to England; for after all there are only two nations, France and England, the rest are nothing."[2] Still more remarkable was his language to Foy. In the midst of the Peninsular War Foy came to Paris and had two or three interviews with the Emperor. One day Napoleon said to him abruptly: "Tell me, are my soldiers fighting well?" "What do you mean, Sire? Of course. . . ." "Yes, yes, I know. But are they afraid of the English soldiers?" "Sire, they respect them but do not fear them." "Well, you see, the English have always beaten them, Cressy, Agincourt, Marlborough." "But, Sire, the battle of Fontenoy." "Ah! the battle of Fontenoy. That

---

[1] *Carnet historique*, i. 175. Cf. Jackson, p. 147.
[2] Rémusat, iii. 287, note.

is a day that made the monarchy live forty years longer than
it would otherwise." [1]

On another occasion, at St. Helena, when Napoleon conceived Lady Malcolm to be saying that he hated England, he
interrupted her with much animation, saying she was mistaken,
he did not hate the English; on the contrary, he had always
had the highest opinion of their character. "I have been deceived, and here I am on a vile rock in the midst of the ocean.
I believe there are more honourable men in England pro-
portionately than in any other country—but then there are
some very bad, they are in extremes." [2] On other occasions he
says: "The English are quite a different race from us, they
have something of the bulldog in them, they love blood." [3]
"They are ferocious, they fear death less than we do, have
more philosophy, and live more from day to day." [4]

He thought well and justly of our blockades ("les Anglais
bloquent très bien"),[5] but ill, and with even more justice, of
our diplomacy.[6] He could not understand, and posterity
shares his bewilderment, why the British had derived so little
benefit from their long struggle and their victory.[7] He thinks
that they must have been stung by the reproach of being a nation of shopkeepers, and have wished to show their magnanimity. "Probably for a thousand years such another opportunity
of aggrandizing England will not occur. In the position of
affairs nothing could have been refused to you." It was
ridiculous, he said, to leave Batavia to the Dutch, and Bourbon
and Pondicherry to the French. He would not have given a

[1] Rémusat, iii. 283, note.   [2] Lady Malcolm, pp. 105–6.
[3] Montholon, ii. 227.   [4] Gourgaud, ii. 218.
[5] Montholon, ii. 201; Gourgaud, ii. 316.
[6] Montholon, ii. 67–70. Note that Lady Malcolm, who was present, records none of this, pp. 97–110, but Montholon's record is
probably correct, as Bertrand complains of the Emperor's having
talked too freely to the Admiral. Gourgaud, i. 446.
[7] Forsyth, ii. 105–8; Gourgaud, ii. 315–6; Las Cases, vii. 207;
Montholon, ii. 67–77; Voice, ii. 83, 232–5.

farthing for either, had it not been for his hope of driving the English out of India. "Your Ministers, too," he says, "should have stipulated for a commercial monopoly in the seas of India and China. You ought not to have allowed the French or any other nation to put their nose beyond the Cape. . . . At present the English can dictate to the world, more especially if they withdraw their troops from the Continent, *relegate Wellington to his estates*, and remain a purely maritime Power. She can then do what she likes." [1] "You want old Lord Chatham for a Prime Minister," he says another day.[2]

Again: "You English have imposed a contribution on France of 500 millions of francs, but after all I imposed one of ten milliards on your country. While you raised yours by your bayonets, I raised mine through your Parliament." [3]

He set himself to learn English, and Las Cases to teach him. The lessons were pursued for a few months, "sometimes with an admirable ardour—sometimes with a visible disgust,"[4] from January to October 1816, and then ceased all but entirely.[5] There had already been an abortive attempt on the voyage.[6] Las Cases, who had himself since his return to France somewhat forgotten the spoken language, says that his illustrious pupil managed to some extent to understand English as he read it, but that his pronunciation was so extraordinary as to constitute to some extent a new language.[7] The longest specimen that we possess of Napoleon's English is thus phonetically given by Henry, who heard it, "Veech you tink de best town?" [8] He wrote an English letter under an assumed name to Las Cases, which the facile courtier declares to have deceived him.[9] We give it here as the only written English of Napoleon's that we possess, and as a proof of the polite credulity of Las Cases.

"Count Lascases. Since sixt wek, y learn the english and y

---

[1] Gourgaud, ii. 316–7.   [2] *Voice*, ii. 189.   [3] Las Cases, iv. 345.
[4] *Ibid*. ii. 163.   [5] *Ibid*. ii. 133, iii. 31.   [6] *Ibid*. i. 148.
[7] *Ibid*. ii. 166. Cf. his letter to Lucien in Forsyth, i. 481.
[8] Henry, ii. 19.   [9] Las Cases, ii. 301–2.

do not any progress. Sixt week do fourty and two day. If might have learn fivty word, for day, i could know it two thousands and two hundred. It is in the dictionary more of foorty thousand; even he could most twenty; bot much of *tems*. For know it or hundred and twenty week which do more two years. After this you shall agree that the study one *tongue* is a great labour who it must *do into the* young aged.

"Longwood, this morning, the seven march thursday one thousand eight hundred sixteen after nativity the yors (sic) (lord) Jesus Christ."

It was thus addressed:

"Count Lascases, chambellan of the S.M., Longwood; into his polac: very press." [1]

He read English history with interest, having read none since he left school.[2] "I am reading Hume," he said one day. "These English are a ferocious race; what crimes there are in their history. Think of Henry VIII marrying Lady Seymour the day after he had had Anne Boleyn beheaded. We should never have done such a thing in our country. Nero never committed such crimes. And Queen Mary! Ah! the Salic law is an excellent arrangement." [3] But the most interesting result of this is that he discourses on the analogies between Cromwell and himself. There is no doubt, he thinks, some resemblance between the reign of Charles I and the French Revolution, but there could be no real comparison between his own position and that of Cromwell. He was thrice chosen by the free election of the people, and the French army had only waged war with strangers.[4] Cromwell had one essential quality, dissimulation; he had also great political talents, and consummate judgment, for there was no action in his life which could be criticized as being ill calculated.[5] Was he a great general? Napoleon does not know enough of him to judge.

On French history he makes one or two interesting and

[1] L. de Brotonne, *Lettres inédites de Napoléon Ier*, p. 605.
[2] Gourgaud, ii. 43. [3] *Ibid.* ii. 392–3. [4] *Ibid.* ii. 43. [5] *Ibid.* ii. 35.

indeed startling remarks. St. Louis he considered an "imbécile." [1] To Lady Malcolm he said that Henry IV was undoubtedly the greatest man that ever sat on the throne of France.[2] But this judgment was only for external use: in his interior circle he spoke very differently. Henry IV, he declared, never did anything great.[3] Voltaire made him the fashion by the "Henriade," and then he was exalted in order to depreciate Louis XIV, who was hated.[4] Napoleon laughed when he saw Henry described as the greatest captain of ancient or modern times.[5] He was, no doubt, a good sort of man; a brave man, indeed, who would charge sword in hand;[6] but, after all, an old greybeard pursuing women in the streets of Paris could only be an old fool.[7]

Louis XIV, in the opinion of the Emperor, was the greatest king that France had possessed. "There are only he and I.[8] He had 400,000 men under arms, and a King of France who could collect such a host could be no ordinary man. Only he or I was able to raise such armies." [9] Had he himself lived under the old monarchy, he thinks he would have risen to be a marshal. For, as it was, he had been remarked as a lieutenant: he would soon have become a colonel and been placed on the staff of a marshal, whom he would have guided, and under whom he would have distinguished himself.[10]

He utters one speculation on contemporary French history which must not be taken too seriously. "Would to God," he says, "that the King and the Princes had remained (in March 1815)! The troops would have come over to me: the King and the Princes would have been massacred; and so Louis XVIII would not be on the throne."[11] Sometimes in his wrath he flies out against France herself: "She has been violated, she

[1] Gourgaud, i. 210.　　　　　　[2] Lady Malcolm, p. 32.
[3] Gourgaud, i. 210.　　　　　　[4] Cf. Montholon, ii. 107.
[5] Gourgaud, ii. 13.　　[6] *Ibid.* ii. 357.　　[7] *Ibid.* ii. 13.
[8] Montholon, ii. 107.　　[9] Gourgaud, ii. 12.　　[10] *Ibid.* ii. 426.
[11] *Ibid.* ii. 301; Montholon, ii. 187. Cf. Montholon, i. lxxxix and ii. 46.

is henceforth only a cowardly dishonoured country. She has only had her deserts, for instead of rallying to me, she deserted me." [1]

He talks freely of his family. And it is perhaps his frankness in this respect that chiefly distinguishes him from a sovereign born in the purple. No one can conceive the contemporary emperors, Alexander or Francis, conversing with their suites on the most intimate family matters. One might almost say that this is the note of distinction between the legitimate and the parvenu sovereign. At any rate, the Empress Catherine, who was born remote from the prospect of a throne, had this surprising candour.

His family was, he says, among the first in Corsica, and he had still a great number of cousins in the island. He reckons them indeed at eighty.[2] He was sure that a number of these were among the band of Corsicans who followed Murat in his mad and fatal attempt at Pizzo; [3] though as a matter of fact the clan Bonaparte in Corsica would have nothing to do with Murat or his expedition.[4] But he did not care to be considered a Corsican at all. In the first place, he was French: "I was born in 1769 when Corsica had been united to France"; though his enemies accused him of having exchanged birthdays with Joseph, who was born in 1768, and so before the union. A tactless mayor of Lyons, under this belief, had innocently complimented him on having done so much for France, though not a Frenchman. But, secondly, putting his French nationality aside, he protested that he was rather Italian or Tuscan than Corsican. Two centuries ago his family lived in Tuscany.[5] "I have one foot in Italy, and one in France." It is obvious to the candid reader that both feet were politically of use to him, for he reigned in France and Italy. His Corsican origin was of no use to him, and was therefore minimized.

[1] Gourgaud, ii. 266–7.   [2] *Ibid.* ii. 170.   [3] *Ibid.* ii. 263, 345.
[4] Maceroni, ii. 288.   [5] Gourgaud, ii. 345.

He makes some curious remarks about his descent. There was a tendency at one time to prove it from the Man in the Iron Mask. It came about in this way. The Governor of Pignerol, where the mysterious prisoner was confined, was named Bompars; he was said to have married his daughter to the captive (who was, in the belief of Napoleon, the brother of Louis XIV),[1] and smuggled them off to Corsica under the name of Bonaparte. "I had only to say the word," said the Emperor, "and this fable would have been believed." [2]

When he married Marie Louise, the Emperor Francis became anxious as to his son-in-law's nobility of birth, and sent him a packet of papers establishing his descent from the Dukes of Florence. Napoleon returned them to Metternich with the remark that he had nothing to do with such tomfoolery; that in any case the Dukes of Florence were inferior to the Emperors of Germany; that he would not be inferior to his father-in-law; and that his nobility dated from Montenotte.[3]

Napoleon himself seems to incline to one illustrious connection, for he says that the name of Bonaparte is the same as Bonarotti or Buenarotti.[4] Did he then believe himself related to Michael Angelo? He regrets, too, that he did not allow an ancestor of his, Bonaventure or Boniface Bonaparte, to be canonized. The Capuchins, to which order the monk belonged, were eager for the distinction, which would have cost a million francs. The Pope, when he came to Paris, spontaneously offered this compliment, which Napoleon was inclined to accept, as it would, he thought, conciliate the priesthood.[5] But it was finally decided that it might afford matter for ridicule, so dangerous anywhere, so fatal in France.[6]

Napoleon seems to have no family secrets from his compan-

[1] Montholon, i. 326. [2] Gourgaud, i. 218; Las Cases, iv. 363.
[3] Gourgaud, ii. 223; "famille souverain à Trévise," says Las Cases, i. 108; *Voice*, ii. 296–7.
[4] Gourgaud, i. 550. [5] *Ibid.* ii. 345; i. 550.
[6] *Ibid.* i. 370. Cf. *Voice*, ii. 297.

ions. His father died at Montpellier at the age of thirty-five,[1] he says at one time, thirty-nine at another.[2] He had been a man of pleasure all his life, extravagant, "wishing to play the great noble;" [3] but at the last he could not have enough monks and priests round him, so that at Montpellier they considered him a saint.[4] Napoleon's great-uncle to some extent restored the family fortunes, and died wealthy: so much so that Pauline thought it worth while to steal the purse from under his pillow as he was dying.[5] The Emperor discusses quite calmly a common report that Paoli was his father, and gives a conclusive but not very refined or decorous reason for disbelieving it.[6] Still Paoli took a semi-paternal interest in him. "You, Bonaparte, are all Plutarch, you have nothing modern about you," the general said to him.[7] And of him to others: "That young man bears the head of Cæsar on the body of Alexander: there is the stuff of ten Sullas in him." [8] Both his father and mother were very handsome.[9] She during her pregnancy followed the army of independence. The French generals took pity on her, and allowed her to come to her own house for her confinement. She availed herself of the permission, and was delivered of Napoleon. "So that I can say I was conceived when Corsica was independent, and born when Corsica was French."[10] This last point was, of course, capital for him, and for his dynasty.

Here perhaps may be noted the singular connection of Napoleon with Corsica. He was born there. He lived there till he was nine. With the first freedom of manhood he returns there. Of the period between January 1, 1786, and June 1793, he spends more than three years and two months in Corsica, so unsuccessfully that he leaves it a penniless and proscribed fugitive, and never again sees the island, of which he could

---

[1] Gourgaud, ii. 166. [2] Ibid. i. 473.
[3] Ibid. ii. 166. See, too, Montholon, ii. 16. [4] Gourgaud, i. 473.
[5] Ibid. ii. 166. Montholon, ii. 17. [6] Gourgaud, ii. 332.
[7] Ibid. i. 189. [8] Chaptal, p. 187. Cf. Pasquier, ii. 73.
[9] Gourgaud, i. 166. [10] Ibid. ii. 331.

have had nothing but bitter and humiliating recollections, except for a moment on his return from Egypt, and in outline from Elba. Nevertheless, Corsica follows him—he could shut his eyes and smell Corsica, he says at St. Helena—and profoundly influences his career. During his early years on the island he had contracted a lifelong feud, after the Corsican fashion, with Pozzo di Borgo. That vendetta was fateful if not mortal. For to Pozzo di Borgo, more, perhaps, than to any other single man, is due the first overthrow of Napoleon.[1] It is strange that a village quarrel in Corsica should have been fought to an issue on so vast a scene, and have decided, maybe, the mastery of Europe.

After her flight from Corsica and her arrival at Marseilles the Emperor's mother was once more, he tells us, in a desperate plight. She and her daughters had not a farthing to live upon. He himself was reduced to an assignat of five francs, and was on the verge of suicide, being indeed on the brink of the Seine for that purpose, when a friend lent him money and saved him.[2] His mother had thirteen children of whom he was the third. "C'est une maîtresse femme." [3]

He receives a letter from his mother, and, though he destroyed it,[4] is sufficiently moved by it to quote it to his companions. Its tenderness indeed might well affect a son; for she wishes, old and blind as she is, to come to St. Helena. "I am very old," she writes, "to make a journey of two thousand leagues. I should die perhaps on the way, but, never mind, I should die nearer you." [5] His nurse, who long survived him, and whom he remembered affectionately in his will, came to Paris for the coronation, where the Pope took so much notice of her that Madame Lætitia was almost jealous.[6] His foster-brother, her son, became captain of a vessel in the British navy.[7]

---

[1] Pasquier, ii. 156–7, 161–3, 173.   [2] Montholon, ii. 413–4.
[3] Gourgaud, ii. 71.   [4] Montholon, i. 292.   [5] Gourgaud, i. 189.
[6] Gourgaud, i. 166; Las Cases, v. 162. See Méneval, i. 379.
[7] A frigate? Gourgaud, i. 166; a storeship? *Voice*, ii. 294.

Even of his wives he is not chary of talking, nor is he sparing of the most intimate details about both.[1] He wonders if he ever really loved anybody. If so, it was Josephine,—a little.[2] She generally lied,[3] but always cleverly, except with regard to her age. As to that she got into such a tangle, that her statements could only be reconciled on the hypothesis that Eugène was twelve years old when he was born.[4] She never asked anything for herself or her children, but made mountains of debt.[5] Her greatest defect was a vigilant and constant jealousy. However, she was not jealous of Marie Louise, though the latter was extremely susceptible as to her predecessor. When the Emperor tried to take his second wife to see his first the former burst into tears, and she endeavoured by every possible ruse and device to prevent his going there.

Marie Louise, he declares, was innocence itself and really loved him. Had she not been influenced by that wretch (canaille) Madame de Montebello, and by Corvisart, who was a scoundrel (misérable), she too would have followed him to Elba. "And then her father has placed that 'polisson' Neipperg by her side." [6] This is perhaps the only avowal which we have from Napoleon, who kept up appearances gallantly to the last,[7] that he was aware of his wife's infidelity; though a letter to Lavallette had informed him of it during the Hundred Days,[8] and his suite were all gossiping about the scandal.[9] Still he always praises Marie Louise, and gives, in sum, the following account of her. She was never at ease with the French, remembering they had killed her aunt Marie Antoinette.[10] She was always truthful and discreet, and courteous to all, even those whom she most detested.[11] She was cleverer than her father, whom alone of her family she loved: she could not bear her step-mother.[12] Different in this from Josephine,

---

[1] Gourgaud, ii. 276, 328, 330, 278.　　[2] Ibid. ii. 8.
[3] Ibid. ii. 330.　　[4] Ibid. i. 414.　　[5] Ibid. ii. 330.
[6] Ibid. ii. 330.　　[7] Voice, ii. 159.　　[8] Lavallette, ii. 147.
[9] Gourgaud, ii. 195.　　[10] Ibid. ii. 196.　　[11] Ibid. ii. 276.
[12] Ibid. i. 338. Cf. Las Cases, ii. 317.

she was delighted when she received ten thousand francs to spend. One could have trusted her with any secret,[1] and she had been enjoined at Vienna to obey Napoleon in everything. She was a charming child,[2] a good woman, and had saved his life.[3] And yet, all said and done, he loved Josephine better. Josephine was a true woman, she was his choice, they had risen together. He loved her person, her grace.[4] "She would have followed me to Elba," [5] he says, with oblique reproach. Had she had a child of his, he would never have left her. It would have been better so for her, and for France. For it was Austria that lost him.[6] But for the Austrian marriage, he would never have made war on Russia.[7] He declares that he has made up his mind, should Marie Louise die, not to marry again.[8] Considering the circumstances in which he was placed, and the area of choice presented to him at St. Helena, there is something half comic, half tragic in the declaration.

To his little son he makes one bitter allusion. Gourgaud, on the 15th of August, the imperial festival, presents the Emperor with a bouquet as if from the King of Rome. "Bah!" says Napoleon rudely, "the King of Rome thinks no more of me than he does of you." [9] But that his thoughts were always with the boy his will and, indeed, his conversations sufficiently prove. It was his intention, he says, to have given the kingdom of all Italy, with Rome as the capital, to his second son, had he had one.[10]

Caroline, who married Murat, was considered, he tells us, in childhood to be the dunce and Cinderella of the family. But she developed favourably, and became a capable and handsome woman.[11] He cannot, however, disguise his fury with her

[1] Gourgaud, ii. 277.   [2] *Ibid.* ii. 276.   [3] *Ibid.* ii. 196, 278.
[4] *Ibid.* ii. 277.   [5] *Ibid.* ii. 330.   [6] Montholon, i. 331.
[7] Gourgaud, ii. 277, 337.   [8] *Ibid.* ii. 8, 25.
[9] Montholon, i. 353; Gourgaud, i. 235.
[10] Gourgaud, ii. 61, 345; Montholon, ii. 277.
[11] Las Cases, vi. 158.

second marriage. He can scarcely believe it—after twenty years of marriage, within fifteen months of the violent death of her husband, with children grown up, that she should marry again, publicly, and, where of all places? at Vienna. If the news be true it will have astonished him more than anything that ever happened. Human nature is indeed strange.[1] And then explodes his inmost thought: "Ah! la coquine, la coquine, l'amour l'a toujours conduite." [2]

We have seen that he considered Louis XIV the greatest of French sovereigns; and this news of Caroline's marriage produces the strangest of analogies between them. Readers of St. Simon will recollect the vivid description he gives of the day when Louis XIV received the tidings that his cherished son, the Duc du Maine, had, on a signal occasion, behaved with something less than conspicuous courage. How the King, then at Marly, perceives a scullion pocketing a biscuit: how his suppressed fury breaks out and wreaks itself on the relatively innocent object: how he rushes up before the astonished court and breaks his stick on the servant's back: how the man flies and the King stands swearing at him, and impotently brandishing the stump of his cane. The courtiers cannot believe their eyes, and the King retires to conceal his agitation.[3] So, on hearing of Caroline's nuptials, Napoleon sits down to dinner bursting with uncontrollable wrath. He declares that the pastry is gritty, and his anger, expending itself on the cook, passes all restraint. Rarely, says Gourgaud, never, says Montholon, has the Emperor been seen in such a rage. He orders that the man shall be beaten and dismissed.[4] The scene is grotesque and painful enough, but it is Caroline, not the cook, that is the cause.

It was not, we may surmise, his sister's marriage alone that provoked this explosion. The news had probably brought back

[1] Gourgaud, ii. 281; Montholon, ii. 176. Cf. *Voice*, ii. 180.
[2] Gourgaud, ii. 285. [3] St. Simon, i. 276.
[4] Gourgaud, ii. 282; Montholon, ii. 177.

to him that day in 1814 when he received the news that Murat had betrayed him and turned his arms against France. The Emperor's feeling for Murat at that time was a bitter contempt for the "barber," as he called him, whom he had raised to be a king. His anger he reserved for his sister, who, as he knew, governed and directed her husband. His language about her, too, was such, as reported by Barras (who is, however, a questionable witness in matters relating to Napoleon), that a French editor, by no means squeamish, is unable to print it.[1] In any case, whether indelicate or not, we may be sure that it was forcible, and that on this day of petulance the misalliance of Caroline brought to his mind a darker tragedy and a direr wrath.

Of his brothers he says little that is worth recording, in view of other and fuller revelations elsewhere. He declares compendiously that they have done him much harm.[2] He made a great mistake, he says, in making Joseph a king, especially in Spain, where a firm and military sovereign was required; whereas Joseph thought of nothing but gallantry at Madrid.[3] Joseph, in his great brother's opinion, was not a soldier, though he fancied himself one, nor was he even brave.[4] It may here be mentioned that as Napoleon's appearance deteriorated at St. Helena it strikingly resembled that of Joseph. Las Cases declares that on at least one occasion he could have sworn that it was Joseph and not Napoleon whom he saw. With regard to Louis and Lucien, their mania for publishing indifferent verses, and dedicating them to the Pope,[5] is a constant perplexity to him. Of both poetasters he remarks at different times: "Il faut avoir le diable au corps." [6] Lucien, says Napoleon, wished, after Brumaire, to marry the Queen of Etruria, and threatened if this were refused to marry a woman of bad character,[7]—a menace which he carried out. He was, in his

---

[1] Barras, iv. 457. [2] Gourgaud, ii. 307.
[3] Montholon, ii. 193. [4] Gourgaud, ii. 306. [5] *Ibid.* ii. 158.
[6] *Ibid.* i. 551–2; Las Cases, vi. 158. [7] Gourgaud, ii. 158.

brother's judgment, useless during the Hundred Days,[1] but aspired after Waterloo to the dictatorship. He pointed out that his relations to the Republican party would make him acceptable to them, and that he would give the military command to the Emperor. Napoleon, without answering this strange rhapsody, turned to Carnot, who declared unhesitatingly that he could speak on behalf of the Republicans, not one of whom would prefer Lucien's dictatorship to the Emperor's.[2] Eliza, the member of his family who most resembled him in character and talents, and whom, perhaps for that reason, he disliked, he scarcely mentions; [3] nor does he say much of the exquisite and voluptuous Pauline.

From the world at large the Bonaparte family has scarcely received sufficient attention. For it was an astonishing race.[4] Born and reared in poverty and obscurity, it assumed a divine right with easy grace.[5] No Bourbons or Hapsburgs were so imbued with their royal prerogatives as these princes of an hour.[6] Joseph believed firmly that he would easily have established himself as King of Spain, if Napoleon would only have withdrawn his troops.[7] Louis had the same conviction with regard to Holland. Murat and Caroline were not less fatuous at Naples. Jérôme promptly established the state and etiquette of a petty Louis XIV. Not less remarkable was their tenacity of character. An unfriendly commentator is forced to admit that their qualities or defects were all out of the common. The women even approached greatness. Caroline and Eliza had striking qualities. And all, brothers and sisters, had something of the inflexibility of their mighty head, and the fullest possible measure of his self-confidence. They frequently defied him. Some did not scruple to abandon him. The two governing sisters tried to cut themselves adrift from his fortunes, and make terms as independent sovereigns with the enemy. Lucien

[1] *Ibid.* ii. 158.   [2] Montholon, i. 11–12.
[3] *Ibid.* ii. 468.   [4] Pasquier, i. 401.   [5] *Ibid.* i. 402.
[6] Chaptal, p. 346.   [7] Pasquier, i. 402.

believed that he could more than fill the place of Napoleon. In this astounding race, says Pasquier, the most binding engagements and the most sacred affections melted away at the first aspect of a political combination.[1]

His confidences do not end with his family, for he likes to talk of his loves.[2] He has had, as he counts on his fingers, seven mistresses in his life: "C'est beaucoup." [3] But, after all, it is not much when we remember that a learned and competent historian is devoting three thick volumes to this side of Napoleon's character. Of the most famous, Madame Walewska, to whom at one time he seems to have been sincerely attached (though he thought all Polish women addicted to intrigue), he speaks with great detachment. She was obtained for him, he declares, by Talleyrand.[4] He avers to Gourgaud, when vexed with the General, that when they started for St. Helena he would have given her to Gourgaud as a wife, but not now, such was the change in his sentiments.[5] He hears with complacency that she has married M. d'Ornano. "She is rich and must have saved, and I settled a great deal on the two children." "Your Majesty," says the tactless equerry, "paid Madame Walewska ten thousand francs a month." The Emperor blushes, and asks him how he knows this. "Lord!" says Gourgaud, "as if I were not too close to your Majesty not to know that sort of thing: your household knew everything." [6] On another occasion Napoleon declares that one of his main grievances against Murat was that King Joachim had sequestrated in 1814 the Neapolitan estates of Madame Walewska.[7]

He speaks with candour of his relations with Mademoiselle Georges [8] and Madame Grassini,[9] with Madame Duchâtel,

---

[1] Pasquier, i. 403; cf. ii. 137.
[2] Gourgaud, ii. 140; Montholon, i. 204.
[3] Montholon, ii. 205.   [4] Gourgaud, i. 136. Cf. Rémusat, i. 121.
[5] Gourgaud, i. 430.   [6] Ibid. i. 423. Cf. Montholon, ii. 60.
[7] Montholon, i. 303.   [8] Gourgaud, i. 60, ii. 53.
[9] Ibid. ii. 52, i. 305, ii. 311; Las Cases, v. 19.

Madame Galliéno, and Madame Pellaprat.[1] Of another lady whose name Gourgaud does not record, but who may easily be identified as Madame Fourés, he says summarily, "She was seventeen, and I was commander-in-chief!"[2] He was supposed when Emperor to disdain female society: he admits the fact and explains it. He declares that he was naturally susceptible, and feared to be dominated by women. Consequently he had avoided them, but in this, he confesses, he made a great blunder.[3] Were he again on the throne he should make a point of spending two hours a day in conversation with ladies, from whom he should learn much.[4] He had endeavoured during the Hundred Days, indeed, to repair the fault of his former indifference.[5] But whatever he may have been in France, he is diffuse on this topic at St. Helena. When he finds himself engaged in a gloomy retrospect, he turns the conversation by saying, "Let us talk about women," and then, like a good Frenchman, he discusses the subject with a zest worthy of Henry the Fourth.[6] During one dinner, for example, the conversation turns entirely on the question whether fat women are more admirable than thin.[7] He discourses on his preference for fair women over dark.[8] Time has to be killed.

Naturally, he likes most to talk of his battles [9]—of which he counts no less than sixty [10]—and speaks of them with simple candour. "War," he says, "is a strange art. I have fought sixty battles, and I assure you that I have learned nothing from all of them that I did not know in the first. Look at Cæsar: he fights in the first battle as in the last." [11]

He takes full responsibility for the Russian campaign. "I was master, and all blame rests on me" [12] (though he cannot bring himself to make the same admission with regard to

---

[1] Gourgaud, i. 81, ii. 169, 353.   [2] *Ibid.* ii. 89.
[3] *Ibid.* ii. 54.   [4] *Ibid.* i. 81; Montholon, i. 175.
[5] *Madame de Montholon*, p. 66; Las Cases, iii. 356.
[6] Gourgaud, i. 60.   [7] *Ibid.* i. 411; Montholon, ii. 57.
[8] Gourgaud, ii. 311; Montholon, ii. 57.   [9] Bertrand, p. xvi.
[10] Gourgaud, ii. 135.   [11] *Ibid.* ii. 424–5.   [12] *Ibid.* ii. 14.

Waterloo). When he knew at Dresden that he would not have the support of Sweden or Turkey, he should not have proceeded with the expedition. But even then, had he not remained in Moscow, he would have been successful. That was his great fault.[1] "I ought to have only remained there a fortnight. After arriving there I should have crushed what remained of Kutusow's army, marched on Malo-Jaroslavetz, Toula, and Kaluga: proposing to the Russians to retire without destroying anything."[2]

He constantly repeats that his marriage with Marie Louise was the cause of the war with Russia, for it made him feel sure of the support of Austria.[3] Prussia, too, was as usual, he says, pining for aggrandizement, and so he reckoned with confidence on these two Powers, though he had no other allies. But "I was in too great a hurry. I should have remained a year on the Niemen and in Prussia, and then devoured Prussia."[4] It is strange, indeed, to observe how heartily, as if by a foreboding, he hates Prussia.[5] He bitterly regrets that at Tilsit he did not depose the King, and proclaim that the House of Hohenzollern had ceased to reign. He is confident that Alexander would not have opposed such a course, provided Napoleon did not himself annex the kingdom. A petty Hohenzollern prince on his staff had, he tells us, asked for the Prussian throne, and Napoleon would have been disposed to give it him had he been descended from the great Frederick (who, by the by, was childless). But his family was a branch which had separated three centuries ago from the royal stock. And then, says the Emperor, with less verisimilitude, I was over-persuaded by the King of Prussia.[6]

He made, he admits, a fatal mistake in not sending Ferdinand back to Spain after the Russian campaign, for that would have restored to him 180,000 good soldiers. The Spanish

[1] Gourgaud, ii. 337.　　　　　　　　[2] Ibid. ii. 13.
[3] Ibid. ii. 115, 277, 337, i. 136.　　　[4] Ibid. ii. 115.
[5] Carnet historique, i. 174.　　　　　[6] Gourgaud, ii. 112.

blunder began, he confesses, from his having said to himself on watching the quarrels of the Spanish Bourbons: "Let us get rid of them, and there will be no more Bourbons left." [1] He apparently counted the Sicilian Bourbons for nothing.

Still it is to Austria, in his judgment, that he owes his fall.[2] Without Essling he would have destroyed the Austrian monarchy, but Essling cost him too dear.[3] Austria is, he thinks, the real enemy of France, and he regrets having spared her. At one moment he had thoughts of causing a revolution there; at another, of carving her into three kingdoms, Austria, Hungary, and Bohemia.[4]

What, does he think, was his most brilliant victory? Austerlitz? Perhaps, he answers. But he has a leaning for Borodino, it was superb, it was fought so far from home.[5] To Bertrand he stated emphatically that it was Borodino—"It was the Battle of Giants"—and took peculiar pride in the intuition which had made him before the battle make himself master of the mamelon and redoubt in front of the enemy's position. At Austerlitz was the best army, and at Wagram the largest army that he had ever commanded in battle.[6] After Austerlitz the quality of his army declined. He recurs with constant pride to the strategy of Eckmühl: "that superb manœuvre, the finest that I ever executed," [7] where with fifty thousand men he defeated a hundred and twenty thousand. Had he slept the previous night he could never have won that victory; as it was, he had to kick Lannes awake. A commander-in-chief should never sleep; it is then that he should work. That is why he used a carriage to avoid unnecessary fatigue in the daytime. Joseph, he declares, lost the battle of Vittoria by his somnolence.[8]

A great general, he says, is rarely found. Of all the generals produced by the Revolution, Desaix and Hoche are the only

[1] *Ibid.* ii. 265.   [2] *Ibid.* ii. 435.
[3] *Ibid.* ii. 112.   [4] *Ibid.* i. 202; Las Cases, iii. 107.
[5] Gourgaud, ii. 115. Cf. Bertrand, p. xxv.   [6] Gourgaud, i. 571.
[7] Las Cases, ii. 151, v. 168-9; *Voice*, ii. 206.
[8] Gourgaud, ii. 159.

ones, he thinks, who had the makings of one.[1] The campaign of Dumouriez in Champagne was extremely fine and bold; he was the only man produced out of the nobility.[2] Kléber, says Napoleon, oddly enough, had the qualities and defects of a tall man.[3] Turenne is the greatest of French generals: he is the only one who became bolder with old age. "He does exactly what I should have done in his place. . . . Had he come to me at Wagram, he would at once have understood the position. So would Condé, but not Cæsar or Hannibal. Had I had a man like Turenne to second me in my campaigns, I should have been master of the world, but I had nobody. When I was absent, my lieutenants were always beaten.[4] . . . Condé was a general by intuition, Turenne by experience. I think much more highly of Turenne than of Frederick. In the place of that sovereign he would have done much more, and would not have committed Frederick's mistakes.[5] Frederick, indeed, did not thoroughly understand artillery." [6]

"I count myself for half in the battles I have won, and it is much even to name the general in connection with a victory, for it is after all the army that wins it." [7] And yet he sets great store by officers. "A perfect army," he says, on another occasion, "would be that in which each officer knew what to do according to circumstances; the best army is that which is nearest to this." [8]

In his judgment of hostile generals, when in active life, he had been politic. A trustworthy associate of his in those days records that Napoleon often said that Alvinzy was the best general that he had ever had opposed to him in Italy, and for that reason he had never mentioned Alvinzy in his bulletins, whereas he constantly commended Beaulieu, Würmser, or the Archduke Charles, whom he did not fear.[9] It seems probable

[1] Gourgaud, ii. 423.   [2] Ibid. i. 327.   [3] Ibid. ii. 186.
[4] Cf. Chaptal, p. 305. [5] Gourgaud, ii. 135–6. Cf. Chaptal, p. 306.
[6] Gourgaud, ii. 335. See, too, ii. 16, 31–4, 136, 337. See, however, Gourgaud, ii. 21.
[7] Ibid. ii. 425.   [8] Ibid. ii. 425.   [9] Chaptal, p. 301.

that he afterwards entertained a higher opinion of the Arch-duke.[1] He declined, as we have seen, to confide his opinion of Wellington to Warden, and at St. Helena he could not be fair to the Duke. But, when on the throne, he had coupled Wellington's name with his own in a strange connection. It was because Wellington had devastated the country in his retreat on Lisbon. "Only Wellington and I are capable of executing such measures." And he adds with perversity that he regards the ravaging of the Palatinate as the greatest act of Louvois.[2]

He regretted Elba. "This day year I was at Elba," he says gloomily.[3] Had the stipulated income been paid, he would have kept open house for the learned men of Europe, for whom he would have formed a centre. He would have built a palace for them, and led a country-house life surrounded by men of mark.[4] He would, too, have enriched the island by throwing open its little ports.[5] Sometimes, again, he speaks of making it a second Gibraltar and an emporium of American commerce. Lucien, who seems not to have thoroughly understood his brother, wished to have the minerals of the island for nothing.[6]

But Bertrand confided to Gourgaud that St. Helena was better than Elba, that at any rate they were more unhappy at Elba. It was terrible to leave the most splendid throne in the world for a tiny island where one was not even sure of a good reception; and for four months they were deeply depressed. At St. Helena the greatness of the fall was less sensible; they had become accustomed to it.[7] Napoleon on this point declared conflicting opinions. Sometimes he regrets Elba: often he abuses St. Helena, but on one occasion he launches into praise of it, at any rate as a residence for his suite. "We are very happy here, we can ride, we have a good

---

[1] But see Rémusat, ii. 235.   [2] Chaptal, p. 304.
[3] Gourgaud, i. 112.   [4] *Ibid.* i. 461.
[5] *Ibid.* ii. 415.   [6] *Ibid.* i. 552.   [7] *Ibid.* ii. 221.

table, we can go away whenever we like, we are well received everywhere, and covered with glory," [1] records the unhappy Gourgaud, at whom this discourse was aimed.

In speaking of Elba the Emperor gives one curious detail. When he left Fontainebleau in 1814 he had little hope of returning. The first hope that he conceived arose from his perceiving that no officers' wives were invited to the banquets at the Hôtel de Ville.[2]

One of his favourite topics, in treating which he reveals the practical character of his mind, is that of private budgets. He is always discussing them. At one time it is the budget of a man of 200,000 francs a year.[3] The imaginary person is French, of course; for a Dutchman, he declares, in a tone of approbation, would with such an income only spend 30,000 francs a year.[4] Another time he reckons up the expenditure of a man with 500,000 francs a year.[5] This is the fortune he would himself prefer; to live in the country with 500,000 or 600,000 francs a year, and with a little house in Paris like the one that he had in the Rue Chantereine.[6] But he could live very comfortably on 12 francs a day.[7] He would dine for thirty sous, he would frequent reading-rooms and libraries, and go to the play in the pit. His room would cost him twenty francs a month. But suddenly he remembers that he must have a servant, for he can no longer dress himself, and so he raises his figure and says that one could be very happy with twenty francs a day—it is only a question of limiting one's wants. He would amuse himself greatly, living only with people of a similar fortune.[8] The most comical result of this habit or game of calculation appears when he rereads *Clarissa Harlowe*. He cannot wade through it, though he devoured it at eighteen,

[1] Gourgaud, i. 342; cf. ii. 309. Cf. Las Cases, ii. 229.
[2] Gourgaud, ii. 302.
[3] *Ibid.* i. 193; Montholon, i. 294.　　[4] Gourgaud, i. 572-3.
[5] *Ibid.* i. 304.　　[6] *Ibid.* i. 572.
[7] Montholon, ii. 80-1. Cf. Méneval, ii. 38.
[8] Cf. Montholon, i. 454.

and so forth.[1] But what really perplexes him is the personal expenditure of Lovelace. "He has only two thousand pounds a year: I made out his budget at once." [2]

In the same practical spirit of detail, when waiting for a moment in Montholon's sitting-room, he hastily values the furniture piece by piece and appraises it at thirty napoleons at most.[3]

[1] Montholon, ii. 99.   [2] Gourgaud, i. 548.

[3] Las Cases, ii. 116.

CHAPTER FOURTEEN

The Supreme Regrets

★

HE seems to concentrate the main regrets of his solitude on three capital points: that he could not have died at some supreme moment of his career; that he left Egypt and gave up his Eastern ambitions; and, of course, Waterloo. As to the first, he discusses the right moment with his suite. "For the sake of history, I should have died at Moscow, Dresden, or Waterloo." Again: "I should have died after my entry into Moscow":[1] or "I should have died at La Moskowa (Borodino)."[2] Gourgaud thinks either Moscow or Waterloo, and only leans to the latter date as including the return from Elba. Las Cases protests against Moscow, as omitting so much.[1]

On another occasion Napoleon again leans to Moscow. Had a cannon-ball from the Kremlin killed him, his greatness would have endured, because his institutions and his dynasty would, he declares, have survived in France. As it is, he will be almost nothing to posterity, unless his son should come to mount the throne.[3] "Had I died at Moscow," he says on another occasion, "I should have left behind me a reputation as a conqueror, without a parallel in history. A ball ought to have put an end to me there."

To Bertrand he said that for the sake of his glory he should have died at Borodino. If a bullet had carried him off on that day his name would have appeared to posterity with unrivalled glory. The imagination would have been unable to place limits to the possibilities of his career.

Again: "To die at Borodino would have been to die like Alexander: to be killed at Waterloo would have been a good death: perhaps Dresden would have been better: but no, better at Waterloo. The love of the people, their regret. . . ."[4]

---

[1] Gourgaud, i. 202.   [2] *Ibid.* i. 165; Bertrand, p. xxv.
[3] Gourgaud, ii. 163; *Voice*, ii. 156.
[4] Montholon, ii. 269. Cf. *Voice*, ii. 107.

The greatest moment in his life, he thinks, was his stay at Dresden in 1812,[1] when every sovereign in Europe, except the Sultan, the Russian Emperor, and the King of Great Britain, was at his feet. What was his happiest? To O'Meara he says the march from Cannes to Paris. But on another occasion he asks his suite to guess. Gourgaud guesses the occasion of his (second) marriage. Madame Montholon thinks his nomination as First Consul. Bertrand the birth of the King of Rome. Napoleon answers, "Yes, I was happy as First Consul, at the marriage, at the birth of the King of Rome, 'mais alors je n'étais pas assez d'aplomb.' Perhaps it was at Tilsit: I had gone through vicissitudes and anxieties, at Eylau amongst others, and I had come out victorious with emperors and kings paying court to me. Perhaps I was happiest after my victories in Italy: what enthusiasm, what cries of 'Long live the Liberator of Italy'—and all at twenty-five. From that time I saw what I might become. I already saw the world beneath me, as if I were being carried through the air." [2]

Then he is sorry that he ever left Egypt.[3] He regrets the career that Asia offered to him, he would rather have been Emperor of the East than Emperor of the West, if only that in the former case he would have been still on the throne. His later dreams as well as his earlier turn to the Orient. At the first glimpse of St. Helena from the ship, he says, criticizing the aspect of the place, that he should have done better to remain in Egypt, for he would now be Emperor of the entire East.[4] That empire, he declares, would have suited him; for the desert had always had a particular attraction for him, and his own name Napoleon means, he says, "lion of the desert." [5] "Arabia awaits a man. With the French in reserve and

[1] Gourgaud, i. 202. Cf. what he says of the eve of Austerlitz, Ségur, ii. 462.

[2] Gourgaud, ii. 55–6. See, too, Montholon, i. 424, ii. 125–6; Méneval, i. 427; Las Cases, vi. 309; Las Cases, i. 162. Cf. Bertrand, p. xxii.

[3] Cf. Rémusat, i. 252, 274. Cf. Ségur, ii. 458.

[4] Gourgaud, i. 67, 82.　　　　　　　　　[5] Las Cases, v. 55.

the Arabs as auxiliaries I should have seized Judæa; I should have been master of the East." [1] "Had I taken Acre I should have gone to India. I should have assumed the turban at Aleppo, and have headed an army of 200,000 men. The East," he goes on repeating, "only awaits a man." [2] "Had I," he says another time, "been able to make allies of the Mamelukes I should have been master of the East. Arabia awaits a man."[3]

It was not, however, because of Arabia or Judæa that Napoleon regretted Egypt. He reveals his secret aim in a laconic sentence. "France mistress of Egypt would be mistress of India." [4] And again: "The master of Egypt is the master of India." [5] And again: "Egypt once in possession of the French, farewell India to the British. This was one of the grand projects I aimed at."[6] He would have constructed two canals— one from the Red Sea to the Nile at Cairo, the other from the Red Sea to the Mediterranean. He would have extended the dominion of Egypt to the south, and would have enlisted the blacks of Sennaar and Darfur. With sixty or seventy thousand of these, and thirty thousand picked Frenchmen, he would have marched in three columns on the Euphrates, and, after making a long halt there, would have proceeded to conquer India. On arriving in India, he would have allied himself with the Mahrattas, and had hopes apparently of seducing the Sepoy troops. The British, he declares, were much afraid of this scheme of his.[7] "Gorgotto, I have been reading three volumes on India. What rascals the English are. If I had been able to get to India from Egypt with the nucleus of an army, I should have driven them from India. The East only wants a man. The master of Egypt is the master of India.[8] But now we shall see what will come to them from Russia. The Russians, already in Persia, have not far to go to reach India." And then he repeats his constant

[1] Gourgaud, i. 52.   [2] Ibid. i. 165.   [3] Ibid. ii. 52.
[4] Ibid. ii. 161.   [5] Ibid. ii. 315.   [6] Voice, i. 375.
[7] Gourgaud, ii. 75, 161.   [8] Ibid. ii. 315; see, too, p. 74.

preoccupation. "Russia is the Power that marches the most surely and with the greatest strides towards universal dominion,[1] . . . for now there is no France and therefore no equilibrium." [2]

He had been in effect Emperor of the West, and Montholon tells Gourgaud that from his instructions as Ambassador he inferred that Napoleon meant to be crowned by that title.[3] The Confederation of the Rhine was being influenced in this direction, and at Erfurt, it is said, the matter would have been settled, had not Alexander demanded Constantinople as a counterbalance. At St. Helena, however, his regrets are not for that position, but for the Empire of the East. And the reason is twofold; as ruler of the East he would have struck a great blow at the British, and would have emulated Alexander the Great. For, here let us note that his real hero and model is Alexander.[4] It is not merely his campaigns that Napoleon admires, for these one cannot, he says, well conceive, but his statesmanship. In his thirty-fourth year he leaves an immense and well-established empire. He had, too, the art of making friends of the peoples that he conquered. It was, continues the Emperor, a great act of policy in him to go to the temple of Ammon, for it was thus that he conquered Egypt. "So I, had I remained in Egypt, should probably have founded an empire like Alexander, by going on a pilgrimage to Mecca." [5] Even as he leaves France in the *Bellerophon* he says to Captain Maitland: "Had it not been for you English I should have been Emperor of the East; but wherever there is water to float a ship, we are sure to find you in our way." [6]

Nor did his admiration for Alexander the Great, his passion for the East, his aims on India, ever forsake him, until he had lost his empire on the plains of Russia and Germany. Not

[1] *Ibid.* ii. 75. [2] *Ibid.* ii. 315; i. 567-8.
[3] *Ibid.* ii. 196. Cf. Montholon, ii. 103-4. See, too, Miot, i. 290.
[4] Chaptal, p. 305.
[5] Gourgaud, ii. 435-6. Cf. Montholon, ii. 246. [6] Maitland, p. 99.

long before he passed the Niemen, in the midst of a conversation with Narbonne, he broke off with a sudden flash in his eyes: "After all," he exclaimed, as if under the inspiration of a vision, "this long journey is the way to India. Alexander had to make as long a march as that from Moscow to India in order to gain the Ganges. I have always said so to myself since the siege of Acre. Without the English filibuster and the French emigrant who directed the Turkish artillery, and who, with the plague, made me raise the siege, I would have conquered half Asia, and come back upon Europe to seek the thrones of France and Italy. I must now do just the reverse, and from the extremity of Europe invade Asia in order to attack England. You are aware of the missions of Gardanne and Jaubert to Persia: there has been no outward result: but I have all the maps and statistics of population for a march from Erivan and Tiflis to India. That would be a campaign less formidable, perhaps, than that which awaits us in the next three months. . . . Suppose Moscow taken, Russia crushed, the Czar reconciled or assassinated in some palace plot, succeeded perhaps by a new and dependent dynasty. Would it not then be possible for a great French army with auxiliaries from Tiflis to attain the Ganges? Once touched by a French sword, the scaffolding of mercantile power in India would fall to the ground. It would be a gigantic expedition, I admit, but practicable in this nineteenth century." [1] Who will maintain, who reads this, that absolute power had not had its usual effect, and that Napoleon had preserved in 1812 the balance and sanity of his judgment?

The third great subject of regret is, of course, Waterloo, over which we sometimes seem to hear him gnash his teeth. "Ah! if it were to begin again!" he exclaims. [2] He cannot understand how he lost it. [3] Perhaps the rain of the 17th? [4] Had he had Suchet at the head of Grouchy's army, [5] had he had Andréossi in

[1] Villemain, *Souvenirs*, i. 175–6.   [2] Gourgaud, i. 62.
[3] *Ibid*. i. 79, 93, 142.   [4] *Ibid*. ii. 159.   [5] *Ibid*. i. 370, 502.

Soult's place, could Bessières [1] or Lannes [2] have commanded the Guard, had he given the command of the Guard to Lobau, [3] had Murat headed the cavalry, had Clausel or Lamarque been at the War Office,[4] all might have been different. Should he have waited a fortnight longer? [5] He would then have had the 12,000 men employed in La Vendée. But who could tell that La Vendée would be so soon pacified? [6] Should he have attacked at all? Should he not have concentrated all his troops under Paris and awaited events? Perhaps then the Allies would not have attacked him. It is noteworthy, he says, that all their proclamations are dated after Waterloo. [7] He should not, he thinks, have employed Ney or Vandamme. [8] More than once he says he lost it because of the fault of an officer who gave Guyot the order to charge with the Horse Grenadiers, for had they been kept in reserve they would have retrieved the day, [9] but Montholon declares that there is no doubt that the Emperor gave the order himself. [10] He had not been able to see the battle well. [11] But the men of 1815 were not the men of 1792: the generals had become timid.[12] He is too apt, indeed, to blame his generals, such as Ney and Vandamme. Gourgaud begs him to be more lenient: he replies, "One must speak the truth." [13] He goes so far as to declare that the whole glory of the victory belongs to the Prince of Orange. Without him the British Army would have been annihilated, and Blücher hurled back beyond the Rhine. [14] This is a good instance of his occasional petulance. He exhausts himself in reasons for his defeat, but begins at last to perceive that some part of the result may have been due to the character of the enemy. "The English won by the excellence of their discipline," he admits, then wanders on to other reasons. But this may be taken to be his summing up: "It was a fatality, for in spite of all I should have

[1] *Ibid.* i. 150.   [2] *Ibid.* i. 196, 347.   [3] *Ibid.* i. 502.
[4] *Ibid.* i. 93.   [5] *Ibid.* ii. 370.   [6] *Ibid.* i. 500.
[7] *Ibid.* i. 577.   [8] *Ibid.* i. 502.   [9] *Ibid.* i. 196-7, 347.
[10] Montholon, ii. 84, 128-9.   [11] Gourgaud, i. 544.
[12] *Ibid.* i. 196.   [13] *Ibid.* i. 200.   [14] Montholon, ii. 184.

won that battle. [1] . . . Poor France, to be beaten by those scoundrels. But 'tis true there had already been Cressy and Agincourt." [2] A thought which, as we have seen, had long been present to his mind.

Then what should he have done after Waterloo? There is only one point on which he is always clear and constant—that he should have had Fouché hanged or shot at once. [3] He had the military commission all ready to try him, it was that which had tried the Duc d'Enghien, men who ran the danger of being hanged themselves. [4] But beyond that it is all darkness. Sometimes he thinks he should have shot Soult, but when or why does not clearly appear. He should, he says at other times, have beheaded Lafayette, Lanjuinais, and a dozen, [5] or thirty, sometimes even a hundred others. [6] Gourgaud and he often discuss this interesting point. On one occasion, Napoleon alludes to the plan of convoking at the Tuileries the Council of State, the 6,000 men of the Imperial Guard in Paris, the faithful part of the National Guard, and the Federates, haranguing them, and marching on the Chambers, which he would have adjourned or dissolved. He thinks he could thus have gained a respite of a fortnight, in which he would have fortified the right bank of the Seine and collected 100,000 men. Gourgaud gloomily replies that in the state of public opinion this would not have been practicable, and hints at a "Decius," who with a pistol shot would have killed the Emperor.[7] Las Cases also felt that this course would have been futile, and have damned the Emperor in history. [8] Gourgaud's own plan was different. He thinks that the Emperor should have gone straight from Waterloo to the Chambers, exhorted them to union, and made them feel that all depended on it. In reply, Napoleon thinks aloud. He had been three days without eating

[1] Gourgaud, i. 197.   [2] Ibid. ii. 370.
[3] Ibid. i. 93, ii. 321–4.   [4] Ibid. ii. 205.   [5] Ibid. ii. 205.
[6] Ibid. ii. 199. Cf. Montholon, ii. 204, who gives thirty as the number.
[7] Gourgaud, ii. 149.   [8] Las Cases, iii. 14–5.

and he was worn out. Had he gone to the Chambers it would have been no use simply to harangue; he must have gone like a Cromwell, and thrown a certain number of deputies into the river. By this means, as he explains more in detail, he would have demanded the purification of the Chamber, and have hanged seven or eight deputies, with Fouché, of course, at their head. But to do this he must have thrown himself into the arms of the Jacobins: it would have been anarchy. [1] Putting that on one side, he doubted of success; he would have disappeared in bloodshed and abhorrence.[2] Another time, he says frankly, he had not the courage to do it. Could one at such a moment revolutionize the populace and raise the guillotine? In 1793 it was the only way, but not then. And indeed he would not have succeeded, for he had too many enemies—it would have been a horrible risk, much blood and little result. He preferred, therefore, to abdicate in favour of his son, and make it clear to the nation that the Allies were the enemies, not of himself alone, but of France. So he said to the Chambers, "Well, gentlemen, you think me an obstacle to peace? Very well, then, get out of the scrape without me." [3]

Gourgaud is not satisfied; he presses the Emperor, and says that his mere presence would have electrified the deputies, and so forth. [4]

Napoleon replies with a sepulchral truth, "Ah! mon cher, j'étais battu." "As long as I was feared," he continues, "great was the awe I inspired, but not having the rights of legitimate sovereignty, when I had to ask for help, when, in short, I was defeated, I had nothing to hope. No. I only reproach myself for not having put an end to Fouché, and he but just escaped." [5] Then he returns again. "Yes, I ought to have gone to the Chambers, but I was tired out, and I could not anticipate that they would turn against me so quickly, for I arrived at eight o'clock and at noon they were in insurrection; they took

[1] Gourgaud, ii. 157.   [2] Ibid. ii. 320–1.
[3] Ibid. ii. 283.   [4] Ibid. ii. 321.   [5] Ibid. ii. 322.

me by surprise." He passes his hand over his face, and continues in a hollow voice: "After all, I am only a man.[1] I might indeed have put myself at the head of the army, which was in favour of my son, and, whatever happened, it would have been better than St. Helena. [2]

"Then again the Allies would have declared that they were only warring against me, and the army would have come to believe it. History will perhaps reproach me for having succumbed too easily. There was a little pique on my part. I offered at Malmaison to place myself once more at the head of the army, but the Government would not have it, so I left them to themselves.[3]

"The fact is that I came back too soon from Elba, but I thought the Congress was dissolved.[4] No doubt I ought then to have declared myself dictator, or have formed a council of dictatorship under Carnot, and not to have called the Chambers together; but I hoped that the Allies would feel confidence in me when they heard of my convoking a parliament; [5] and that the Chambers would give me resources that as dictator I could not obtain. But they did nothing for me; they were mischievous before Waterloo, and abandoned me after it. In any case, it was a mistake to trouble myself about a constitution, as had I been victorious I should soon have sent the Chambers to the right-about.[6] I was wrong, too, to quarrel with Talleyrand. But this sort of talk puts me out of temper. Let us go into the drawing-room and talk of our early loves." [7]

---

[1] Montholon, ii. 203; Gourgaud, ii. 322. [2] Gourgaud, ii. 322.
[3] Ibid. ii. 322–3.   [4] Ibid. i. 499.   [5] Ibid. ii. 323.
[6] Ibid. i. 93.   [7] Montholon, ii. 204.

CHAPTER FIFTEEN

Napoleon and the Democracy

★

ONE point is clear in all these discussions on Waterloo and its sequel: so clear and yet so unnoticed that it seems worth a short digression. Whatever Napoleon may occasionally say in retrospect, with regard to placing himself at the head of a popular and revolutionary movement after Waterloo, we are convinced that he was only deluding himself, or toying with his audience. "The recollections of my youth deterred me," [1] he said with truth at St. Helena. He had seen too much of the Revolution to face any such contingency. He had been the friend of Robespierre, or rather of Robespierre's brother, but after having reigned over France as a sovereign he entertained, it is clear, the profoundest repugnance to anything resembling revolution or even disorder. No eye-witness of the Terror was affected by a more profound reaction than Napoleon.[2] It had left him with a horror for excess, and a passion for order. He could have uttered with absolute truth the proud words which his dynastic successor uttered with more imperfect fulfilment: "Pour l'ordre, j'en réponds."

This was no secret to his intimates. He feared the people, said Chaptal; [3] the least discontent or disturbance, the slightest rising affected him more than the loss of a battle. He was perpetually vigilant on this point. He would send for his Ministers and say that there was not enough work, that the artisans would lend an ear to agitators, and that he feared an insurrection from loss of bread more than a battle against 200,000 men.[4] He would then order stuffs or furniture, and he would advance money to the principal manufacturers. One of these crises cost him in this way more than two million sterling.[5]

[1] Montholon, i. 228.
[2] Gourgaud, i. 416–8; Pasquier, iii. 178; Las Cases, vi. 68.
[3] Chaptal, pp. 221, 291.
[4] *Ibid.* p. 285.   [5] *Ibid.* 286. Cf. Beausset, iv. 149.

When I hear people, writes Madame de Rémusat, saying how easy it is to govern by force, I think of the Emperor: of how he used to harp on the difficulties arising from the use of force against citizens: of how when his Ministers advised any strong measures he would ask, "Will you guarantee that the people will not rise against it?" He would take pleasure in talking of the emotions of battle, but would turn pale at the narration of the excesses of a revolted people.[1] The Revolution had indeed set her seal on him; he had never forgotten it. He represented and embodied it, but was always silently contending against it.[2] And he knew it to be a hopeless battle. "I, and I alone, stand between society and the Revolution," he would say. "I can govern as I like. But my son will have to be a Liberal."[3] And he was right, for in the ten months during which he was absent at Elba the Revolution reared its head once more. It was always present to him, not as his source or inspiration, but as a nameless terror to be averted at any cost. He was indeed the child of the Revolution, but a child whose one object was parricide.

He dreaded the idea of firing upon the people; he preserved a lifelong regret for his action in the Vendémiaire outbreak, which he feared the people would never forget: he was prepared, as we have seen, at almost any cost to avert and buy off the material discontent of the people. But his horror of the Revolution and its methods went far beyond such demonstrations as these, considerable though they be. For he would not touch the Revolution even to save his crown or himself. Hostility to the Revolution could not go beyond this. He had seen, and seen with bitter outspoken contempt, Louis the Sixteenth bow to the multitude from the balcony of the Tuileries with the cap of liberty on his head. Not to preserve his liberty or his dynasty would Napoleon for a moment assume that cap.

After Waterloo the multitude ("canaille" as Napoleon gener-

---

[1] Rémusat, iii. 355.   [2] *Ibid.* iii. 225; Lamarque, i. 130.
[3] Rémusat, ii. 126. Cf. Chaptal, pp. 312, 320.

ally called them at St. Helena)[1] thronged round his palace and begged him to lead them; for they considered him the only barrier against feudalism, against the resumption of the confiscated property, and against foreign domination. "What do these people owe me?"—Napoleon, as he hears them, breaks out with sudden candour—"I found them poor, I leave them poor." [2] Montholon preserves for us one of these scenes. Two regiments and a vast multitude from the Faubourg St. Antoine come to demand that he shall lead them against the enemy. One of their spokesmen alludes to the 18th of Brumaire. Napoleon replies that circumstances are changed, that what then expressed the unanimous wish of the people would now require an ocean of French blood, and that he would shed none on behalf of a personal cause. And when the multitude is dispersed he explains himself more fully to Montholon. "Were I," he said, "to put into action the brute force of the masses, I should no doubt save Paris, and assure the crown to myself without having recourse to the horrors of civil war, but I should also risk a deluge of French blood. What power would be sufficient to dominate the passions, the hatred, the vengeance that would be aroused? No! I cannot forget that I was brought from Cannes to Paris amid sanguinary cries of, Down with the Priests! Down with the Nobles! I prefer the regrets of France to her crown." [3] During that famous march, the passion of the people, stirred by the brief government of the Bourbons, had made the deepest impression on him.[4] "I have," he said on arriving in Paris, "only to give the signal or even to turn my eyes away, and the nobles would be massacred in every province in France. But I will not be the King of the mob." Had he consented to associate himself with the popular fury

---

[1] *E.g.* Gourgaud, i. 208, 499, 579; *Voice,* ii. 379, note, *et passim;* Hobhouse, ii. 136, note.

[2] B. Constant, *Mémoires sur les Cent Jours,* ii. 139.

[3] Montholon, i. 16–18, 380–1.

[4] D'Hérrisson, *Cabinet Noir,* 183, note. Cf. Montholon, i. lxx.

at the suspected attempt to resume the land and privileges which were lost in the Revolution, he could, he was convinced, have arrived in the capital at the head of two millions of peasants.[1] But he would not be the leader of a jacquerie: his whole being, he declared, revolted at the thought.[2]

Once indeed at Longwood he is said to have abandoned himself for a moment to a different dream. "Were I to return," he said, "I should found my empire on the Jacobins. Jacobinism is the volcano which threatens all social order. Its eruption would be easily produced in Prussia, *and by the overthrow of the throne of Berlin I should have given an immense impetus to the power of France. Prussia has always been since the time of Frederick, and will always be, the greatest obstacle to my projects for France.* Once the red cap of liberty supreme at Berlin, all the power of Prussia would be at my disposal. I would use it as a club to smash Russia and Austria. I should resume the natural frontier of France, the Alps and the Rhine; and, having effected that, I should set about the great work of founding the French empire. By my arms and by the force of Jacobinism, by availing myself of every favourable circumstance and conjuncture of events, I should convert Europe into a federation of small sovereigns over which the French Emperor should be paramount. I should fix its limits at the Niemen: Alexander should only be the czar of Asiatic Russia. Austria would be only one of three kingdoms—Hungary and Bohemia being the other two—into which I should divide the empire of Maria Theresa. Then Europe would be protected from Russia, and Great Britain would become a second-rate Power. Only thus can peace be secured for Europe." [3] Montholon records this strange rhapsody, and declares that it was spoken on March 10, 1819, two years before the Emperor's death. It is very unlike his other estimates of Prussia, or his

[1] Las Cases, vi. 152. Cf. *Henry de Chaboulon,* i. 392; ii. 19.
[2] Montholon, i. 380–1; Las Cases, vi. 67; Hobhouse, ii. 354.
[3] *Carnet historique,* i. 173–5. Cf. Gourgaud, ii. 378–9.

real views as to Jacobinism. If we accept it as genuine, we must take it to be a sort of meditation as to the possibilities of an alternative policy. Possibly, indeed, he may have come to the conviction, after the experience of the Hundred Days, that were he ever again to find himself in France there was no other way of maintaining himself. He had, however, made an allusion of the same kind to Metternich in their famous interview at Dresden. "It may be that I shall succumb, but if so I shall drag down with me all other crowns and the whole structure of society itself." [1]

Talleyrand, with his cold instinct of judgment, had seen at the very outset of the Hundred Days that the one chance for Napoleon was to nationalize the war. His army would not suffice him; he must rely on the party from which he sprang, on the ruins of which he had raised himself, and which he had so long oppressed.[2] Nor was Alexander insensible to the danger. He pointed out to Lord Clancarty that it was necessary to detach the Jacobins from Napoleon,[3] though that would not seem to have been an easy task for a Russian emperor. Still it is well to note that the clearest and best-informed among the assembled princes at Vienna realized that the one chance for Napoleon was to become again what he had been at the outset of his career—the Revolution incarnate.

Lavallette tells us the truth in one pregnant sentence—the eleven months of the regin of Louis XVIII had thrown France back into 1792.[4] Even during that short period discontent had crystallized into conspiracies. But their object was to place Louis Philippe as a constitutional monarch on the throne, not to bring back the banished despot.[5] On his return the Emperor was alarmed. He found that the face of Paris was changed—respect and regard for him had visibly waned.[6] Had he realized

---

[1] Metternich, *Mémoires*, i. 153.   [2] *Mémoires*, iii. 170.
[3] *Ibid*. iii. 172.   [4] Lavallette, ii. 139. Cf. Montholon, i. 302.
[5] Pasquier, iii. 155; Méneval, iii. 521.
[6] Las Cases, vii. 135; Pasquier, iii. 178.

at Elba, he said, the change which had taken place in France he would have remained on his island. He would send for Lavallette—sometimes two or three times a day—and would discuss the new situation for hours.[1] Even had he returned victorious, he would, says Lavallette, have had to face great danger from internal troubles.[2] Indeed, it was soon evident that what the country desired was less the return of the Emperor than the departure of the Bourbons. When these had gone, enthusiasm promptly cooled.[3] Napoleon, with characteristic perception, had seen this at once. To a Minister who congratulated him on the miracle by which he, almost alone, had reconquered France, he replied, "Bah! the time for compliments is past: they let me come as they let the others go." [4] One instance will perhaps suffice. Napoleon had resumed his former title of Emperor by the Grace of God and the Constitutions of the Empire. This was repugnant to the new spirit, and the Council of State replied by proclaiming the sovereignty of the people, a decree not less distasteful to the Emperor, but which he could not resent.[5] He had to put up with slights, and a peremptory insolence from his Chambers. Nevertheless he faced this new situation with imperturbable calm.[6] He felt, no doubt, that in case of victory he could easily put things right.[7] But in case of defeat? He was conscious that in that case the new spirit would overwhelm him, unless he could summon a mightier power still to outbid it, and proclaim a new revolution. Why, then, did he not accept the last alternative? Why did he not put himself at the head of an uprising of revolutionary France? [8] Once, no doubt, in earlier days, the personal leadership of a revolution would have been a dazzling object of desire. The First Consul would not have hesitated. But the Emperor saw

---

[1] Lavallette, ii. 139.   [2] Ibid. ii. 140.   [3] Ibid. ii. 140–1.
[4] Mémoires d'un ministre du trésor publique, iv. 18. Cf. Pasquier, iii. 135.
[5] Lavallette, ii. 143.   [6] Ibid. ii. 140.
[7] Pasquier, iii. 218.   [8] Hobhouse, ii. 35, note.

clearly, we think, that there would in that case have been no question of a dynasty, that the dictatorship would have been a personal one, that he would have been Marius or Sylla, not Augustus or Charlemagne. It will be observed that in his remark to Montholon, cited above, he says, "I should secure the crown to myself:" there is no mention of, or illusion as to, a succession. Such a position seemed degrading after that which he had filled;[1] and, as we have seen, everything connected with revolution was odious to him. It was consequently impossible for him to become the prophet or general of a new Revolution after Waterloo. Had he known what awaited him— St. Helena, its sordid miseries, its petty gaolers, its wearisome and hopeless years of living death—he might possibly have overcome his repugnance. But all this he could not foresee; and no less would have moved him; so he preferred to fold his arms and watch the inevitable catastrophe of the rhetoricians: to fold his arms and await events. Better, he thought, the life of an American farmer than the presidency of a committee of public safety.

Between Napoleon and the Chambers there reigned from the first a scarcely disguised hostility. Appearances were to some limited extent maintained. But both parties were playing a part, with little, if any, disguise; and neither was the dupe of the other.[2] The Chambers were willing to use Napoleon as a consummate general to resist invasion and the return of the Bourbons, hoping to be able to subordinate or get rid of him when the victory was won. "As soon as he is gone to the army," said Fouché, "we shall be masters of the situation. I wish him to gain one or two battles. But he will lose the third, and then it will be our turn." [3] This was the complacent calculation of the Chambers. But they were in the position of the mortal in the fairy tale who summons a genie which he cannot control. Napoleon, on the other hand, submitted to the Chambers, as a pledge to the world of his reformed

[1] Montholon, i. lxx.   [2] Pasquier, iii. 195.   [3] *Ibid*. iii. 195.

character, and with the hope of obtaining supplies through them, but with the fixed intention of getting rid of them, should he be victorious.[1] After Ligny he stated categorically his intention of returning to Paris and resuming absolute power when he had defeated the English.[2] Each party was perfectly aware of the policy of the other. There were no doubts and no illusions. It seems certain that the temper of the Parliament was such that many of its members hoped that their arms might be defeated, and were able to rejoice over Waterloo. And it was Napoleon's consciousness of the hostility of the Chambers that compelled his return to Paris after the disaster. He has been blamed for not remaining on the frontier and endeavouring to rally his shattered troops. But of what avail would this have been if behind him his own Parliament were deposing and disavowing him? Yet no one can doubt that these would have been the first acts of the Chambers on hearing of his defeat. Outlawed by all Europe and by his own country, he could hardly have continued to struggle, even with much greater military forces than any that he could have collected.

This digression leads inevitably to another. The relations of the Emperor and his Parliament are clear and patent. What is more difficult to understand is that, in spite of this last sombre struggle between Constitutionalism and Napoleon, his name should have been cherished as a watchword for some thirty years by the Liberals of the Continent. For with liberty and its aspirations he had no sympathy; he relegated them to those whom he contemptuously termed ideologues. Order, justice, force, symmetry, these were his administrative ideals;— tempered always by the personal equation. The legend of his liberalism can only be explained by the fact that, the Constitution-mongers of 1815 having disappeared on the return of the Bourbons in a storm of contempt, this episode of the Hundred Days was forgotten. All that was remembered was the fact

[1] Gourgaud, i. 93, 99; ii. 323.   [2] Pasquier, iii. 227, note.

that Napoleon was the child of the Revolution, who had humbled and mutilated the old dynasties of Europe, without regard to antiquity, or prescription, or title. To the people he stood for the Revolution, and to the army for glory. No one remembered, or at any rate cared to recall, that he had knowingly ceded his throne and yielded himself a prisoner rather than place himself at the head of a popular insurrection.

But had it been remembered, it would have been held to be expiated by the martyrdom of St. Helena. Napoleon was quite aware of the advantage that his memory and cause would derive from his imprisonment. His death in lonely captivity cancelled all his errors and all his shortcomings. His memory, purged of all recollection of his iron rule, of his insatiable demands on the blood and resources of France, of the two invasions of her territory which he had brought about, became a tradition and a miracle. The peasantry of France had always been, next to the army, his main support, for they had considered him their sure bulwark against any return of feudal rights or feudal lords, against any restitution of the estates confiscated during the Revolution. The peasantry then were the jealous guardians of his fame.[1] Among them long lingered the tradition of his supernatural achievements. Béranger, it has been remarked, was able to condense the popular conception in the narrative of an old peasant woman who does not mention a single one of his victories.

"Long, long," says the poet in that exquisite piece, "will they talk of his glory under the thatched roof; in fifty years the humble dwelling will know no other history." And he goes on to give the keynote in a couplet. "Children, through this village I saw him ride, followed by kings."

It is too much to say, perhaps, that Napoleon received the honours of apotheosis, but short of that point it is difficult to exaggerate. He received, at any rate, the most singular and sublime honour that has ever been awarded to humanity. For

[1] Chaptal, p. 293.

he was known in France not as General, or Consul, or Emperor, or even by his name, but simply as "The Man" (l'homme).[1] His son was "the Son of the Man," he himself was always "The Man." He was, in fact, the Man of the popular imagination, and it was thus that Liberals swore by him. His intense individuality, even more than his horror of anarchy, had made him an absolute ruler. But as the product of the Revolution, as the humbler of kings, a glamour of liberty grew round his name. He had gratified the passion for equality by founding the fourth dynasty, though sprung from nothing; he had kept out the Bourbons; he had, above all, crushed and abased the chiefs of that Holy Alliance which weighed so heavily on Europe, which endeavoured to tread out the last embers of the French Revolution, and which represented an embodied hostility to freedom. So regarded, it is not wonderful that the image of Napoleon became the idol of Continental Liberalism. Later on, again, it was stamped on a more definite plan. Authoritative democracy, or, in other words, democratic dictatorship, the idea which produced the Second Empire in France, which is still alive there, and which, in various forms, has found favour elsewhere, is the political legacy, perhaps the final message, of Napoleon.[2]

[1] As early as 1814. Cf. Montalivet, *Fragments et souvenirs*, i. 6.
[2] Montholon, i. 271.

CHAPTER SIXTEEN
The End

★

It is unnecessary to dwell further on these last scenes or glimpses of the great drama of Napoleon's life. It is strange, however, to note that, in spite of the atmosphere of vigilance in which he lived, the end was unexpected. His death came suddenly. This we gather from the scanty record of Arnott; for Antommarchi we put, for reasons already explained, entirely on one side. Arnott was evidently unaware of his patient's grave condition.[1] Though he was called in on April 1, only thirty-five days before Napoleon's death, he did not then or for some time afterwards suspect the gravity of the illness. Indeed it was not till April 27 or 28, a bare week before the end, that he realized that the malady was mortal. Nor had the Governor or the British Government any suspicion that the end was near, though on May 3, within the last two days of life, Montholon had a long interview with Sir Hudson, in which he gave painful details of his master's condition.

For the last nine days of his life he was constantly delirious; he would not be touched, he would not be moved. On the morning of May 5, he uttered some incoherent words, among which Montholon fancied that he distinguished, "France . . . armée . . . tête d'armée." [2] As the patient uttered these words he sprang from the bed, dragging Montholon, who endeavoured to restrain him, onto the floor. It was the last effort of that formidable energy. He was with difficulty replaced in bed by Montholon and Archambault, and then lay quietly till

[1] Forsyth, iii. 275.
[2] Antommarchi, characteristically enough, states that three hours afterwards he heard Napoleon say "tête . . . armée," and that these were his last words. Montholon expressly states that Antommarchi was not in the room at two o'clock when Napoleon said "tête d'armée." The point is of little importance except as showing the difficulty of ascertaining the exact truth at Longwood up to the last instant.

near six o'clock in the evening, when he yielded his last breath.[1]
A great storm was raging outside, which shook the frail huts
of the soldiers as with an earthquake, tore up the trees that the
Emperor had planted, and uprooted the willow under which
he was accustomed to repose.[2] Within, the faithful Marchand
was covering the corpse with the cloak which the young
conqueror had worn at Marengo.[3]

The Governor and his staff were waiting below to hear the
last news. On learning the event Lowe spoke a few manly
and fitting words.[4] But the inevitable wrangling soon broke
out again over the corpse. Lowe insisted on an immediate
autopsy, which the French strenuously resisted. He also
declined to allow the removal of the remains to France. Here,
he had no choice. The unexpected arrival of the dead Napoleon in Europe would have been second only in embarrassment
to the arrival of the living. Lastly, as we have seen, he insisted
that the name "Bonaparte" should be appended if "Napoleon," as was proposed, were engraved on the coffin. Comment
on this is superfluous.

During the next morning the body lay in state, and Montchenu obtained his only view of the captive. Four days afterwards the funeral took place with such simple pomp as the
island could afford. The coffin, on which lay the sword and
the mantle of Marengo, was borne by British soldiers to a car
drawn by four of the Emperor's horses, and thence again by
relays of British soldiers to a spot which he had himself chosen,
should burial in France be refused. It was in a garden at the
bottom of a deep ravine. There, under the shade of two
willows, by the side of a spring which had supplied the
Emperor with water to drink, had the grave been dug. The

[1] Montholon, ii. 548-9.

[2] Watson (*Story of Napoleon's Death Mask*, p. 7) denies that there
was a storm, on the authority of ships' logs, which it is difficult to
controvert. Yet it has hitherto been universally accepted. Forsyth,
iii. 287.

[3] Montholon, ii. 555.　　　　　　　[4] Henry, ii. 80.

inmates of Longwood followed as chief mourners. Then came Lowe, Montchenu, and the officials, civil, naval, and military, of the island. As the body was lowered into the earth there were salvoes of musketry and cannon.

Nineteen years afterwards a French frigate, under the command of the Prince of Joinville, anchored at Jamestown. It had come for the purpose of conveying back to France the Emperor's remains. They had been surrendered in the hope expressed by the British Government that all traces of national animosity would be buried in the tomb of Napoleon. But before the vessel had returned with her precious burden the two countries were on the very brink of war. In the *Belle-Poule* there returned on this last pious pilgrimage to St. Helena, Bertrand and Gourgaud, the young Las Cases, and Arthur Bertrand ("the first French visitor who entered St. Helena without Lord Bathurst's permission"). There, too, were Marchand, the most faithful and trusted of the Emperor's attendants, Noverraz, Pierron, and Archambault; as well as St. Denis, who, disguised under the name of Ali, had acted as a second Mameluke with Rustan, and whom Napoleon had often used as an amanuensis at St. Helena. Together these sombre and devoted survivors visited the scene of their exile, and amid the shame and embarrassment of the British authorities, witnessed the degradation of Longwood into a stable. Together they surrounded their master's grave at midnight on October 15, 1840 (the twenty-fifth anniversary of his arrival at St. Helena); and, when, after ten hours' strenuous labour, the coffin was disinterred, together they beheld once more the features of the Emperor, unaltered and unimpaired. Together they followed the corpse to Paris in a procession which savoured less of a funeral than a triumph. It was then that the dead conqueror made the most majestic of his entrances into his capital. On a bitter December morning the King of the French, surrounded by the princes and ministers and splendours of France, sat in silent state under the dome of the Invalides, awaiting the arrival of the corpse. Suddenly a chamberlain appearing at the door announced in a clear and resonant voice, "l'Empereur," as if it were the living sovereign: and the vast and illustrious assembly rose with a common emotion as the body was borne slowly in. The spectators could not restrain their tears as they realized the pathos and significance of the scene.[1] Behind the coffin walked the surviving exiles of St. Helena; it was the undisputed privilege of Bertrand to lay his master's sword upon the pall.

One point in the Emperor's last illness should be noticed once for all. The policy of Longwood, actively supported by O'Meara, was to declare that there was a deadly liver complaint, indigenous to the island, to which Napoleon was a victim, and which could of course only be cured by his removal.[2] We think that the Emperor himself, who combined a shrewd interest with a rooted disbelief in the art of medicine,[3] knew better. He would, for example, put his hand on the pit of his stomach, and say, with a groan, "Oh! mon pylore! mon pylore!"[4] He, however, as we have seen, gravely condoled with Gourgaud, who was in the best of health, on being another victim of this insular malady.[5] Within two months of his own death he wrote to Pauline that the "liver complaint with which he has been afflicted for six years, and which is endemic and mortal at St. Helena, has made alarming progress during the last six months." Within a month of his death he made the same complaint to Arnott. Montholon, on his return to Europe, in spite of the post-mortem examination, still gallantly maintained the theory of a liver complaint. But Napoleon's liver was found to be quite sound; he died of the cancer in the stomach which had killed his father.[6]

His last days, before the agony began, were tragical enough,

[1] *Souvenirs du Marquis de Massa*, p. 18.
[2] Gourgaud, ii. 344; Montholon, ii. 352.
[3] Las Cases, ii. 303; iv. 128.   [4] Henry, ii. 78.
[5] Gourgaud, ii. 530; cf. p. 360.   [6] Forsyth, iii. 289–90, 293.

as we gather from the jejune chronicles of Montholon; which, moreover, do not give the impression of having been really written from day to day, but retrospectively, perhaps from notes. Bertrand, in a letter to King Joseph,[1] says that after August 1820, the Emperor remained almost always in his chair, and in his dressing-gown, able to read and talk, but not to work or dictate. After the middle of March 1821 he scarcely left his bed; he could hardly eat; and he became extremely emaciated. He and his suite would sometimes build castles in the air of a new life in America, but he well knew that he was dying. He devoted much time to his will, and was extremely anxious that the collection of letters from European sovereigns to himself, as well as a few that Madame de Staël had written to him from Italy, should be published. On this point he was strenuous and insistent.[2] He believed them to be in the hands of Joseph. But they had been stolen, and had been offered to and refused by Murray the publisher. The Russian Government had intervened and purchased for a large sum the letters of Alexander: the fate of the others is not known.[3] He would still read aloud, and would still discuss the past. But it is strange how little we know of it all; and we infer that Napoleon's suite were as much in the dark as the rest of the world with regard to their master's approaching end. Otherwise they would surely have recorded with pious care these remarkable moments.

It is these last months that we chiefly grudge to oblivion. Otherwise one may well ask: What is the use of recalling these sere records of the captivity of St. Helena? They can scarcely be called history; they are not, unhappily, romance; they can hardly be held to possess any healthy attraction. They

---

[1] *Mémoires du Roi Joseph*, x. 254, etc. See in Didot, 307-15, the conversation between Lowe and Montholon of May 3, 1821, with strange details of Napoleon's state.

[2] *Mémoires du Roi Joseph*, x. 259, 269.

[3] *Memoirs of John Murray*, i. 279, 280.

only narrate with obtrusive inaccuracy an episode which no one has any interest in remembering, and which all would fain forget. Why, then, collate these morbid, sordid, insincere chronicles? Does not history tell us that there is nothing so melancholy as the aspect of great men in retirement—from Nebuchadnezzar in his meadow to Napoleon on his rock?

The first answer to this question is incidental and personal. To the present writer Lord Beaconsfield once explained why he wrote *Count Alarcos;* a drama nearly, if not quite, forgotten. It was produced, he said, not in the hope of composing a great tragedy, but of laying a literary ghost. The story haunted him, and would, he felt, haunt him until he should have put it into shape. And so it is with this little book. It cannot help embodying a tragedy, but it was written to lay a literary ghost, dormant for years, only quickened into activity by the analysis of Gourgaud's last journals, and by stimulating leisure.

Secondly, it is an episode on which History has yet to record her final judgment. Nor is it clear that she is yet in a position to do so. The actors, indeed, have long passed away; the blood heated by twenty years of warfare is now cold enough; on the one side the faint inextinguishable hopes, on the other the apprehensions and the suspicions, all are dead. And yet—the subject still seems warm. It is doubtful if one side is yet cool enough to own any error, it is doubtful if the other side has wholly forgiven. Nations have silent, stubborn memories. The fires of Smithfield have left in England embers that still smoulder. Ireland has remembered much which it would be for her own happiness to forget. The Scots are still Jacobites at heart.

Again, we have more chance of seeing the *man* Napoleon at St. Helena than at any other period of his career. In the first years of the consulate the man was revealed, but then he was undeveloped. On the throne he ceased to be human. At Elba he had no present existence; he was always in the past or the future.

Moreover, what was published about him during his life
and for long after his death has little value. A sure test of
greatness in men of action is the absence of lukewarmness with
regard to them. They are detested or adored. The idolatry
and hatred which Napoleon inspired survived him too long to
allow of the play of reason. No one seemed able then or for
long afterwards to put on a pair of smoked glasses and gaze
dispassionately at this dazzling luminary. Nor is it easy now.
One has to sift evidence and passion, and make allowance for
opposing frenzies. His correspondence, especially that part
which was suppressed, furnishes, of course, the great picture
of his manifold activities and methods. This is, however, but
a small fraction of the literature which concerns him. Of
books and memoirs about Napoleon there is indeed no end. Of
veracious books, which give a sure or even remotely impartial
picture of the man, there are remarkably few.

Some judicious observers, who knew Napoleon well, wrote
their real impressions, but wrote them very secretly, and the
result is only now oozing out. Of these witnesses we incline
to put Chaptal first. He was for some time Napoleon's confidential Minister, and he analyzes his character with the dispassionate science of an eminent chemist. Pasquier we are
inclined to place next, as being on the whole unfavourably fair.
With him we should perhaps bracket Ségur, whose memoirs,
which include the classical history of the Russian expedition,
give a brilliant portrait, the work of an admirer, but by no
means a blind admirer. We should put him as a pendant to
Pasquier, and say that he is favourably fair. And the beauty
of his style, the exquisite eloquence of some of the passages,
would lure on the sternest and sourest critics of the hero.
Lavallette, though he does not tell us much, and though the
Duke of Wellington on the slightest grounds stigmatized him
as a liar,[1] seems sufficiently trustworthy, on the partial side.
Roederer, from among a number of massive volumes contain-

[1] Stanhope's *Wellington*, p. 31.

ing his unreadable works, yields some pure gold: priceless notes of Napoleonic conversation. The three books of Fain fancifully called *Manuscripts*, are valuable, not merely for the state papers they contain, but as the work of a man who was always with Napoleon, and who had received, moreover, the valuable co-operation of Maret. Fain's personality is always kept in the background, a notable peculiarity in this class of literature; and to his not less exceptional accuracy even Wellington testifies. Madame de Rémusat, with heavy deductions, leaves something of value. But we can never forget that she burned her real, contemporary memoirs in 1815; and that those now published were composed three years afterwards, during the bitterest reaction of the Restoration, when it was considered indecent to allude to the Emperor, much less pronounce his name, in polite society. Moreover, she was the close friend of Talleyrand, Napoleon's unremitting enemy; was lady-in-waiting to Josephine, whose wrongs she resented; and, worst of all, was a woman who could not forgive Napoleon's clumsiness and deficiency in courtesies and gallantries. On a lower scale we may mention Méneval and Beausset. On a lower still there is Constant. Constant (the valet, not Benjamin) gives many details of interest: though the memoirs which bear his name were probably written by another hand from his notes. To him, in despite of the proverb, his master was a hero, though one to be abandoned as soon as fortune frowned. We place some confidence in Miot de Melito and in the dry humour of Beugnot. Nor do we desire to disparage the authors, some of them conspicuous, whom we do not name; we only desire to indicate those who seem most worthy of trust. Scores of memoirs throw here and there a flash of light on the man. But the light is usually accidental, as the writers are generally idolaters or enemies. To Marbot and Thiébault we owe the most vivid snapshots of Napoleon. The extraordinarily lifelike scene of Napoleon at the masked ball mopping his hot head with a wet handkerchief and murmuring

THE END

"Oh! que c'est bon, que c'est bon!" is recorded by Marbot.[1] The fleeting vision of Napoleon galloping homewards through Spain alone with an aide-de-camp, whose horse the Emperor is flogging with a postilion's whip, is the little masterpiece of Thiébault.[2] We wish we felt sure of the conscientious accuracy of either author.

At length, in this final phase, we have some chance of seeing something of the man. The artifice and drapery still encompass him, but not always; and through the perplexed and adulatory narratives there come glimpses of fact. From one there even comes illumination. Had Gourgaud remained till the end, it is scarcely too much to say that we should have known from him more of the naked Napoleon than from all the existing library of Napoleonic literature. But Gourgaud leaves before we most require him. The remaining records tell us little or nothing of that period when there might well have been most to be learned; at that supreme opportunity for self-revelation when the vanities and passions of life were paling before the infinite shadow of death. It was then that, left alone with history and with eternity, the *Man*, as apart from the warrior and statesman, might possibly but not probably, have revealed himself, and confessed himself, and spoken what truth was in him. Indeed, the declaration about the Duc d'Enghien's death, made five weeks before his own, shows, if it be authentic, that the dying man did assert himself with passionate impatience to clear others and to put an end to the fables which he had countenanced.

But, even without the last revelations, which he may have made, but which we have not got, it is to St. Helena that the world must look for the final glimpse of this great human problem. For a problem he is and must ever remain. Mankind will always delight to scrutinize something that indefinitely raises its conception of its own powers and possibilities. For this reason it loves balloons and flying machines, apparatus that

[1] Marbot, ii. 313-4.   [2] Thiébault, iv. 280.

245

moves below earth or sea, the men who accomplish physical or intellectual feats which enlarge the scope of human achievement. For this reason also it seeks, but eternally in vain, to penetrate the secret of this prodigious human being. In spite of all this delving, mining, and analysis, what secret there is will probably evade discovery. Partly, it may be argued, because it is so complex. Partly, it may be contended, because there is none: there are only the play and procession of destiny.

As to the complexity of the problem, as to the variety of the man, there can be no doubt. But the study, even if illusory, will always remain absorbing. There will always be alchemists, and always investigators of Napoleon's character. Nor can this be considered surprising. He is so multifarious, luminous, and brilliant that he gives light from a thousand facets. Sometimes he invents, sometimes he talks something perilously like nonsense; sometimes he is petty, theatrical, or outrageous; but in the main, where you get at the man himself, he is intensely human and profoundly interesting. Study, then, of Napoleon's utterances, apart from any attempt to discover the secret of his prodigious exploits, cannot be considered as wasted; whether it be pursued with the view of imitating, or avoiding, or simply of learning, it can scarcely fail to be stimulating. His career, partly perhaps because it is not scientifically divided into acts or phases, gives rise to a number of questions, all obvious and pertinent, but seldom admitting of a direct or satisfactory reply. What was his conception of life? What was his fixed object? Had he any such deliberate conception or object? Was he always sane? Was he in any degree a charlatan? Was he simply a lucky fatalist of vast natural powers? Or was his success due to the most remarkable combination of intellect and energy that stands on exact record?

To all these questions, and scores of others, many capable men will be ready with a prompt reply. But the more the student examines the subject, the less ready will he be with an answer. He may at last arrive at his own hypothesis, but

it will not be a confident one; and he will find without surprise that his fellows, equally laborious and equally conscientious, will all supply excellent solutions, totally at variance
with his own and with each other.

By the philosopher, and still more by the philosopher who
believes in the divine guidance of human affairs, the true
relation of Napoleon to the world's history will be reduced
to a very simple conception: that he was launched into the
world as a great natural or supernatural force, as a scourge
and a scavenger, to effect a vast operation, partly positive, but
mainly negative; and that when he has accomplished that
work he is withdrawn as swiftly as he came. Cæsar, Attila,
Tamerlane, and Mahomet are forces of this kind; the last a
much more potent and abiding factor in the universe than
Napoleon; another proof, if proof were needed, of how small
is the permanent effect of warfare alone on the history of mankind. These men make great epochs; they embody vast transi-
tions; they perplex and appall their contemporaries; but when
viewed at a distance they are seen to be only periodical and
necessary incidents of the world's movement. The details of
their career, their morals, their methods, are then judged,
interesting though they may be, to be merely subordinate
details.

Scavenger is a coarse word, yet it accurately represents
Napoleon's first function as ruler. The volcano of the French
Revolution had burned itself out. He had to clear away the
cold lava; the rubbish of past destruction; the cinders and
the scoriæ; the fungus of corruption which had overgrown
all, and was for the moment the only visible result. What he
often said of the Crown of France is absolutely true of its
government. "I found it in the gutter, and I picked it up on
my sword's point." The gutter government he replaced by a
new administrative machine, trim, pervading, and efficient;
efficient, that is to say, so long as the engineer was a man of
extraordinary energy and genius.

Then he is a scourge. He purges the floor of Europe with fire. As the sword and spirit of the Revolution, though in all the pomp of the purple, he descends upon the ancient monarchies, and compels them to set their houses in order. True, after his fall they relapse. But it is only for a space, and reform if not revolt is soon busy among them. Had it not been for Napoleon this could not have happened; for, when he assumed the government, Europe seemed at last to have stemmed the Revolution.

We do not discuss his military greatness; that is universally acknowledged. It would, moreover, require an expert and a volume to discuss it with authority. To the civilian eye he seems, at his best, the greatest of all soldiers. His rapidity of movement and apprehension, his power of inspiring his armies to perform extraordinary feats, his knowledge of detail combined with his gigantic grasp, his prodigious triumphs, make cool judgment difficult. Later on, even civilians may see faults —the Grand Army, for example, becoming, before it struck a blow, little more than a mob, without discipline and without provisions, for want of practical foresight and commissariat.[1] There is a disposition, too, among historians, perhaps a growing one, to attribute a larger share of credit to his lieutenants for some of his great victories; to Desaix, for instance, at Marengo, to Davoust for Jena. But, let what will be subtracted, there remains an irreducible maximum of fame and exploit. After all, the mass of mankind can only judge of results. And, though there may be no one achievement equal to Cæsar's victory at Alesia, the military genius of Napoleon in its results is unsurpassed.

We do not, of course, imply that the negative and warrior work of Napoleon, immense though it was, represents anything like his whole career. He was a great administrator. He controlled every wheel and spring, large or small, of his vast machinery of government. It was, as it were, his plaything.

[1] Ségur, iv. 111, etc., 165.

He was his own War Office, his own Foreign Office, his own Admiralty, his own Ministry of every kind. His Minister of Police, when he was Fouché, had no doubt a department of some independence; but then Napoleon had half-a-dozen police agencies of his own.[1] His financial management, by which he sustained a vast empire with power and splendour, but with rigid economy and without a debt, is a marvel and a mystery. In all the offices of state he knew everything, guided everything, inspired everything. He himself aptly enough compared his mind to a cupboard of pigeon-holes; to deal with any subject he opened the pigeon-hole relating to it and closed the others; when he wished to sleep, he closed them all.[2] Moreover, his inexhaustible memory made him familiar with all the men and all the details as well as with all the machinery of government. Daru, one of Napoleon's most efficient Ministers, told Lamarque a curious story which illustrates the Emperor's unflagging thoroughness of administration as well as anxiety to learn. One day, in the Eylau campaign, Daru left the Emperor, saying that he had to open his letters. "What letters can you receive," asked the Emperor derisively, "in this Arab camp, where we live on the country as we march?" "Your Majesty shall see," replied Daru, and in a short time returned, followed by half-a-dozen secretaries laden with papers. Napoleon opened the first at hazard; it contained a demand from the hospital at Mayence for a hundred syringes. "What! Do you provide syringes for the hospital at Mayence?" "Yes, and your Majesty pays for them." The Emperor spent four hours opening and reading all the letters; he continued to do so for eight successive days; then he said: "For the first time I understand the mechanism of an army." On his return to Paris after Tilsit he pursued the same course with all the other Ministers successively. After this process, which lasted six weeks, he carried a similar investiga-

---

[1] Chaptal, pp. 379, 381; Stendhal, *Napoléon*, p. 21; Pasquier, i. 430.
[2] Méneval, i. 423.

tion into the ranks of the subordinates.[1] What a force in itself was this quick yet laborious apprehension, this detailed probing of his vast administration! The inherent defect of such an executive was that no less an energy or intellect could have kept it going for a week. So completely did it depend on the master that it was paralyzed by the least severance from him.[2] Had Napoleon been ill for a week the whole empire would have sickened. The conspiracy of Mallet in 1812, and the conduct of affairs by the Council of Regency in 1814, are eminent instances of this.

Then he was a great legislator. The positive and permanent part of his work is, of course, the Code.[3] Wars end, and conquests shrink—so much so, that Napoleon after all left France less than he found it. Indeed, the only trace of his reign now visible on the face of Europe is the Bernadotte dynasty in Sweden, which was not the direct result of conquest, nor the direct work of Napoleon. All that of this kind he planned and fashioned passed away with him. But the Code remains, and profoundly affects the character of the nation, as well as of the other races to which it has been extended. Few enactments, for example, have had a more potent effect in moulding the social and political life of a community than the provision of the Code for the compulsory division of property. It checks population, it enforces equality, it constitutes the most powerful and conservative of landed interests.

To achieve such work required a puissant organization, and indeed his physical constitution was not less remarkable than his intellectual mechanism. His digestion endured for a lifetime, without resentment, hearty meals devoured in a few moments at odd times.[4] His first tooth was extracted at St. Helena, and then, it seems, unnecessarily.[5] But this opera-

---

[1] Lamarque, i. 420–1.   [2] Méneval, iii. 225, etc., 99.
[3] Montholon, i. 401.   [4] Chaptal, pp. 328–9.
[5] Montholon, ii. 225–6.

tion was the only one that he ever underwent. It appeared in other ways that his exceptional mind was lodged in an exceptional body.[1] In his prime, before his passion for hot baths had weakened him, he was incapable of fatigue. He fought Alvinzy once for five consecutive days without taking off his boots or closing his eyes; when he had beaten the Austrian he slept for thirty-six hours.[2] On arriving at the Tuileries after his breathless journey from Valladolid, when he had paused only for a few hours at Bayonne, he insisted on at once inspecting, without an instant's delay, the entire palace, and the Louvre, where new constructions were proceeding.[3] He would post from Poland to Paris, summon a council at once, and preside at it with his usual vigour and acuteness.[4] And his councils were no joke. They would last eight or ten hours.[5] Once at two o'clock in the morning the councillors were all worn out; the Minister of Marine was fast asleep: Napoleon still urged them to further deliberation, "Come, gentlemen, pull yourselves together; it is only two o'clock; we must earn the money that the nation gives us." [6] Throughout these sittings his mind was always active and predominant.[7] Never did a council separate without being the wiser, either from what he taught or from the close investigation which he insisted upon. He would work for eighteen hours at a stretch, sometimes at one subject, sometimes at a variety.[8] "Never," says Roederer, "have I seen his mind weary; never have I seen his mind without its spring; not in strain of body, wrath, or the most violent exercise." [9]

Sometimes he carried physical force to an extreme point.[10] He kicked Volney in the stomach for saying that France wanted

[1] Las Cases, v. 167.   [2] Chaptal, p. 327.
[3] Beausset, iv. 187.   [4] Chaptal, p. 327.
[5] *Ibid*. p. 328; cf., too, Pasquier as to the work, i. 233.
[6] Roederer, iii. 382.
[7] Stendhal, *Napoléon*, pp. 67, etc. In later days he sometimes dozed at the Conseil d'État. Las Cases, iv. 245; Roederer, iii. 444.
[8] *Ibid*. iii. 382.   [9] *Ibid*. iii. 382.   [10] See Miot, ii. 243.

the Bourbons, and the philosopher was carried away senseless.[1] On another occasion he knocked down his Chief Justice and belaboured him with his fists.[2] He is said to have attacked Berthier with the tongs.[3] These were the rare eruptions of a nervous system occasionally yielding to continuous strain. Nor was the primitive Corsican altogether smothered under the robe of Empire.

Again there were reactions.[4] Witness that strange scene at the little mansion of Düben, where he sits for two days on a sofa, heedless of the despatches which are massed on his table calling for reply, engaged in vacantly tracing capital letters on sheets of paper, in a prostration of doubt whether he should yield to the dumb revolt of his generals against the march to Berlin.[5] Witness the apathy at Malmaison after Waterloo.

One other positive result, which is in truth scarcely less substantial than the Code, may be laid to his account. He left behind the memory of a period of splendour and dominion, which, even if it does not keep the imagination of his people in a perpetual glow, remains a symbol, as monumental and visible as the tomb in the Invalides, to stimulate the national ambition. The terrible sacrifices which he exacted are forgotten, and, if they be remembered, compare not unfavourably (on paper, at all events) with those entailed by the modern system, even in time of peace; without continental supremacy or the Empire of the West to be placed to the credit side. And so they may obliterate the eagles and the initials if they will, it avails nothing. France in chill moments of disaster, or even of mere material and commercial well-being, will turn and warm herself at the glories of Napoleon. The atmosphere is still imbued with the light and heat of the imperial era, with

---

[1] Taine, *Rég. Mod.*, i. 54. [2] Stendhal, *Napoléon*, p. 58.
[3] *Ibid.* p. 59. [4] Méneval, i. 424.
[5] Constant, v. 268; De Sor, *Souvenirs du Duc de Vicence*, i. 247, 256. There was a mysterious illness of eight days after Wagram. Ségur, iii. 387.

the blaze of his victories, and with the lustre of those years when Europe was the anvil for the hammer of France.

The details of methods and morals are, in cases like Napoleon's, as we·have said, subordinate matters—subordinate, that is, for History, which only concerns itself with his effect and result. But, none the less, they are profoundly interesting for mankind. They will not, indeed, enable us to discover his secret. We study them as we would the least facts concerning a supernatural visitant; a good or bad spirit, something alien to ourselves, and yet linked to ourselves by the bond of humanity—not merely human shape and human utterance, but human failing and human depravity.

What, after all, is the story?

Into a career of a score of years he crowded his own dazzling career, his conquests, his triumphant assault on the old world. In that brief space we see the lean hungry conqueror swell into the sovereign, and then into the sovereign of sovereigns. Then comes the catastrophe. He loses the balance of his judgment and becomes a curse to his own country and to all others. He cannot be still himself, or give mankind an instant of repose.[1] His neighbours' landmarks become playthings to him, he cannot leave them alone, he manipulates them for the mere love of moving them. His island enemy is on his nerves; he sees her everywhere; he strikes at her blindly and wildly. And so he produces universal unrest, universal hostility, the universal sense of his incompatibility with all established society. But he pursues his path as if possessed, as if driven by the inward sting of some burning devil. He has ceased to be sane. The intellect and energy are still there, but as it were in caricature: they have become montrosities. Body and mind are affected by the prolonged strain to be more than mortal. Then there is·the inevitable collapse; and at St. Helena we are watching with curious compassion the reaction and decline.

[1] See St. Marsan's remarks in Pasquier, ii. 193.

The truth we take to be this. The mind of man has not in it sufficient ballast to enable it to exercise, or endure for long, supreme uncontrolled power. Or, to put it in other words, the human frame is unequal to anything approaching omnipotence. All history from the Cæsars onwards teaches us this. Strong as was the intellect of Napoleon, it formed no exception to the rule.

For in the first period of his consulate he was an almost ideal ruler.[1] He was firm, sagacious, far-seeing, energetic, just. He was, moreover, what is not of less importance, ready and anxious to learn.[2] He was, indeed, conscious of extreme ignorance on the civil side of his administration. But he was never ashamed [3] to ask the meaning of the simplest word or the most elementary procedure; and he never asked twice. He thus acquired and assimilated all necessary information with extraordinary rapidity. But when he had learned all that his counsellors could teach him, he realized his immeasurable superiority to all men with whom he had been brought into contact. He arrived at the conclusion, probably a just one, that his genius was as unfailing and supreme in the art of statesmanship as in the art of war, and that he was as much the first ruler as the first captain of the world. That discovery, or conviction, backed by the forces and resources of France, inspired him with an ambition, at first vague, but growing as it was fed; at last immeasurable and impossible. Nothing seemed impracticable, nothing illusory. Why should it? He had never failed, except perhaps at Acre. He beheld around him incapable monarchs, incapable generals, incapable ministers, the languid barriers of a crumbling society. There seemed nothing in the world to check a second Alexander, even one more reckless and enterprising than he whose career had inspired his own boyish dreams.

Had he proceeded more slowly, had he taken time to realize

---

[1] Cf. Pasquier, i. 145.   [2] *Ibid*. i. 359, note.
[3] Chaptal, p. 225; Pasquier, i. 359.

and consolidate his acquisitions, it is difficult to limit the extent
to which his views might have been realized. But the edifice
of his empire was so prodigiously successful that he would not
pause, even a moment, to allow the cement to harden. And,
as he piled structure on structure, it became evident that he
had ceased to consider its base. That base was France, capable of
heroic effort and endurance, of all, indeed, but the impossible.
The limit at last was reached. Great as were her resources,
she could no longer supply the reckless demands of her
ruler. In 1812 he left 300,000 French men amidst the snows
of Russia. In 1813 he summoned 1,300,000 more under
arms.[1] And these were only the culminating figures of a long
series of overdrafts, anticipations of the annual conscription,
terrible drains on the population of France proper—a population of some thirty millions. Taine calculates that during
his Empire (1804–1815) there had been slain for him 1,-
700,000 Frenchmen from within the ancient limits of France
—besides 2,000,000 allies drawn from without.

He, no doubt, had convinced himself with that faculty of
self-persuasion which is at once the weakness and the strength
of extraordinary minds, that he had in reality enlarged his
foundation; that it had increased in exact proportion to the
increase of his dominions; that the Germans and Italians and
Dutchmen and Spaniards who served under his banners
formed a solid accretion to it; that his empire rested on an ho-
mogeneous mass of eighty millions of equally loyal subjects.
He seemed to consider that each annexation, however pro-
cured, added as many valid instruments of his policy as it did
human beings to his realm. It added, as a rule, nothing but
veiled discontent and expectant revolt. Frederick the Great was
wont, it is true, to compel the prisoners whom he captured in
battle to serve in his ranks. But he was under no illusions as
to the zeal and fidelity of these reluctant recruits. Napoleon,
however, considered, or professed to consider, that the popu-

[1] Pasquier, ii. 118.

lations that he had conquered could be relied upon as subjects and soldiers. This strange hallucination indicated the loss of his judgment and, more than any other cause, brought about his fall.

Whom the gods would destroy, says the adage, they first deprive of sanity. And so we see Napoleon, with incredible self-delusion, want of insight, or both, preparing his own destruction by dealing with men as if they were chequers, and moving them about the board according to his own momentary whim, without a thought of their passions, or character, or traditions; in a word, by ignoring human nature. Take, for one example, the singular apportionment of souls, in a despatch of February 15, 1810:—"I approve of this report with the following modifications—1. Only to take from the Italian Tyrol 280,000 souls, a population equal to that of Bayreuth and Ratisbon. 2. That Bavaria should only give up for the Kingdom of Würtemburg and the Duchies of Baden and Darmstadt a population of 150,000 souls. So that, instead of 188,000 souls, Bavaria should gain 240,000 or 250,000. Out of the 150,000 souls ceded by Bavaria, I think one must give 110,000 to Würtemburg, 25,000 to Baden, and 15,000 to Darmstadt." [1] It is only fair to add that the congress of his enemies at Vienna proceeded with flattering imitation on the same principles. [2]

But the exasperation of the transferred and retransferred souls was not the only result of this mania for cutting and carving. It produced a moral effect which was disastrous to the new Empire. The founder of such a dynasty should have attempted to convince the world of the stability of his arrangements. He himself, however, spared no exertion to prove the contrary. Moving boundaries, shifting realms, giving and taking back, changing, revising, and reversing, he seemed to have set before himself the object of demonstrating that his founda-

---

[1] Brotonne, *Lettres inédites de Napoléon I*er*, p. 550.
[2] See *Corresp. inédite de Talleyrand et de Louis XVIII, passim.*

tions were never fixed, that nothing in his structure was definite or permanent. It was the suicide of system. His bitterest enemies could hardly have hoped to suggest that conquests so dazzling were transient and insecure, had he not taken such infinite pains to prove it himself.

Austria and Prussia he had conquered; Spain and Italy he had annexed: he reckoned these, therefore, as submissive auxiliaries. Russia he had both defeated and cajoled; so all was at his feet. He never seems to have given a thought to the storm of undying hatred, rancour, and revenge that was chafing and raging below.

He added a Spanish contingent to his Grand Army, when the Spaniards were cutting the throat of every Frenchman whom they could find. He added a Prussian contingent, when he must have known, had he been sane, that no Prussians could ever forgive him the humiliations which he had heaped upon their country. He added an Austrian contingent at a time when a much less clear-sighted observer must have been aware that it was merely a corps of hostile observation.

Supreme power, then, destroyed the balance of his judgment and common sense, and so brought about his fall. But it was not the only cause. There was another factor. He was deeply imbued with the passion of warfare. It is difficult to realize the full strength of this fascination, for, though all soldiers feel the fever of the field, it is rarely given in all the countless generations of the world, to experience it in its full strength, as one who enjoys as absolute ruler the sole direction, responsibility, and hazard of great wars. But if common men love to risk chances in the lottery or with the dice, on the racecourse or the Stock Exchange, if there they can find the sting of excitement, war is the gambling of the gods. The haunting risk of disaster; the unspeakable elation of victory; the gigantic vicissitude of triumph and defeat; the tumult and frenzy and divine sweat; the very scorn of humanity and all that touches it, life and property and happiness; the anguish of the dying, the horror of the dead; all these sublimated passions not merely seem to raise man for a moment beyond his fellows, but constitute a strain which human nerves are not able long to endure. And Napoleon's character was profoundly affected by these ecstasies of fortune. The star of his destiny, which bulked so largely in his mind, was but the luck of the thrower of world-wide dice. He had indeed his full measure of the gross and petty superstition which ordinarily accompanies the vice. And so, even in his most desperate straits, he cannot bring himself to close the account and sign a peace; for he always cherishes the gambler's hope that fortune, or the star of destiny, or whatever it be called, may yet produce another transformation, and restore all his losses by a sudden stroke.

Generals, as a rule, are, fortunately, controlled by governments in matters of policy. But when the supreme captain is also the supreme ruler, there is nothing to restrain him from the awful hazard: he stakes once too often, and ruins his country, having already lost himself. Charles XII was often in the mind and on the lips of Napoleon during the Russian campaign.[1]

Of scarcely any sovereign warrior but Frederick can it be said that he sheathed the sword at the right time, and voluntarily kept it in the scabbard. But his case was peculiar. He had had terrible lessons. He had been within an ace of ruin and suicide. No conqueror had ever seen so much of the horrors of defeat. There are not many examples in history of annihilation so complete as that of Kunersdorf: there are few indeed of triumphant resuscitation after such a disaster. And when Frederick had recovered the material waste and loss of his long war, his blood had cooled; he had the good fortune to have passed, and, what was more important, to know that he had passed, that season of war in the life of man which Napoleon defined. So he consolidated his conquests and died in peace.

[1] Ségur, iv. 305, v. 302–3; Beausset, ii. 154.

Napoleon sometimes spoke lightly of him as a general when at St. Helena. We doubt, however, if he thought lightly of Frederick as a man.[1] Frederick had been his immediate prototype. Had Frederick never lived, Napoleon might have had a different career. And indeed, as it was, he might have learned other lessons from the Prussian king; for Frederick, though inferior to Napoleon in all else, in force and scope and scale, was his superior in two respects. Had Napoleon possessed the astute moderation and the desperate tenacity of Frederick, the destinies of France and of Europe would have taken a different turn.

We hold, then, that the Emperor had lost the balance of his faculties long before he finally fell. But this is not to say that he was mad; except, perhaps, in the sense of Juvenal's bitter apostrophe to Hannibal. Sanity is a relative term. Napoleon at his outset was phenomenally sane. His cool, calculating shrewdness and his intense common sense were at least in proportion to his vast, but still bounded, ambition. From such singular sanity to the limits of insanity there is an immeasurable distance. Napoleon's impaired sanity was superior to the judgment of the vast majority of mankind; but—here lay the fatal change—it had ceased to bear any proportion to, or exercise any control over, his ambition. When that check was removed he was a lost man.

At what precise period the overbalancing of this great intellect took place it is of course impossible to say, for the process was of necessity gradual and almost imperceptible. Some may incline to think that it was apparent even before he became emperor; that the lawless abduction and wanton execution of Enghien may mark the beginning. That proceeding, no doubt, denotes not merely a criminal lawlessness, but an irritability, a want of decency and control, a recklessness of cause and effect which were new in Napoleon. Ségur marks a great change after Jena.[2] Some may surmise that there is a visible

[1] See Rémusat, i. 324–5; Gourgaud, ii. 20. [2] Ségur, iii. 44, 53.

alteration after Wagram.[1] That period seems too late; though he was then standing on a pinnacle, from which he saw all the kingdoms of the earth spread out before him; a pinnacle, lofty and sublime, but with a foothold both giddy and insecure. Any attempt, however, to fix exact dates for a psychological change would need a volume in itself. It is sufficient for our purpose to point out that the alteration did occur, and that the Napoleon of 1810, for example, was a very different being from the Napoleon of 1801. The Napoleon who declared at one time that all the countries of Europe should keep their archives in Paris,[2] and at another that the French Empire should become the mother country of all sovereignties,[3] that all the kings of the earth should have palaces of residence in Paris, and attend in state the coronations of the French Emperors; the Napoleon who refused to make peace in 1813 and 1814, had obviously lost the balance of his reason. So obvious was this that, in the last days of his first reign, there was a conspiracy in Paris to dethrone him on the ground of insanity.[4] It is easy, too, to pronounce with absolute certainty that the loss of balance and soundness had occurred at Bayonne in 1808, and on the Niemen in 1812. He had then ceased to calculate coolly, and to see any bounds—moral, physical, or international—to any freak ambition that might occur to him. In the Russian campaign there is visible a feverish, reckless desire to strain his fortune to the utmost, to push his luck, as gamblers say, and to test, as it were, the extreme limits of his destiny. He himself said of the Treaty of Leoben that he had played at vingt-et-un and stopped at twenty.[5] Later in life he demanded twenty-one at every coup.

And in another way this overbalanced, overweening individuality contributed to his fall. He had no check or assistance from advice, for his Ministers were cyphers. It is not too much

[1] Ségur, *Mélanges*, pp. 268–70.   [2] Metternich, i. 106.
[3] Rémusat, ii. 127, 276; *ibid.* i. 407.
[4] Méneval, iii. 222.   [5] Rémusat, ii. 227.

to say that the blind idolatry of Bassano had much to do with the imperial catastrophe. Great responsibility, too, may be attributed to the compliance and deference of Berthier.[1] Napoleon was apparently safe from all rivalry. But yet he could not endure that there should be approved merit or commanding talent near him to share the lustre of his government.[2] That government, indeed, was so conducted as to render it impossible for men of independent ability to serve under it. For such an adminstration mediocrity was a necessity, and high capacity an embarrassing superfluity. Had he died suddenly, he would have left behind him a vast number of trained subordinates and a few brilliant malcontents. In itself this fact sufficiently proves the weakness of his government, without taking into account its morbid centralization. His system, putting his impracticable ambition on one side, must have brought the Empire to ruin at his death, unless he had been able, which for a man of his temperament was in the last degree improbable, to make a complete change, and fashion a new system which would give ability fair play and which might exist without himself. Some young men of promise, such as Molé and Pasquier [3] (though this last was, it must be added, forty when Napoleon took him up), he did indeed train, but he secured none of their devotion. It is probable that they perceived that as they rose in the hierarchy they would lose his patronage, and that brilliancy could not in the long run be otherwise than distasteful to him. It is strange that jealousy, if jealousy it were, should enter into the composition of so rare a supremacy.

One feature of this attitude was that he was always on his guard, says one who knew him well, against the ambition of his generals.[4] That and popular discontent were what he most

<hr>

[1] Stendhal, *Napoléon*, p. 48, note; Méneval, iii. 47.
[2] Rémusat, iii. 15, 173; Stendhal, *Napoléon*, pp. 53, 61.
[3] *Ibid.* ii. 67, 315.
[4] Chaptal, pp. 218, 246; Rémusat, ii. 205-6, 207 note, 370.

feared. So he kept his generals at arm's length, blamed them easily, commended them parsimoniously.[1] It was only the dead, such as Desaix and Kléber, whom he praised with warmth. Thus, except two or three who had known him in his youth, they approached him with fear and trembling.[2] And even these early friends loved him in spite of themselves. Lannes would deplore, between smiles and tears, in Napoleon's presence, his unhappy passion for "cette catin," and the Emperor would laugh at his rueful tirades, being sure of his Lannes.[3] The awe of the others was not ill-founded. Take for example, this authentic incident: One day at a levee Napoleon sees St. Cyr, one of his ablest lieutenants. He goes up to him and says, placidly: "General, you come from Naples?" "Yes, Sire, after giving up the command to General Pérignon whom you had sent to replace me." "You have, no doubt, received the permission of the Minister of War?" "No, Sire, but I had nothing more to do at Naples." "If within two hours you are not on the road to Naples, I will have you shot on the plain of Grenelle before noon," replied Napoleon, in the same tranquil tone.[4] He rewarded them with titles and appanages, but not with credit. Indeed, "he would have no glory but his own, he only believed in his own talents."

Stendhal, who was a man of genius, and whose opinions are, therefore, worth noting, thinks that one of the two main causes of the fall of the Emperor was this taste for mediocrity. The mediocrity for which Mirabeau is said to have prayed, Napoleon avowedly loved. For of this preference he made no secret. What he wanted was instruments and not Ministers. What he feared and disliked was not so much the competition as the ambition and criticism of superior ability. Two men of eminent parts were long in his employment and necessary to

[1] Chaptal, p. 248.   [2] Taine, *Rég. Mod.*, i. 20-1, 78.
[3] Chaptal, p. 252; Las Cases, iv. 371. Cf. Méneval, ii. 440; Pasquier, i. 362.
[4] Chaptal, p. 251.   [5] Stendhal, *Napoléon*, p. 54, note.   [6] Balzac

his Empire. When he discovered that they were considered indispensable to him, his vigilant egotism took alarm, and he got rid of them. It is difficult in all history to cite a personage more infamous and more loathsome than Fouché. But he was a master of those vile arts which despotism requires in a Minister of Police. He was in truth a pestilent instrument which it was equally dangerous to utilize or to neglect. Napoleon did both, a course which combined all disadvantages.[1] Talleyrand, cynical and ignoble as he was in many respects, stands on a higher level, and may find some excuse, not merely in the laxity and exigencies of a revolutionary epoch, but in a cool foresight which gives colour to the plea that, while doing his best for himself, he was doing the best for France. That question does not concern us. But, in spite of indolence,[2] and in spite of corruption,[3] he was a consummate Foreign Minister and an unrivalled diplomatist. Up to the time of the Spanish imbroglio he was Napoleon's close confidant, as he had been one of the earliest associates of his fortunes. Napoleon charged him with advising the policy with regard to Spain and then denouncing it.[4] Talleyrand denied the charge. We are inclined to think that both were right. Talleyrand, as we learn from his intimate friend, Madame de Rémusat, openly declared, and had no doubt advised the Emperor, that "a Bourbon was an inconvenient neighbour to Napoleon, and it was doubtful whether such a neighbour could be tolerated." [5] But he entirely disapproved of Napoleon's proceedings. In a word, he probably gave the impulsion and inspired the idea, while Napoleon found the methods. Possibly something of the same kind occurred with regard to the Enghien affair. The fact, however, that we have to deal with is the rupture, not its

[1] See his own criticism. Gourgaud, i. 578. Cf. Pasquier, iii. 195; Lavallette, ii. 149.
[2] Méneval, iii. 442.
[3] Gourgaud, i. 485; Pasquier, i. 248–9.   [4] Ségur, iii. 313.
[5] Rémusat, iii. 264. Cf. Pasquier, i. 329, 351; Méneval, ii. 136. As to Napoleon's view, see Gourgaud, ii. 265.

cause. For we are persuaded that, had Napoleon been able to retain and work with Talleyrand, his fall would not have taken place. He quarrelled with both Talleyrand and Fouché, and was never able to replace them.[1]

His relations to both these officials throws an instructive light on the cynical side of his character. He grossly and publicly insulted Talleyrand [2] on more than one occasion, outrages in essence and style so intolerable that no man could forgive them. Yet Napoleon in his troubles sent for Talleyrand, and began talking to him confidentially about politics. In the midst of their conversation, Talleyrand calmly remarks, "But, by the by, I thought we had quarrelled." [3] Napoleon dismisses the remark as irrelevant. Talleyrand, however, had then been long in close relations with Russia, and was not to be won back. Fouché, too, was dismissed with disgrace. He openly hated Napoleon, and passed his exile in intriguing against him.[4] Napoleon was ignorant neither of the hatred nor of the intrigues.[5] But, in 1815, as we have seen, he whistles him back, and entrusts him with one of the most delicate and important offices at his disposal, the one which gives the best opportunity for betrayal.

Many other causes for his overthrow have been alleged, but, in our judgment, they are ancillary to those that we have cited. And, as a rule, they are, strictly considered, rather effects than causes; it was the causes of his overthrow which produced these disastrous errors. His faults of policy were, no doubt, in his later reign, numerous and obvious enough. But they were not, as is often popularly stated, the causes which effected his ruin, but rather the effects and outcome of the causes which produced his ruin. And this much more must be said in fair-

[1] See Napoleon on the pair (Gourgaud, ii. 324), and his cool judgment on Talleyrand at Fontainebleau (Pasquier, ii. 364).

[2] Pasquier, i. 357-8; Ségur, iii. 313; Pasquier, ii. 142; Méneval, ii. 228.

[3] Rémusat, i. 107 (not told according to this version).

[4] Chaptal, p. 314.   [5] Méneval, iii. 525.

ness for them, that, viewing them from their political aspect, and putting aside all moral tests, they were grand and not wholly extravagant errors. Life was too short for his plans. The sense of this made him impatient and violent in his proceedings. And so his methods were often petty—not so his policy. His gigantic commercial struggle with England was an impossible effort, but it was one which distinguished economists have, on a smaller scale, often since endeavoured to repeat. Nor is it easy to see, in the absence of an efficient fleet, what other weapon was available with which to attack his world-wide enemy. Agan, the Spanish expedition was a blunder in method, but not necessarily in policy. Louis XIV had carried out the same policy with conspicuous success. And Napoleon could not foresee that a people which had long supported dynasties so contemptible would rise like one man against his own. Again, the Russian expedition was a blunder, but Russia was the fatal leak in his continental system, and he might well refuse to believe that the Russia which had succumbed after Friedland would burn her ancient capital and her secular shrines rather than again submit. Again, the contest with the Pope was a blunder, so grave that some thinkers believe that it mainly contributed to his fall. But it was the blunder of the Holy Roman Emperor and Most Catholic King, Charles V, the chief guardian and stay, almost the secular arm, of the Church. Napoleon's methods toward the Holy See were brutal, but Charles sacked Rome.

We have no doubt that Napoleon, after bringing Russia into his system, and crippling or crushing Great Britain, aspired vaguely to becoming in some way Lord Paramount of Europe. We question, however, whether the idea ever assumed actual shape, except in regard to the West, or was ever more than a dream of dominion. He must have known that he could not bequeath so personal a power to his son, but he probably thought that a mere remnant of his empire would be a rich inheritance for his posterity. For himself, he would have outstripped those dead rivals who looked back on him from the page of history, and lured him on; his only rivals, on whom his inner eye was always emulously fixed. And he would have bequeathed a name before which all others would pale, and all future generations yield unquestioned homage.

There is one question which English people ask about great men, which one cannot put with regard to Napoleon without a sense of incongruity which approaches the grotesque. Was Napoleon a good man? The irresistible smile with which we greet the question proves, we think, not the proved iniquity, but the exceptional position of this unique personality. Ordinary measures and tests do not appear to apply to him. We seem to be trying to span a mountain with a tape-line. In such a creature we expect prodigious virtues and prodigious vices, all beyond our standard. We scarcely remember to have seen this question seriously asked with regard to Napoleon, though Metternich touches on it in a fashion;[1] it seems childish, discordant, superfluous. But asked nakedly in the ordinary sense, without reference to the circumstances of the time, it can admit but of one prompt reply. He was not, of course, good in the sense that Wilberforce or St. Francis was good. Nor was he one of the virtuous rulers: he was not a Washington or an Antonine. Somewhere or other he has said that he could not have achieved what he did had he been religious, and this is undoubtedly true. In England his name was a synonym for the author of all evil. He was, indeed, in our national judgment, a devil seven times worse than the others. But then we knew nothing at all about him. He, had he been himself asked the question and understood it, would at once have discriminated between the public and the private man. He would have said that private morality had nothing to do with statecraft, and that statecraft, if it had a morality at all, had a morality of its own. His own morals, he would have said, and indeed thought, were extremely creditable to so altogether

[1] *Mémoires*, i. 289.

exceptional a being. To use a common vulgarism, he was not, we think, so black as he is painted. The tone of his age, the accepted and special latitude accorded to monarchs in the eighteenth century, the circumstances and temptations of his position, must be taken into account. Men must judge men not absolutely but relatively, as they would themselves be judged. Circumstance, epoch, environment, training, temptation, must all be taken into account if you would test the virtues of mankind. An abstinent man when starving will choke himself with a meal from which a glutton would shrink. A temperate man in extreme weakness will swallow without injury draughts of brandy which would drown a drunkard. And so with Napoleon. His lot was not cast in a monastery or in a pulpit. He came from Corsica a little Pagan, viewing the world as his oyster. He was reared in the life of camps and in the terrors of revolution. He was raised to rule a nation which, in the horrors of a great convulsion, had formally renounced and practically abjured Christianity. He had to fight for his own hand against the whole world. It was breathless work, which gave little time for reflection.

What he said of religion we have seen. What he thought of religion we do not know.[1] He grasped, no doubt, its political force. He would have understood the military value of the loyal piety of the Tyrolese, or the stern fanaticism of the Covenanters. That he deemed religion essential to a nation he proved by his bold achievement of the Concordat. It is clear, too, that he thought the same of morality, of the sanctity of the family, of public and even private virtue. He was never weary of inculcating them. But it never even occurred to him that these rules were applicable to himself, for he soon regarded himself as something apart from ordinary men. He did not scruple to avow his conviction. "I am not a man like other men," he would say; "the laws of morality and decorum could not be intended to apply to me."[2] He was, it

[1] Ch. Chaptal, pp. 236, 239, etc. [2] Rémusat, i. 115, 206.

may be fairly alleged, indulgent and affectionate to his family,[1] particularly in his first, better years; dutiful to his mother; kind to his early friends.[2] He wished to be a good husband according to his lights. He would have cherished his son had he been allowed. He was a tender brother in his early years, especially to Louis,[3] who rewarded him by the grossest suspicions of a hypochondriac; and to Joseph, who, in the hour of his agony, made love to his wife. He was specially kind to his old tutors and school associates. He was free from the sordid cares of personal wealth or personal avarice. He was quick to wrath, but, according to the best and keenest judges, easily appeased.[4] In another place we have cited the testimonies of Rapp and Drouot to this effect. "Always kind, patient, and indulgent," says Méneval.[5] Chaptal recalls the Emperor's kindness to his old tutors and schoolfellows, and his constant generosity to men of genius and merit in distress. Madame de Rémusat, a hostile and observant chronicler, narrates several instances of his consideration and tenderness,[6] as well as of his susceptibility to the pleading fondness of Josephine.[7] M. de Rémusat witnessed in 1806 a scene of almost hysterical and insurmountable emotion when Napoleon embraced Talleyrand and Josephine, declaring that it was hard to part from the two people that one loved the most; and, utterly unable to control himself, fell into strong convulsions.[8] This was no comedy. There was nothing to gain. It was the sudden and passionate assertion of his heart.

But, it must be admitted, this was an exceptional case. In the final deteriorated phase of his character there is no trace of friendship. In one or two instances he may have felt it. But

[1] Chaptal thinks differently (p. 343). See, however, Méneval, iii. 11.

[2] Chaptal, pp. 179, 184, 195. See, too, p. 339.

[3] Méneval, ii. 369.   [4] Fain, *Manuscrit de 1814*, p. 112.

[5] Méneval, i. 402. Cf. *Madame de Montholon*, p. 62; Bertrand, Preface, p. xxxiv.

[6] *E.g.* Rémusat, i. 237, 264.

[7] *Ibid.* iii. 294, 312; Ségur, iii. 428.   [8] *E.g.* Rémusat, iii. 61.

he had no friends.[1] Duroc most nearly approached to that
intimate character. Napoleon on assuming the crown had
bade Duroc continue to call him "thou": a rare if not a singular privilege.[2] Duroc he called his conscience.[3] From Duroc he
was said to have no secrets.[4] But Duroc stood alone. Great
masses, who knew him only in his public capacity, chiefly as
a general, adored him to the last. The private soldiers who
marched from France to Waterloo were inspired with an
enthusiasm for him which at least equalled that of the soldiers
at Marengo or Austerlitz.[5] But that enthusiasm diminished in
proportion to remoteness from the rank and file. Officers felt
it less in an ascending scale, and when the summit was reached
it was no longer perceptible.[6] It had long since ceased to be
felt by those who knew the Emperor most intimately. Friendship, as we have seen, he had deliberately discarded as too
close a relation for other mortals to bear to himself.[7] Many,
too, of his early friends had died on the field of battle: friends
such as Lannes, Desaix, and Duroc. But some had survived
and left him without ceremony or even decency. Berthier, his
lifelong comrade, the messmate of his campaigns,[8] his confidant, deserted him without a word, and did not blush to become captain of Louis XVIII's bodyguard. His marshals, the
companions of his victories, all left him at Fontainebleau, some
with contumely. Ney insulted him in 1814, Davoust in
1815.[9] Marmont, the petted child of his favour, conspicuously
betrayed him. The loyal Caulaincourt found a limit to his
devotion at last. Even his body attendants, Constant and

---

[1] See, however, Méneval, ii. 409, who does not, however, convince
me; also iii. 540 as to the singular devotion with which Napoleon
inspired Carnot.

[2] Stendhal, *Napoléon*, p. 64. Cf. Ségur's account of Napoleon's
emotion on Duroc's death, vi. 114–7.

[3] Beausset, ii. 176 (Beausset says Duroc was Napoleon's conscience).

[4] *Ibid.* ii. 176.   [5] *Vie muitaire du General Fory*, p. 269.

[6] Miot, iii. 429.   [7] Chaptal, pp. 251, 319. Cf. Méneval, 440.

[8] Méneval, iii. 47–9.   [9] Villemain, ii. 425.

Rustan, the valet who always attended him, and the Mameluke who slept against his door, abandoned him. It was difficult to collect a handful of officers to accompany him to Elba, much more difficult to find a few for St. Helena. The hopeless followers of ungrateful masters, the chief mourners of misfortune, who haunted the barren antechambers of the Bourbons and the Stuarts, had no counterpart in the exile of Napoleon. We need not reproach a nation, for that nation found many faithful adherents for their ancient kings. Moreover, his wife, who left him without a sigh, who wrote, when under his roof, that she was only happy by his side,[1] and who, after his death, wrote that she had never felt any real affection for him,[2] was an Austrian. We must regretfully attribute this alienation, discreditable as it is to the deserters, as more discreditable to Napoleon himself. Bertrand, as we have seen, who, if alone, can claim the halo of fidelity, avowed the truth at St. Helena, not in anger, but in sorrow: "The Emperor is what he is, we cannot change his character. It is because of that character that he has no friends, that he has so many enemies, and indeed that we are at St. Helena."[3]

And yet we must not distribute this judgment over his whole career; it applies only to that part of it which was essentially imperial and partially insane. Until he chose to make a demigod of himself and deliberately cut himself off from humanity, he was kind, generous, and affectionate; at any rate, if that be too partial a judgment, he was certainly not the reverse.

But in the full swell of his career it would never have crossed his mind that these attributes, any more than veracity or sympathy, had any relation to him. They were right and proper for others, but for him something more or something less was required. They were qualities for mere men; and the ordinary restraints, like the ordinary objects of mere men, had ceased to have any meaning for him.

[1] *Correspondance de Marie Louise, 1799–1847* (Vienna, 1887), p. 158.
[2] *Ibid.* 226.   [3] Gourgaud, i. 223.

THE END

Was he a great man? That is a much simpler question, but it involves definitions. If by "great" be intended the combination of moral qualities with those of intellect, great he certainly was not. But that he was great in the sense of being extraordinary and supreme we can have no doubt. If greatness stands for natural power, for predominance, for something human beyond humanity, then Napoleon was assuredly great. Besides that indefinable spark which we call genius, he represents a combination of intellect and energy which has never perhaps been equalled, never, certainly, surpassed. He carried human faculty to the farthest point of which we have accurate knowledge. Alexander is a remote prodigy, too remote for precise comparison. To Cæsar the same objection is applicable. Homer and Shakespeare are impersonal names. Besides, we need for comparison men of action and business. Of all these great figures, it may be said that we do not know enough. But Napoleon lived under the modern microscope. Under the fiercest glare of scrutiny he enlarged indefinitely the limits of human conception and human possibility. Till he had lived, no one could realize that there could be so stupendous a combination of military and civil genius, such comprehension of view united to such grasp of detail, such prodigious vitality of body and mind. "He contracts history," said Madame d'Houdetot, "and expands imagination." [1] "He has thrown a doubt," said Lord Dudley, "on all past glory; he has made all future renown impossible." [2] This is hyperbole, but with a substance of truth. No name represents so completely and conspicuously dominion, splendour, and catastrophe. He raised himself by the use, and ruined himself by the abuse, of superhuman faculties. He was wrecked by the extravagance of his own genius. No less powers than those which had effected his rise could have achieved his fall.

[1] Rémusat, iii. 162.
[2] Raikes' *Journals*, ii. 168. See also Gronow, i. 177, ed. 1867.

APPENDIX

I. CAPTAIN MAITLAND

NAPOLEON BUONAPARTE, when he came on board the *Bellerophon*, on the 15th of July 1815, wanted exactly one month of completing his forty-sixth year, being born the 15th August, 1769. He was then a remarkably strong, well-built man, about five feet seven inches high, his limbs particularly well formed, with a fine ankle and very small foot, of which he seemed rather vain, as he always wore, while on board the ship, silk stockings and shoes. His hands were also very small, and had the plumpness of a woman's rather than the robustness of a man's. His eyes light grey, teeth good; and when he smiled the expression of his countenance was highly pleasing; when under the influence of disappointment, however, it assumed a dark gloomy cast. His hair was of a very dark brown, nearly approaching to black, and, though a little thin on the top and front, had not a grey hair amongst it. His complexion was a very uncommon one, being of a light sallow colour, differing from almost any other I ever met with. From his having become corpulent, he had lost much of his personal activity, and, if we are to give credit to those who attended him, a very considerable portion of his mental energy was also gone. . . . His general appearance was that of a man rather older than he then was. His manners were extremely pleasing and affable; he joined in every conversation, related numerous anecdotes, and endeavoured, in every way, to promote good humour: he even admitted his attendants to great familiarity; and I saw one or two instances of their contradicting him in the most direct terms, though they generally treated him with much respect. He possessed, to a wonderful degree, a facility in making a favourable impression upon those with whom he entered into conversation: this appeared to me to be accomplished by turning the subject to matters he supposed the person he was addressing was well acquainted with, and on which he could show himself to advantage.

APPENDIX

II. SENHOUSE

July 15, 1815.

His person I was very desirous of seeing, and I felt disappointed. His figure is very bad; he is short, with a large head, his hands and legs small, and his body so corpulent as to project very considerably. His coat, made very plain, as you see it in most prints, from being very short in the back, gives his figure a more ridiculous appearance. His profile is good, and is exactly what his busts and portraits represent; but his full face is bad. His eyes are a light blue, with a light yellow tinge on the iris, heavy, and totally contrary to what I expected; his teeth are bad; but the expression of his countenance is versatile, and expressive beyond measure of the quick and varying passions of the mind. His face at one instant bears the stamp of great good humour, and immediately changes to a dark, penetrating, thoughtful scowl, which denotes the character of the thought that excites it.

III. BUNBURY

July 31, 1815.

Napoleon appears to be about five feet six inches high. His make is very stout and muscular. His neck is short, and his head rather large; it is particularly square and full about the jaw, and he has a good deal of double chin. He is bald about the temples, and the hair on the upper part of his head is very thin, but long and ragged, looking as if it were seldom brushed. In the management of his limbs Napoleon is ungraceful; but he used very little gesture, and the carriage of his head is dignified. He is fat, and his belly projects; but this is rendered more apparent by the make of his coat, which has very short lapels turned back, and it is hooked tight over the breast to the pit of the stomach, and is there cut away suddenly, leaving a great display of white waistcoat. He wore a green uniform with scarlet collar and scarlet edging to the lapels, but without lace or embroidery; small gilt buttons, and gold epaulettes. He had a white neckcloth, white waistcoat and breeches, silk stockings, and shoes with small gilt buckles. A very small old-fashioned sword, with a worked gold hilt, was buckled tight to his hip. He wore the ribbon of the Legion of Honour over his waistcoat, and the star, in silver embroidery, on his coat. There were also three very small orders hanging together at one of his button-holes. His hat, which he carried most of the time under his arm, was rather large, quite plain, and having an *extremely small* tricolour cockade. Napoleon took snuff frequently during the interview; the box was not showy; it was rather long, and appeared to have four coins or medals set in its top.

. . . .

Napoleon's eyes are grey, the pupils large; not much eye-brow; hair brown; complexion sallow, and the flesh sodden. His nose is finely formed, his upper lip very short, and the mouth beautiful. His teeth are bad and dirty, but he shows them very little. The general character of his countenance was grave and almost melancholy; but no trace of severity or violent passion was allowed to appear. I have seldom seen a man of stronger make, or better fitted to endure fatigue.

IV. LADY MALCOLM

June 25th, 1816.— ... The following is Lady Malcolm's idea of his figure: His hair of a brown-black, thin on the forehead, cropped, but not thin in the neck, and rather a dirty look; light blue or grey eyes; a capacious forehead; high nose; short upper lip; good white even teeth, but small (he rarely showed them); round chin; the lower part of his face very full; pale complexion; particularly short neck. Otherwise his figure appeared well proportioned, but had become too fat; a thick, short hand, with taper fingers and beautiful nails, and a well-shaped leg and foot. He was dressed in an old threadbare green coat, with green velvet collar and cuffs; silver buttons with a beast engraven upon them, his *habit de chasse* (it was buttoned close at the neck); a silver star of the Legion of Honour; white waistcoat and breeches; white silk stockings; and shoes with oval gold buckles. She was struck with the kindness of his expression, so contrary to the fierceness she had expected. She saw no trace of great ability; his countenance seemed rather to indicate goodness. . . .

V. HENRY

Sept. 1, 1817.

He was dressed in a plain dark green uniform coat without epaulettes, or anything equivalent, but with the star of the Legion of Honour on the breast, which had an eagle in the centre. The buttons were gold, with the device of a mounted dragoon in high relief. He had on white breeches and silk stockings, and oval gold buckles in his shoes; with a small opera hat under his arm. Napoleon's first appearance was far from imposing, the stature was short and thick, his head sunk into the shoulders, his face fat, with large folds under the chin; the limbs appeared to be stout and well-proportioned, complexion olive, expression sinister, forbidding, and rather scowling. The features instantly reminded us of the prints of him which we had seen. On the whole, his general look was more that of an obese Spanish or Portuguese friar, than the hero of modern times. . . .

A fascinating prestige, which we had cherished all our lives, then vanished like gossamer in the sun. The great Napoleon had merged in an unsightly and obese individual; and we looked in vain for that overwhelming power of eye and force of expression which we had been taught to expect by a delusive imagination.